Research Methods in H

Research Methods in Human Rights introduces the reader to key methodological approaches to Human Rights research in a clear and accessible way.

Drawing on the expertise of a panel of contributors, the text clearly explains the key theories and methods commonly used in Human Rights research and provides guidance on when each approach is appropriate. It addresses such approaches to Human Rights research as qualitative methods, quantitative analysis, critical ethnography and comparative approaches, supported by a wide range of geographic case studies and with reference to a wide range of subject areas. The book suggests further reading and directs the reader to excellent examples from research outputs of each method in practice.

This book is essential reading for students with backgrounds in law as well as political and social sciences who wish to understand more about the methods and ethics of conducting Human Rights research.

Dr Lee McConnell is Lecturer in Law at University of Bristol Law School.

Dr Rhona Smith is Professor of International Human Rights and Head of School (Law) at Newcastle University.

Research Methods in Human Rights

Edited by Lee McConnell and
Rhona Smith

LONDON AND NEW YORK

First published 2018
by Routledge
2 Park Square, Milton Park, Abingdon, Oxon OX14 4RN

and by Routledge
711 Third Avenue, New York, NY 10017

Routledge is an imprint of the Taylor & Francis Group, an informa business

© 2018 Lee McConnell and Rhona Smith

British Library Cataloguing in Publication Data
A catalogue record has been requested for this book

Library of Congress Cataloging in Publication Data
Names: McConnell, Lee, editor. | Smith, Rhona K. M., editor.
Title: Research methods in human rights / [edited by] Lee McConnell and Rhona Smith.
Description: Abingdon, Oxon ; New York, NY : Routledge, 2018. | Includes bibliographical references and index.
Identifiers: LCCN 2017051557| ISBN 9781138943230 (hbk) | ISBN 9781138943247 (pbk)
Subjects: LCSH: Human rights—Legal research. | Human rights—Research—Methodology.
Classification: LCC K3240 .R4727 2018 | DDC 342.08/520721—dc23
LC record available at https://lccn.loc.gov/2017051557

ISBN: 978-1-138-94323-0 (hbk)
ISBN: 978-1-138-94324-7 (pbk)
ISBN: 978-1-315-67263-2 (ebk)

Typeset in Garamond
by Keystroke, Neville Lodge, Tettenhall, Wolverhampton

Contents

Contributors

Suzanne Egan is Assistant Professor at the Sutherland School of Law, University College Dublin, Ireland and Director of the UCD Centre for Human Rights. She has served two terms as a member of the Irish Human Rights Commission, worked with the Law Reform Commission in Ireland and worked with an independent research centre on refugee law and policy in Canada. Her research spans a number of human rights themes, including the UN human rights treaty body system, refugee law and human rights education.

Sue Farran is Professor of Laws at Northumbria University Law School and an Associate of the Centre for Pacific Studies, St Andrews University. Sue's main area of interest is the impact development has on economic, social, cultural and human rights. She is particularly interested in the complexities of plural legal systems, the use of comparative methodology to address new and emerging legal issues and the interface of different legal systems. Much of her research uses Pacific Island case studies to explore wider and more global themes such as the rights of indigenous people to determine their own futures, women's and children's rights and the challenges posed by the different and often conflicting agendas of global players and state sovereignty in the context of small island developing states.

Lindsey Raisa Feldman is a doctoral candidate in sociocultural anthropology at the University of Arizona in the United States. Her research is focusing on the role of labour in the prison rehabilitative process with ethnographic research on the inmate wildfire fighting programme in Arizona. Photography is a central component of the research. Previous work has included research on the social effects of the Deepwater Horizon oil spill.

Todd Landman is Professor of Political Science and Pro-Vice-Chancellor of the Faculty of Social Sciences at the University of Nottingham in the UK. His research focuses on analyses of problems in development, democracy and human rights with quantitative and qualitative methodologies. He has written several books and numerous articles, as well as authoring a number of research reports and consultancy reports.

Lee McConnell is a Lecturer in Law at the University of Bristol in the UK. His principal research combines public international law and legal theory, focusing in particular on the regulation of non-state actors such as multinational corporations and non-state armed groups. He also researches in the field of animal law.

William Paul Simmons is Professor of Gender & Women's Studies and Director of the online Human Rights Practice graduate program at the University of Arizona. His research is highly interdisciplinary; using theoretical, legal, and empirical approaches to advance human rights for marginalized populations around the globe. His books include Human Rights Law and the Marginalized Other (Cambridge UP, 2011) and the forthcoming Joyful Human Rights (University of Pennsylvania Press). With Michelle Téllez, he has conducted ethnographic research on sexual violence against migrant women and he has published articles and a book chapter exploring legal remedies for the feminicides in Ciudad Juárez, Mexico. He is currently working on a project in Niger, Nigeria, and Mozambique to empower people affected by leprosy using international human rights documents.

Lorna Smith was Senior Lecturer in Social Sciences at James Watt College in Scotland and is now Teaching Enhancement Lecturer at West College Scotland. She currently teaches across a range of social sciences including research methods. She has previously worked as a researcher in education, drawing on her background in psychology.

Rhona Smith is Professor of International Human Rights and Head of Law at Newcastle University in the UK. She has researched and written across a range of human rights issues. Her consultancy projects and human rights capacity building work has focussed mainly on academic and justice sector partnerships and projects, particularly in China and South East Asia.

1 Introduction to human rights research methods

Rhona Smith and Lee McConnell

This book will provide an overview of the core methods utilised in human rights related research. While the book is aimed at a broad audience of academics, senior undergraduate and postgraduate students, NGO and civil society workers, each chapter will be pitched at an introductory level. The central aim is to equip newcomers to human rights based research with a basic understanding of the core elements of the dominant research methodologies in the field. Each chapter will enable readers to determine the suitability of a particular method in relation to their particular projects. It is hoped that the book will empower readers to adopt new approaches in their research activities. Perhaps at the outset, it is useful to clarify the difference between methods and methodologies as the terms are often used interchangeably. 'Method' is defined in the Oxford English Dictionary as

> a special form of procedure or characteristic set of procedures employed (more or less systematically) in an intellectual discipline or field of study as a mode of investigation and inquiry, or of teaching and exposition.

'Methodology' is defined as

> the branch of knowledge that deals with method generally or with the methods of a particular discipline or field of study . . . . Subsequently also: the study of the direction and implications of empirical research, or of the suitability of the techniques employed in it; (more generally) a method or body of methods used in a particular field of study or activity.

This book seeks to explain several methods which can be used in human rights research. In doing so, it explores a methodology in the sense of the body of methods used in the field of human rights. It is not, however, exhaustive in this endeavour.

Human rights affect everyone and pervade all aspects of society. No person is excluded from the protective remit of human rights and no state can avoid international responsibility for ensuring at least a minimum standard of human rights within their jurisdiction. This process began with the General

Assembly adopting the Universal Declaration of Human Rights in 1948.[1] Today there are hundreds of treaties giving effect to human rights. These are concluded under the auspices of the United Nations[2] and the principal regional organisations.[3] States elect which of these treaties to accept. All rights and freedoms should be given effect to in national laws and policies. It is left to a variety of (international) committees, courts, commissions, experts and even other states to determine whether the standards are realised. However, it can be difficult to measure compliance with human rights. Moreover, individuals and states may differ in their understanding and expectations of human rights. Since human rights are not necessarily static, and may evolve over time, it can be ever more difficult to ascertain the extent of human rights obligations and duties.

Are falling mortality rates proof of an increased respect of the right to life? When is the right to an adequate standard of health realised? Can degrading treatment be defined? Is country K better than country M at respecting human rights? How can true equality be measured? Is human rights education having a positive impact on society? Do journalists understand human rights issues? What are the barriers to combatting trafficking in persons? What is it really like to live in a country that is being subsumed by the surrounding seas?

When researching human rights, a number of diverse questions emerge. How can they best be answered? This book seeks to demonstrate that there is no single method which offers an approach for answering all human rights questions. Rather a range of approaches may be used. Human rights are a common focus of international development aid and partnership funding. All funds and resources must be accounted for. This brings a unique challenge. Proof of progress and success is required. For human rights strategies, this can be interesting. Many human rights projects aim at long term, even generational, change. It is difficult to demonstrate and quantify change in the shorter term as is often required to satisfy funders. Human rights present extensive opportunities for research. Greater understanding of human rights is needed for states so they can give effect to the obligations accepted. Groups and individuals deserve better awareness of those rights and freedoms to which they are entitled. Courts and tribunals need to be able to adjudicate on whether rights and freedoms have been infringed. With the pervasiveness of human rights, students, academics, governments, non-governmental organisations, civil society actors and individuals engage in human rights research.

---

1 General Assembly resolution 217(A) III, 10 December 1948.
2 See http://www.ohchr.org/EN/ProfessionalInterest/Pages/UniversalHumanRightsInstruments. aspx
3 Principally Council of Europe (see www.coe.int/en/web/conventions), Organisation of American States (www.oas.org/en/sla/dil/inter_american_treaties.asp), African Union (au.int/ en/treaties).

The **human rights based approach** is, in effect, a conceptual framework for human development. It originally focussed on development, and attempts to ensure more sustainable third-party interventions in states. Accordingly, the human rights based approach sought to rationalise development work, focussing on sustainability of results and addressing root causes of poverty. The principles have evolved to become a recognised standard. As the international community focussed more strongly on development of states, a greater understanding of the causes of inequality and wealth and power imbalance emerged. This was simultaneous to a series of particularly ill-conceived aid attempts and linked more positively to the millennium development goals and the inherent calls for stronger relationships and support. Emerging postcolonial theories questioned the 'them and us', 'north and south' divisions and approaches. Capacity building and empowerment became the new buzzwords. The UN sought to capitalise on this and strive for agreement that assistance should respect and promote human rights principles. A human rights based approach should respect human rights principles and aim at securing the better fulfilment of human rights. Moreover, such an approach must work towards strengthening the capacities of either rights holders, once they and their entitlements are identified, or duty bearers, once they and their obligations are identified. A strict legal approach, however, does not necessarily accurately explain a particular situation. **Human rights in context** advocates placing human rights and law in their natural setting, considering a range of factors including historical, cultural, religious and socio-economic, which influence the interpretation and application of the law. Traditional practices may shape relationships and limit state action. A deeper level of understanding of the real position in a state is thus achieved by examining law in its actual context. Law in context developed in popularity in the 1960s and some aspects evolved into socio-legal studies. This contribution will focus on those elements of a situation which need to be considered in order to properly understand the actual human rights situation. States and rights holders both need an understanding of law in context to maximise the opportunity for human rights to be meaningfully realised in the state.

As rights are currently expressed in legal forms, there remains a tendency to use legal methods for analysing and explaining human rights. Cases, statutes, treaties and related instruments and associated documentation are undoubtedly a primary source of information on human rights. Such a traditional approach offers an insight as to how human rights standards are interpreted and applied. This approach is of course also relied on in many court processes. Lawyers need to use cases and documentation to make arguments; judges need them to make decisions. A substantive chapter thus examines the traditional **doctrinal legal approach** to research. It is expected that legal researchers will find this familiar but the chapter will serve as an introduction to the different legal sources required for international human rights. The emphasis will be on legal analyses using textual analysis of cases, treaties, instruments and commentaries. Many of these sources are now readily available to the researcher online and in local languages as well as official UN languages.

Of course, the realisation of human rights raises a number of philosophical questions. There are a range of **theoretical approaches** which offer different ways to understand and apply international human rights. These include naturalist, positivist, liberal, cosmopolitan, feminist, critical and postmodern theoretical perspectives, among others. Each offers a different window through which problems can be viewed and responses conceptualised. Different theoretical models can help researchers to view human rights situations differently. Students often adopt a particular theoretical tradition to frame their research questions. For external actors, understanding different theoretical approaches can help explain the application of human rights in specific country situations. Ultimately, all human rights research raises questions of a theoretical nature. This chapter aims to challenge readers to externalise and confront the seemingly natural theoretical presumptions embedded in their work, in the hope of fostering self-aware, reflexive future scholarship.

Proving progress and regress in human rights often requires a credible and reliable evidence base. Many funders now prefer statistical evidence. This brings unique challenges of how to measure human rights. What indicators can be used? Are they reliable? Do they reflect the reality? There are a number of strategies for gathering, analysing and presenting empirical evidence. The best choice in a particular situation depends on what is being measured or researched.

A **qualitative analysis of data** is based on a systematic method of analysis of textual matter. Human rights obviously affect humans. Accordingly, it is often necessary to establish the impact of particular practices on individuals. Often such data will be collected through interviews. These may be structured or semi-structured, depending on the research questions and the time available and scope of the research. Data can also be collected through face-to-face interviewing or through a more remote survey of some type. There are clear ethical issues which have to be considered when dealing with individuals. A human rights based approach to such research demands that the process must do no harm; individuals cannot be re-traumatised by being asked to relive and relate experiences of torture for example. The actual analysis of the resultant data can be undertaken in different ways. Much depends on the volume of material and on what questions are being addressed.

In contrast, **quantitative analysis** is a method often used for analysing material which is reduced to a set of digits or symbols. It is particularly useful for identifying trends and patterns which are statistically significant. Thus, this analysis could be used to indicate improvement in human rights conditions. Quantitative research can also be used to objectively analyse phenomenon. Increasingly, human rights are defined in terms of indicators – the millennium development goals are a prime example – and thus quantitative methods are required to populate progress charts and demonstrate compliance with standards. As noted above, funding agencies often require evidence of progression in human rights standards to be presented in statistical formats.

Critical ethnography: lived experiences evolve from the understanding that human rights obviously affect people. Accordingly, researchers focus on analysing human rights issues through case studies. Lived experiences of individuals are of key importance, as are ethical considerations. Some aspects of this approach are drawn from anthropological studies. The emphasis is usually on empowerment of the rights holders or informing the duty bearers, with the goal of improving the situation. An understanding of the specific situation can be achieved through a variety of media including texts, images, drama and music.

As human rights problems are common to all countries, it is often useful to compare experiences in different countries and situations. However, comparisons need to be made carefully. An understanding of the different legal, political and cultural systems being compared is necessary. **Comparative approaches** can be used to contextualise knowledge and understanding. They can offer cross-cultural or transcontinental understandings. Comparative research can involve researching on the same questions, using the same methods and can even use a similar schedule. The European Union has funded a wide range of projects examining phenomena across member states. Some of these are initially explanatory or descriptive in nature.

Any single method has its limitations and strengths. Different research questions and different funders require different methods to be used. Perhaps unsurprisingly, a lot of human rights research thus follows a **mixed approach**. Hence, different methods are blended to ensure the research questions are fully addressed. This can produce more credible results as a degree of 'testing' is inbuilt by using a second or third method to corroborate or cross-check findings. Accordingly, this is a good 'method' with which to conclude the text.

It is not possible in a book this size to comprehensively explore each method. Rather, the authors introduce each method, and seek to explain its value and possible contribution in human rights terms. Further reading options are presented to advance knowledge and skills if required. A range of textbooks are available, particularly in social sciences which can provide a thorough grounding for many of the approaches outlined in this text. Courses and training are also widely available. This book intends to whet appetites for a diversity of approaches to human rights research and, in so doing, promote a greater degree of understanding of human rights issues, and better ensure all rights and freedoms are adequately respected, protected, and promoted for the benefit of everyone.

2 Human rights based approaches to research

Rhona Smith

Research on human rights issues takes a variety of different forms. The various chapters of this book look at some of the popular options engaged by legal academics as well as social and political scientists when researching human rights. The language of human rights has evolved dramatically since 1948 and the adoption of the Universal Declaration of Human Rights by the General Assembly of the United Nations. In 1993, member states attending the World Conference of Human Rights in Vienna agreed the Vienna Declaration and World Programme of Action.[1] This emphasised the indivisibility of rights, their interdependence and their interrelatedness as well as linking human rights with democracy, sustainability and development.[2] As the global power shifted with decolonisation tapering off, having been largely achieved, and the ideological divisions of the Cold War easing, human rights discourse gained more prominence. Contemporaneously with technological and travel advancements, human rights concerns became increasingly linked to, and drawn on, in development literature, strategies and practice. Indeed, the current UN Secretary-General, Antonio Guterres, has identified human rights as central to his vision for the UN organisation, emphasising the need for an inclusive approach to conflict prevention, peace and development.[3]

Prioritising the application of human rights became a cornerstone of UN activities in 1997 when the then Secretary-General called upon all UN agencies to mainstream human rights in their activities.[4] This call was, in

---

1 Vienna Declaration and Programme of Action adopted by the World Conference on Human Rights in Vienna on 25 June 1993, http://www.ohchr.org/EN/ProfessionalInterest/Pages/Vienna.aspx, accessed 7 February 2017.
2 Vienna Declaration, n1, paras 5, 8–11.
3 Antonio Guterres, Vision, outlined in January 2017, Secretary-General's remarks to the Security Council Open Debate on 'Maintenance of International Peace and Security: Conflict Prevention and Sustaining Peace', https://www.un.org/sg/en/content/sg/statement/2017-01-10/secretary-generals-remarks-security-council-open-debate-maintenance, accessed 7 February 2017.
4 Renewing the United Nations: A Programme for Reform, report of the Secretary General, UN Doc A/51/950, paras 78–79.

effect, rebadged and relaunched in 2013, with former Secretary-General Ban Ki-Moon's Human Rights Up Front initiative.[5] This initiative seeks to ensure that human rights are at the forefront of all UN activities and inform the work. Echoing the UN World Programme for Human Rights Education and the UN Declaration on Human Rights Education and Training,[6] activities should do no harm to human rights and should be delivered in a manner consistent with respect for human rights, and conducive to the implementation of human rights. For development activities, the Millennium Development Goals[7] served as a focal point and led to re-evaluations of the operation of development activities. A growing awareness of the nature of development as cooperation and partnership rather than simple donation was also prominent at this time.[8] Whilst working on the Millennium Development Goals, with real targets and indicators of progress for development goals, each of which in turn linked clearly to human rights, several UN agencies came together to adopt the UN Common Understanding on a Human Rights Based Approach to Development Cooperation (HRBA).[9] The Common Understanding operates as a guide for agencies on how human rights standards and principles can, and should, be put into practice during everyday activities. Ensuring marginalised, excluded and discriminated against peoples are included, and that development interventions reach these people is the main goal.

A human rights based approach to development dramatically changed the nature of development. Rather than a focus on the needs of beneficiaries (e.g. a requirement of clean water was identified so a project was initiated to deliver a clean water supply), a human rights based approach will focus on not only the outcome (e.g. clean water supply), but how that outcome is achieved (coordination with stakeholders, both duty bearers and rights holders). The

---

5 Human Rights Up Front, Ban Ki-Moon's commitment statement and associated documentation, https://www.un.org/sg/en/content/ban-ki-moon/human-rights-front-initiative, accessed 7 February 2017.

6 UN World Programme for Human Rights Education, proclaimed by General Assembly resolution 59/113 (2004) and the UN Declaration on Human Rights Education and Training, General Assembly resolution 66/137 (2011).

7 UN Millennium Development Goals, adopted World Summit United Nations Millennium declaration, General assembly resolution UN Doc A/RES/55/2, further information and reports on progress available http://www.un.org/millenniumgoals, accessed 17 February 2017.

8 M. Langford, A. Summers and A. Yasmin (eds) *The Millennium Development Goals and Human Rights: Past, Present and Future* (Cambridge: Cambridge University Press, 2013); Philip Alston and Mary Robinson (eds) *Human Rights and Development: Towards Mutual Reinforcement* (Oxford: Oxford University Press, 2010) and perhaps slightly controversial, OECD and World Bank (eds) *Integrating Human Rights to Development: Donor Approaches, Experiences and Challenges* (Washington: OECD/WB, 2013).

9 UN Common Understanding on a Human-Rights-Based Approach to Development Cooperation 2003, http://hrbaportal.org/the-human-rights-based-approach-to-development-cooperation-towards-a-common-understanding-among-un-agencies, accessed 10 February 2017.

language of rights was then employed and development was intended to shift focus to building capacity to secure and protect rights and freedoms whilst simultaneously supporting individuals and groups with claiming rights. Obviously, progress was slow and there is still a reluctance amongst many development agencies in the UN to use the language of human rights due to perceived sensitivities.[10] Consistency of approach was an aim of the Common Understanding, but is arguably yet to be fulfilled. Yet there is ever more operational connections and coordination, especially in countries with multiple agency field presences.

According to the Common Understanding,

> all programmes of development cooperation, policies and technical assistance should further the realisation of human rights as laid down in the Universal Declaration of Human Rights and other international instruments; human rights standards contained in, and principles derived from, the Universal Declaration of Human Rights and other international human rights instruments guide all development cooperation and programming in all sectors and in all phases of the programming process; Development cooperation contributes to the development of the capacities of 'duty-bearers' to meet their obligations and/or of 'rights-holders' to claim their rights.[11]

The human rights based approach has been adopted across a number of development agencies outside the UN including the Foreign Ministries of countries such as Sweden.[12] Those involved in programming and reporting will be familiar with the deployment of HRBA in activities and reports, to a greater or lesser extent depending on context.

It is argued that all good research on human rights issues, even when not directly related to programming activities, could and should meet the requirements of a human rights based approach. What does this mean in practice? Well first, human rights research should advance the realisation of human rights, second, research should respect human rights standards and principles, and third, research should ideally contribute to capacity development of duty bearers or rights holders.

---

10 UNDP in some field offices downplays rights terminology though still works hard delivering on human rights.
11 UN Common Understanding, http://hrbaportal.org/the-human-rights-based-approach-to-development-cooperation-towards-a-common-understanding-among-un-agencies, accessed 7 February 2017.
12 SIDA Sweden, Human Rights Based Approach at SIDA, http://www.sida.se/English/partners/resources-for-all-partners/methodological-materials/human-rights-based-approach-at-sida, accessed 10 February 2017.

1 Research should advance the realisation of human rights

A HRBA to research should result in research which advances the realisation of human rights. This is normally relatively straightforward as much human rights research aims at deepening understanding of human rights and freedoms, their monitoring and enforcement or their implications in reality. Doctrinal analyses, theoretical analyses, empirical data analyses – all contribute to the understanding of what human rights standards are, what they mean in practice and/or how protection can be strengthened. In development, it is usually necessary for a programme to be directly linked to one or more specific rights or freedoms and the realisation thereof. For research, the more 'blue-sky' and conceptual research can also contribute towards understanding so may be more abstract than would necessarily be the case for development programmes.

A degree of forethought allows the intended beneficiary to be identified. A new theoretical understanding of a particular right could be used to re-conceptualise how a particular culture or legal system deals with violations, for example. The token beneficiary could therefore be a particular community or the state authorities. Naturally, doctrinal analyses can deepen understanding of how law can be used to protect human rights and/or action violations. Lawyers and activists could therefore be notional beneficiaries of this research as they will have stronger legal tools to use when protecting human rights or when advocating for strengthening of laws and policies to better protect human rights and fundamental freedoms.

Quantitative and qualitative approaches can provide strong empirical data supporting findings that respect for human rights is strengthening. For example, measuring progress against the human rights indicators in the UN sustainable development goals can indicate advancements in development and strengthening of human rights in practice

2 Research should respect human rights standards and principles

A human rights based approach to research should ensure that the research does no harm, the golden rule of human rights work. This is particularly important when empirical work and case studies are used. As the chapters on qualitative methods and ethnographical research make clear, researching with and on people, particularly vulnerable peoples, bring specific challenges. Respecting human rights standards can have an impact on sample selection (ensuring the views or experiences of everyone in a group is appropriately represented). Consideration must also be given to free prior informed consent of all participants with due regard to confidentiality of interviewees and/or anonymising data when necessary or requested. In addition, human rights researchers may have additional considerations in the field – ensuring the risk of reprisals against those being interviewed, translating, and assisting otherwise in the research is minimised and ensuring that the risk of retraumatisation of individuals is minimised. Being guided by respect for human rights principles can also manifest itself in respect for different cultures, so cultural sensitivity, tolerance of differences and awareness of reality is important. Examples can include being sensitive to gender dimensions in interviewing – it is often advisable to have females interviewing female rape victims or victims of violence, for example. Respecting human rights standards can also mean cultural sensitivity – clothes, materials and tools used in the field, for example. All need to be carefully selected for function, to minimise offence and to ensure mutual respect, trust and understanding.

Just as with development, human rights principles can guide the research at all stages – conceptualisation, planning, information/data gathering, analysis and writing up and dissemination. Arguably this can also mean ensuring any outputs meet human rights standards. Consideration may have to be given to the funding of research (if applicable) and the human rights credibility of the dissemination strategy. Few academic researchers do undertake human rights impact studies in advance of planned research and few delve into the background of funders and/or outlets of dissemination. Bias in funded research should be avoided or, at least, acknowledged and its possible impact on the work recognised. The potential for unconscious bias should also be considered as objectively as possible.

A number of guidelines exist to ensure respect for human rights standards and principles. The 1999 Istanbul Protocol and the OHCHR Manual on the Effective Investigation and Documentation of Torture and Other Cruel, Inhuman or Degrading Treatment or Punishment,[13] for example, is the UN standard for assessing claims of those alleging torture, and reporting such findings to official bodies. Many international professional organisations (e.g. Bar Associations), civil society organisations and non-governmental organisations have their own guidelines for gathering information on human rights violations.

3 Research should ideally contribute to capacity development of duty bearers or rights holders

If research follows a human rights based approach, then it should result in strengthening the capacities of duty bearers and/or the capabilities of rights holders. For many researchers, this is relatively straightforward. Developing an understanding of human rights standards, or the impact of human rights

---

13 OHCHR, *Istanbul Protocol, Manual on the Effective Investigation and Documentation of Torture and Other Cruel, Inhuman or Degrading Treatment or Punishment* (OHCHR: Geneva, Professional training series, No 8/Rev.1 1999), http://www.ohchr.org/Documents/Publications/training 8Rev1en.pdf, accessed 17 February 2017.

in reality, monitoring, enforcement and so on can indelibly strengthen capacity of duty bearers or rights holders. Where this becomes important is in dissemination. Most academics are required to produce publications, usually in academic journals. However, for a human rights based approach, the practical impact has to be considered. Can the research achieve greater impact by being repackaged and sent in a policy paper to a government ministry, for example? Could a special procedure mandate holder benefit from having a theoretical approach to a particularly thorny issue outlined? Could the government of state R benefit from a better comparative understanding of the experiences of a particular issue of other states in the region? Many countries are now adopting the language of 'impact' to ensure that academic research translates to making a difference on the ground: translational or transformative work. Securing an impact is undoubtedly a major goal in a human rights based approach. As with all such work, the impact may be incremental and build up progressively. Accordingly, the first piece of work may not produce a major impact but may lead to another piece of work which does have an impact. A holistic approach can be taken of impact but its importance cannot be underestimated in a HRBA to research. A dissemination strategy, or pathway to impact, can be useful to frame and shape the impact of the research. After all, most researchers on human rights ultimately want to make a difference and improve human rights on the ground in some shape or form.

Ultimately the HRBA moves away from the hitherto predominant welfare model approach to development and the key difference lies in the shift from donor/beneficiary conceptualisations to capacity building and partnerships. Rather than giving 'charity' to those deemed poorer or less fortunate (with clear echoes of post-colonialism[14]), human rights discourse is used to frame a moral imperative for actors to build capacity and develop tangible results progressing human rights and freedoms.

Many engaged in human rights research are doing programme evaluations or base line studies. This can be the first exposure to HRBA for legal academics and other non-empirical research trained researchers. The move towards a rights based approach has brought a sharp focus on the tangible results of programmes and other initiatives. Several chapters in this book explain the mechanics, benefits and challenges of relevant methods of research. Twenty-first-century development programming relies heavily on deliverables and tangible outputs. This can be relatively straightforward for some projects, but infinitely more challenging for others. Proving a cultural change towards respect for rights, for example, can be difficult to measure. Similarly, proving a programme of human rights education has changed attitudes is infinitely harder than gathering evidence that the programme has increased knowledge and understanding or developed skills.[15] However,

---

14 See generally, E. Said, *Orientalism* (London: Routledge and Kegan Paul, 1978).
15 The head, heart and hands of human rights education, for example.

there is a considerable challenge in effecting the shift from recipient of training/programmes/infrastructure to independent capacity for sustainable and progressive use thereof. The sustainable development goals which, as noted, are currently very influential in development work, emphasise sustained results. Rights holders have as much responsibility to build capacity on the nature of their rights and freedoms and develop tools to better claim them and hold states to account as do the states to better respect, protect and promote human rights.

4 Law in context

A human rights based approach to research means researching human rights issues with due consideration as to the surrounding circumstances. This can mean ensuring an appropriate historical, cultural, religious, legal and political understanding of the issues which shape the subject. An understanding of the relevance of individual rights as opposed to group rights differs from state to state. The African Charter on Human and Peoples' Rights, for example, reflects the broad African understanding of collective rights to development, enjoyment of natural resources and international security and peace.[16] The exposition of the corollary of duties to family, community and country, likewise.[17] Development status of a country is also relevant, especially when considering the progressive development of rights and evaluating resource mobilisation. Demographics, geography, religion, legal system (common law, civil law, mixed) and politics remain important to understand when evaluating the human rights situation.

The final chapter of this book reflects on mixing and blending methods. There are undoubtedly benefits to drawing on different approaches as, ultimately, a deeper understanding of human rights will require a holistic understanding of how a situation arose or developed and how it can be addressed. This section notes some of the common approaches which can help illuminate human rights issues in particular contexts. There are of course many other contexts which can be of relevance. As is so often the case, it depends on the particular facts and circumstances of the issue being studied/researched.

4a History

Human rights research can benefit from historical approaches to research. Understanding why things are as they are, learning from past experiences of a situation, identifying trends and providing perspectives on current issues are examples of the richness historical approaches can bring to human rights research. Historical research can empower people – decision makers, for example,

16 Respectively, Articles 22, 21 and 23 African Charter on Human and Peoples' Rights.
17 Duties of every individual are enshrined in Articles 27–29 of the Charter.

can learn from the experiences of predecessors; rights holders can learn from the experiences of others in a similar position. Generally, primary historical sources are first-hand accounts or records of the issue being studied; secondary sources are at least one step removed – the difference between an autobiography and a biography for example.

A better understanding of the evolution of the right, for example, drawing on the travaux preparatoires or other archival material, can help. This can feed in directly to doctrinal approaches, supporting a better understanding of the intention of high contracting parties, and so aiding understanding of the meaning of the particular text. Suzanne Egan discusses a doctrinal approach later in this book.[18] Dominic McGoldrick, Sarah Joseph and Melissa Casten draw heavily on travaux preparatoires and historical context when analysing the International Covenant on Civil and Political Rights and its monitoring mechanism;[19] Manfred Nowak does likewise on the Convention Against Torture.[20] Travaux preparatoires are increasingly pulled together and published[21] as well as being made available and searchable online. The UN website, for example, now contains the early resolutions and documentation of the main organs. Archives of the UN and the League of Nations are being expanded online. This facilitates the accessibility of historical research materials, though in some instances recourse to physical archives may still be needed. Understandings gained from the official record of debates leading to the adoption of major treaties or simply institutional debates on major human rights issues can be useful. So too can national archives, which are increasingly digitalised, and can reveal insights into the specific approaches of states to situations. In many countries, legislation covers the rules on release of national archival material, some of which may be time sensitive or potentially incriminating. However, there is in human rights a more general freedom of information which, though rebuttable on grounds inter alia of national security, can be a useful tool for the researcher.

Post-colonial states may share particular challenges, especially if they share the same former colonial occupier. For example, the legal system may have been left by the colonial power and be progressively tempered by new laws introduced post-independence. Some research on that colonial system

---

18 Suzanne Egan, 'The doctrinal approach in international human rights scholarship', below.

19 Dominic McGoldrick, *The Human Rights Committee – Its Role in the Development of the International Covenant on Civil and Political Rights* (Oxford: Oxford University Press, 1994); Sarah Joseph and Melissa Castan, *The International Covenant on Civil and Political Rights – Cases, Materials, and Commentary* (3rd edn) (Oxford: Oxford University Press, 2013).

20 Manfred Nowak, *The United Nations Convention Against Torture, A Commentary* (Oxford: Oxford University Press, 2008).

21 For example, consider Ben Saul (ed.) *The International Covenant on Economic, Social and Cultural Rights - Travaux Préparatoires* (Oxford: Oxford University Press, 2016) or William Schabas (ed.) *The Universal Declaration of Human Rights: The Travaux Préparatoires* (3 volumes) (Cambridge: Cambridge University Press, 2013).

may assist analysis of the post-colonial system. Gaps in legal protection may be linked to the dawn of independence and change in laws – for example, appeals to the former colonial power supreme court may no longer exist.[22] Understanding this can help the researcher identify potential protection gaps. Many states have undergone dramatic legal and political change at different phases of their history, all exert influences on the present. Consider perhaps the extent to which understanding apartheid allows current challenges in human rights in South Africa to be better understood.

Post-conflict societies may similarly evidence particular challenges traceable to the restoration of peace and the reestablishment of infrastructure, political stability, law and order. Understanding the historical legacy of conflict and any peace and reconciliation process deepens the understanding of the human rights situation, both the imperatives the duty bearers work under and certain expectations of the rights holders. Historical imperatives may have been a factor in the conflict, as indeed may historical political or economic situations. Countries with an historic tradition of slavery, either as slaves or slavers, may approach forced labour, debt bondage and trafficking in a manner shaped by the experiences of slavery in the nineteenth century.

From a legal perspective, an understanding of the legal history of a country may also aid understanding of legal protection, or lack thereof, in a state. States with relatively new legal systems, perhaps introduced post conflict, may have gaps in protection or have disparate, piecemeal laws, depending on how the new legal system was created and drafted. So too, perversely, states with very old established legal systems – there may be gaps as the law has evolved over time and may be applied in situations never envisaged. Applying old laws to modern communications methods such as Whatsapp, Facebook and Twitter as well as the internet is proving problematic in many states. Understanding common law systems may require knowledge of old case law and the evolution of precedent; understanding civil law systems may require understanding of older codified versions of the law to trace the current law; understanding mixed legal systems can help the researcher understand the interaction of the plurality of systems in the state.

The present is in part shaped by the past, and in turn the present will influence the future. Consideration of the implications of the timing of human rights, political or economic development can ensure a more accurate understanding of the situation.

4b Culture

Culture is obviously protected by international human rights laws.[23] However, cultural traditions of a people (or state) may also shape understanding of human

---

22 See, for example, Statute of Westminster, 1931, from the UK.
23 Article 15, International Covenant on Economic, Social and Cultural Rights; see also the minority provision of article 27, International Covenant on Civil and Political Rights.

rights and freedoms. UNESCO is clear that 'no one may invoke cultural diversity to infringe upon human rights guaranteed by international law, nor limit their scope'.[24] Cultural traditions can also be viewed through an historical lens, or even through an understanding of religion. Much depends on the right, freedom, community and indeed culture involved. Of course, human rights based research may be aiming at challenging behaviours of rights holders, illuminating the problems with particular cultural practices. Obvious examples include work on combatting female genital mutilation. The Norwegian Ministries action plan draws on culture, history and religion when shaping education and opinion changing towards the practice.[25] Changing the culture towards violence against women and children is another area in which cultural understanding predates successful, if incremental, changes in human rights protection. Understanding cultural perceptions of roles in families, for example, can help the researcher's work develop action plans to effect change. A culture sensitive approach can also secure the researcher access to the relevant actors – for example, working with relevant organisations supporting women and child victims of violence.

Culture can be a dominant factor in many instances of discrimination. In India, Pakistan and several surrounding states, the caste system is regularly implicated in the abuse of human rights. Working on rights issues in the region requires an understanding of the system to better understand the cultural and indeed legal implications of different cases. Similarly, an appreciation of the traditionally 'macho' culture of some Latin American states can aid understanding of how certain practices and laws evolved.

Indigenous people around the world have distinct cultural traditions, many of which are under threat. Their relationship with land and their understanding of who can use land and enjoy usufructory rights reflect this. Understanding this and the historical abuse and misuse of indigenous lands can ensure a more holistic approach by duty bearers to land titling, exploitation of natural resources and such like.[26] Land rights, for example, are indelibly linked to the traditional connections the people have to the land on which they live. Similarly with forestry, mountains and rivers. These traditional connections come to the fore particularly when non-indigenous peoples are proposing land use, e.g. mining, hydroelectric dams, forestry or tourism.

24 UNESCO Universal Declaration on Cultural Diversity, 2001.
25 Norwegian Ministries, *Action Plan for Combating Female Genital Mutilation, Action Plan 2008–2011*, https://www.politi.no/vedlegg/skjema/Vedlegg_668.pdf, accessed 10 February 2017.
26 See, for example, Alexandra Xanthaki, *Indigenous Rights and United Nations Standards: Self-Determination, Culture and Land* (Cambridge: Cambridge University Press, 2006); James Anaya, *International Human Rights and Indigenous Peoples* (New York: Aspen Publishers, 2009).

Problems can also arise with changes in housing, healthcare or education and indeed with other rights and freedoms.

In a HRBA, understanding culture also has a prominent role when approaching qualitative and ethnographic work. A researcher from a cold northern country turning up in shorts and T-shirt in a tropical country may indicate a lack of respect for the community, or may be deemed friendly and accessible – which depends on an understanding of the cultural context, including possibly the gender of the interviewer/observer and interviewee/observed. Similarly, wearing expensive clothes and carrying a lot of expensive equipment in an area with high poverty levels may be culturally inappropriate. The old adage of 'dress to impress' means very different things in different cultural settings.

Language is a relevant cultural consideration, both when undertaking interviews, and when engaging in human rights discourse. The core international human rights UN instruments are only authentic in the official UN languages; all regional instruments are only authentic in some of the languages spoken within the territory covered by the instrument. This problem is compounded by the fact that some languages do not have the vocabulary for human rights in everyday usage. This can cause diverse problems for the human rights researcher. Even a skilled interpreter may struggle to ensure that questions are correctly understood by the interviewee when the language of human rights is not commonly employed in a particular setting. In a HRBA, supporting right holders and duty bearers requires each to have an understanding of the rights and freedoms at issue. Individuals and communities need to be fully informed of their rights and their right to participate in decisions affecting them. Similarly, duty bearers need to understand what should be done to ensure adequate protection of human rights.

Understanding culture is crucial for sustainable development and therefore progressive realisation and strengthening respect for human rights. The UN sustainable development goals emphasise this. The Rio+20 conference and associated activities were sub-headed 'the future we want'[27] emphasising the need for sustained development. The final outcome document recognised that

> people are at the centre of sustainable development and, in this regard, we strive for a world that is just, equitable and inclusive, and we commit to work together to promote sustained and inclusive economic growth, social development and environmental protection and thereby to benefit all.[28]

27 See General Assembly resolution A/RES/66/288, The Future We Want, endorsing the outcome document of the same name of the United Nations Conference on Sustainable Development.
28 UN Doc A/RES/68/288, annex para 6. The final outcome document and associated materials are available online, https://sustainabledevelopment.un.org/rio20, accessed 10 February 2017.

A cross-cutting cultural understanding can also assist the work of the researcher towards strengthening respect for universal human rights.[29]

4c Religion, ideology and philosophy

Culture is often linked to religion, ideologies and philosophies. Notwithstanding the oft-proclaimed universality of rights, different religions, ideologies and philosophies can offer different prisms through which to understand human rights. Some protagonists argue that human rights draw primarily on a Christian model, though obviously the UN has regularly proclaimed and accepted the universality of all rights and freedoms in core treaties. In states adhering to particular ideologies or state religions, this can shape human rights in the country. For example, Islamic feminist scholars and civil society organisations can contribute towards a rights compatible approach to equality of men and women, or civil society organisations can draw on Christian theologians to strengthen claims for sexual and reproductive rights of women in Roman Catholic countries. The religious imperatives were therefore acknowledged and respected whilst interpreted in a manner consistent with the realisation of human rights. Abdullahi Ahmed An-Na'im, for example, has spoken and written widely on reconciling international human rights standards with the writings of Islam and the implementation of shari'a laws.[30] Other authors too write on human rights and Islam, exploring potential challenges and gaps as well as articulating compatibility.[31] This is of clear benefit to both duty bearers as well as rights holders when, respectively, seeking to ensure international standards are met in a manner consonant with religious tenets or seeking to claim rights and freedoms in a secular environment.

There is growing evidence of some UN treaty bodies taking cognisance of these factors in concluding observations as well as in general comments and recommendations. Obviously, UN treaty bodies comprise independent unpaid experts and therefore even with the work of the committee of chairpersons, there is not necessarily consistency of approach across all committees on such matters. However, there is often a breadth of cultural and religious understanding brought to the table when discussing sensitive matters.

There is literature on the interaction of human rights with different ideologies, religions and so on. As noted above, many authors explore the recognition and implementation of human rights in Islamic doctrine and thence inform the recognition and protection of human rights in Islam. There is also writing

---

29 See, for example, Abdullah An Na'im (ed.) *Human Rights in Cross-Cultural Perspectives: A Quest for Consensus* (Philadelphia: University of Pennsylvania Press, 1992).
30 See for example, *Toward an Islamic Reformation: Civil Liberties, Human Rights and International Law* (Syracuse, NY: Syracuse University Press, 1996).
31 See for example, Shahram Akbarzadeh and Benjamin MacQueen (eds) *Islam and Human Rights in Practice: Perspectives Across the Ummah* (Abingdon: Routledge, 2008).

on human rights and Buddhism, and on religions generally.[32] Religion is an important element of culture, so understanding at least the basic tenets of a particular faith is important when considering the intersection of different rights and freedoms. Religious beliefs can impact on approaches to work, family, law and many other interactions.

The Marxist approach to human rights is also well covered in the literature.[33] Different ideologies can emphasise the relative importance of different rights. It was ideological differences which led to the Universal Declaration of Human Rights being divided into two covenants – the International Covenant on Economic, Social and Cultural Rights and the International Covenant on Civil and Political Rights.

There is evidence of states increasingly claiming that rights and freedoms have to be given effect in terms of specific country characteristics – China's oft reiterated arguments on human rights with Chinese characteristics, for example. Foreign Minister Hong Lei, speaking at a press conference in 2016, commented

> The Chinese government attaches great importance to promoting and protecting human rights, integrates the universality of human rights with the realities of China, blazes a trail of human rights development with Chinese characteristics and has made notable progress. There is no one-size-fits-all approach for the development of human rights. Every country has the right to advance its human rights cause in light of its national conditions, realities and people's requirements.[34]

This statement links to both philosophy and, of course, development.[35] Diverse positions of states are frequently reiterated in public. Generally, no state refutes human rights. This leads to each state striving to justify its actions (and omissions) in terms of human rights. Over the years, Asian values, Chinese characteristics, African understanding, global south, post-conflict

---

32 For example, Irene Bloom, J. Paul Martin and Wayne Proudfoot (eds) *Religious Diversity and Human Rights* (New York: Columbia University Press, 1996); Leroy Rouner (ed.) *Human Rights and the World's Religions* (Indiana: University of Notre Dame Press, 1988).

33 For example, L. MacFarlane, 'Marxist Theory and Human Rights' 1982 (17.4) *Government and Opposition* 414; George Brenkert 'Marx and Human Rights' 1986 (24.1) *Journal of the History of Philosophy* 55.

34 See http://www.fmprc.gov.cn/mfa_eng/xwfw_665399/s2510_665401/2511_665403/t134 7202.shtml, accessed 7 February 2017. See also comments made by Chinese delegates within universal periodic review at the UN Human Rights Council and before the UN treaty bodies. See also internal discussion in, for example, China Society for Human Rights, *Human Rights Magazine*, 2012, Hainian Liu, 'On Building Theoretical System of Human Rights with Chinese Characteristics', http://www.chinahumanrights.org/CSHRS/Magazine/ Text/t20110520_746459.htm, accessed 7 February 2017.

35 Discussed below.

transition have all been argued as evidence of particular approaches to human rights. Obviously, the conceptualisation of universal human rights is predicated on all rights and freedoms applying everywhere.

Other philosophical approaches are covered in the McConnell's chapter below on theory.

4d Legal

Modern human rights are given effect through law. Remedies are available, or should be available, through national law. Although the international regime is the same for all states, the national implementation mechanisms may differ. Whether a state has a monistic or dualistic approach to international law, for example, will shape the manner in which a country gives effect to its treaty obligations. Are international human rights standards accepted by the state directly enforceable in the courts and tribunals of the state? An understanding of the approach of a particular state to international treaties is essential when looking at how rights holders can best claim their rights.

Similarly, an understanding of the justiciability of constitutional rights may help when a programme of research aims to build capacity of rights holders in accordance with the HRBA. Constitutional rights may be directly claimed in courts. However, equally, they may not be justiciable, existing primarily as a restriction on the activities of the state (all, or certain organs). For rights holders, a lack of locus standi to bring complaints based on the constitutional enshrinement of rights can be a major issue, especially when no other national remedies are available for constitutionally enshrined international human rights standards. Using a HRBA necessitates an understanding of the opportunities for challenging the state and seeking remedies.

Civil law and common law countries approach rights and freedoms differently. In common law countries, the language of liberties and freedoms historically predominates. This frequently manifests itself in laws and judgments which focus on examining state interference in the enjoyment of freedoms, a more passive approach. Not interfering with rights and freedoms rather than actively establishing them in law and protecting them. Common law traditions also emphasise case law, with at times lengthy judicial reasoning contained in judgements. In contrast, and simplifying the situation somewhat, many civil law systems display more familiarity with the rhetoric of rights, having a legal system based on codes or similar legal encapsulation of laws and processes. In such systems, the concept of enshrining rights and freedoms then having courts give effect to them is more easily construed. Civil law systems often have less lengthy legal reasoning in decisions, in part due to the reliance on codified laws. Several countries have legal systems drawing primarily, or for specific areas of law (particularly family law), on Islamic precepts. Islamic jurisprudence includes various source of shari'a (religious law) including the Qur'an and Hadith. Of course, there are also mixed jurisdictions which draw on common law and civil law,[36] traditional and customary systems.[37]

International and regional legal systems can and frequently do develop and use their own vocabulary, meaning that challenges can arise when trying to translate the obligations accepted by a state at the regional or international level into a legally viable, justiciable form in terms of national law. In HRBA this can mean that training of lawyers, law enforcement officers and judicial officers is necessary to foster a common understanding of how national law gives effect to international norms. The duty bearers at all levels need to be aware of the international framework within which many laws are adopted. There are also problems when the legal norms themselves are alien to the culture of a society. Land rights and indigenous peoples have been mentioned above, intellectual property rights can similarly pose problems. Forsyth and Farran discuss the challenges in importing the global intellectual property regime into Pacific Island countries, noting the transplantation of legal ideas and norms and highlighting some of the challenges this causes.[38]

As human rights are usually given effect in the legal systems of states, it is useful to understand that context further. Even an understanding of rights to remedies, the parliamentary/governance, court and administration system can inform applications of human rights in a state. The approach of the state to the rule of law can also be useful when considering how a state reacts to international and regional norms.

4e Economics and development

Considering the stage of development of a particular state or its economical position can be instructive in fostering an understanding of rights priorities and government action (or inaction). This is true not only of economic, social and cultural rights when there is a requirement incumbent on states to ensure rights and freedoms are progressively realised to the maximum of the state's available resources.[39] There are a number of challenges and tensions when addressing development issues.[40] Whilst cost is not a defence to

36 See, for example, Esin Orucu, 'What is a Mixed Legal System: Exclusion or Expansion?' 2008 (12.1) *Electronic Journal of Comparative Law*, http://www.ejcl.org, accessed 17 February 2017.

37 See also, V. Palmer, M. Mattar and A. Koppel (eds) *Mixed Legal Systems, East and West* (Abingdon: Routledge, 2015); S. Farran, E. Orucu and S. Donaln (eds) *A Study of Mixed Legal Systems: Endangered, Entrenched or Blended* (Abingdon: Routledge, 2014).

38 Miranda Forsyth and Sue Farran, *Weaving Intellectual Property Policy in Small Island Developing States* (Cambridge: Intersentia, 2015).

39 Article 2(1) International Covenant on Economic, Social and Cultural Rights.

40 An interesting report which highlights (from a particular perspective) some issues is The Nordic Trust Fund of the World Bank commissioned report Human Rights and Economics: Tensions and Positive Relationships (Geneva: World Bank, 2012), http://siteresources. worldbank.org/PROJECTS/Resources/40940-1331068268558/Report_Development_

non-realisation of accepted human rights standards, a better understanding of economics can help the researcher address cost arguments. For example, when faced with a duty bearer claiming realising a right would be too expensive and therefore not viable, an understanding of the economics of the state and its relative state of development can help the researcher explore options for securing the necessary funds, either through redistribution of budgets or through exploring technical assistance and partnership options. Using a HRBA would mean considering the development of the state and how best to strengthen the capacity of the state to protect actively the rights and freedoms it accepts. A doctrinal approach to human rights standards can help a HRBA researcher better inform the duty bearers of rights and obligations in economic, social and cultural rights. There are arguments that the range of duty bearers is wider for development orientated rights than others – multinational businesses,[41] non-state actors, donor states and such like.[42]

One of the most prominent authors focussing on economics and development is Amartya Sen.[43] His capabilities approach is an economic theory with strong resonance for human rights given it relates to social welfare. This was developed with and by others including Martha Nussbaum,[44] and found support within the UN, influencing the UN Human Development Index.[45] This annual index was created as a summary measure of achievement in key areas of human development. For examples, health is measured by life expectancy at birth; education by average years of schooling. This is a longitudinal measurement as well as a snapshot. It is drawn on in other work by the UN Development Programme (UNDP) including the millennium development goals and now the sustainable development goals.

An awareness of economics and the status of development of a state can also have an impact on understanding the feasibility of a rights holder claiming his or her rights, or even being in a position vulnerable to possible violations

Fragility_Human_Rights.pdf, accessed 17 February 2017. This in itself is controversial as the World Bank has been declared a human rights free zone by the UN Special Rapporteur on extreme poverty and human rights – see for a detailed analysis, Philip Alston, *Report of the Special Rapporteur on Extreme Poverty and Human Rights*, UN Doc A/70/274, 4 August 2015.

41 The UN Guiding Principles on Business and Human Rights: Implementing the United Nations 'Promote, respect, remedy' Framework, annexed to the report of the Special representative of the Secretary-General on Human rights and Business, UN Doc A/HRC/17/31, endorsed by the UN Human Rights Council in Resolution A/HRC/RES/17/4 (2011).

42 Margot Salomon, Arne Tostensen and Wouter Vandenhole (eds) *Casting the Net Wider: Human Rights, Development and New Duty-Bearers* (Cambridge: Intersentia, 2007).

43 Amartya Sen, *Development as Freedom* (Oxford: Oxford University Press, 2001); *Commodities and Capabilities* (New York: Elsevier, 1985).

44 Martha Nussbaum, *Creating Capabilities: The Human Development Approach* (Boston: Harvard University Press, 2013).

45 See www.hdr.undp.org, accessed 7 February 2017.

of human rights.[46] This context is important when trying to evaluate vulnerability. It can also be a reality indicator when determining the possibility of an individual claiming his or her rights. Lack of money when claiming rights through an expensive court process indicates a problem, for example, and a researcher using HRBA needs to be aware of this if the (or an) objective of the research is to focus on supporting rights holders.

5 Balancing approaches

As the foregoing comments and the following chapters demonstrate, there is almost no limit to the methods which can be used for human rights research. New theories emerge from reflecting on history, reconceptualising the present and developing towards the future. The influential work on the capabilities approach to development by Amartya Sen[47] and Martha Nussbaum alluded to above is an example.[48]

Human rights is inevitably interdisciplinary and research on it can be interdisciplinary or even multidisciplinary. This offers substantial benefits for those seeking to build research. There is as much to be gained by exploring an issue from a range of different perspectives as from integrating a mixed methods approach. For example, exploring the early twenty-first-century challenges of violence against women and children, trafficking in human beings or irregular migration practices could be undertaken using any of the methods in this book, or any number of methods not discussed or only touched upon briefly. Each approach brings its own strengths and weaknesses; each contributes to an understanding of human rights, the capacities and capabilities of rights holders or duty bearers and each can be guided by the principles of human rights embodied in the core instruments. What is important for a HRBA research project is the time and care taken to reflect on the research, its purpose, its conduct and its impact.

What perhaps can be identified as particular (if not unique) to a HRBA research is the end goal of making a tangible difference, whether by influencing government or strengthening the capacities and understanding of rights holders whose rights may be compromised. From the development based human rights approach, the do no harm principle obviously prevails as does the idea of leaving no one behind.[49]

46 Paul Hunt, Manfred Nowak, and Siddiq Osmani, *Human Rights and Poverty Reduction: A Conceptual Framework* (Geneva: OHCHR, 2004), http://www.ohchr.org/Documents/Publications/PovertyReductionen.pdf, accessed 17 February 2017.
47 Amartya Sen, *Development as Freedom* (Oxford: Oxford University Press, 1999).
48 Martha Nussbaum, *Women and Human Development: The Capabilities Approach* (New York: Cambridge University Press, 2000).
49 UN Sustainable Development Goals (www.un.org/sustainabldevelopment/sustainable-development-goals, accessed 17 February 2017), in *UN Transforming our World: the 2030 Agenda for Sustainable Development*, UN Doc A/RES/70/1.

Further reading

UN Common Understanding on Human Rights Based Approaches to Development Co-operation, http://hrbaportal.org/the-human-rights-based-approach-to-development-cooperation-towards-a-common-understanding-among-un-agencies, accessed 17 February 2017.

3 The doctrinal approach in international human rights law scholarship

Suzanne Egan

1 Introduction

Studies reveal that academics who engage in doctrinal research in the discipline of law rarely describe their reasons for doing so or how they go about it.[1] Perhaps this is because doctrinal research does not lend itself to straightforward explanation but rather is a genre of research 'that is largely intuitively, rather than rationally, understood amongst lawyers and researchers'.[2] Doctrinal legal research in the field of international human rights scholarship appears to be no different: while this method of research infuses a great deal of human rights scholarship, there is a dearth of reflection on its intrinsic value, or indeed purpose in the field, and even less concrete instruction on what it entails in terms of its methodological requirements. In an attempt to fill this lacuna, this chapter begins with an overview of the doctrinal method in general terms, highlighting its strengths as well as its weaknesses. It goes on to consider the specific challenges facing the doctrinal analyst when researching in the field of international human rights, before analysing some concrete examples of the doctrinal method in action in this context.

2 What is the doctrinal method?

The doctrinal method of legal research has been described as the 'core legal research method'[3] and indeed the 'core of legal scholarship'[4] generally. Closely derived from methods of legal training developed since the Middle Ages,[5] the

---

1 See Terry Hutchinson and Nigel Duncan, 'Defining and Describing What We Do: Doctrinal Legal Research' (2012) 17 *Deakin Law Review*, 83, 98–101.
2 Brendon Murphy and Jeffrey McCabe, 'Phronetic Legal Inquiry: An Effective Design for Law and Society Research' (2015) 24 *Griffith Law Review*, 288–289.
3 Hutchinson and Duncan (n 1) 85.
4 Richard Posner, 'The Present Situation in Legal Scholarship' (1982) *Yale Law Journal*, 1113.
5 Terry Hutchinson, 'Doctrinal Research: Researching the Jury' in Dawn Watkins and Mandy Burton (eds), *Research Methods in Law* (Abingdon: Routledge, 2013) 7, 10 and see generally 9–15.

doctrinal method emphasizes the concept of 'doctrine' as a source of law that can only be discovered through close analysis of authoritative texts intrinsic to the discipline of law. At its most basic level, the doctrinal scholar's endeavour in diverse legal contexts can be expressed very simply in the research question: *'what is* the law?'[6] His or her focus is consequently aimed in the first instance at parsing the law from the density of rules, legislation, case law and possibly scholarly materials that may apply to a particular issue being examined. At a practical level, the method involves 'the careful reading and comparison of appellate opinions with a view to identifying ambiguities, exposing inconsistencies among cases and lines of cases, developing distinctions, reconciling holdings, and otherwise exercising the characteristic skills of legal analysis'.[7]

These 'skills of legal analysis' that are regarded as necessary in applying the doctrinal method to a mass of assembled legal materials include a number of logical reasoning techniques. Where the legal principle is relatively clear from a statute, a process of *deductive* reasoning may be used (i.e. reasoning from one or more legal rules to reach a logically certain conclusion). Where it is not so clear whether an identified legal principle applies to a particular set of facts or hypothetical facts, a process of reasoning by *analogy* may be used whereby the researcher examines whether there are other factually similar cases in which the rule has been applied such that it can be concluded that the case under consideration would be treated in a similar way. In the course of such a process, the researcher may notice that a large number of cases have been decided on similar grounds such that a general principle can now be identified from those cases. Reaching such a conclusion involves a process of *inductive* reasoning (i.e. reasoning from a series of cases to generate a general principle or rule).[8] Owing to the fact that legal rules are usually expressed in very general language, there is always room for competing interpretations of particular phrases or indeed the rule itself. For this reason, the skill of the doctrinal analyst lies in applying the above techniques alone or in combination as well as applying the general canons of interpretation[9] or 'recognized patterns

---

6 Paul Chynoweth, 'Legal Research' in Andrew Knight and Les Ruddock, *Advanced Research Methods in the Built Environment* (Hoboken: Wiley-Blackwell, 2008) 28, 30.
7 This preoccupation with detail has prompted Posner to describe doctrinal scholars as 'law's talmudists': Posner (n 4).
8 Chynoweth (n 6) 32–34.
9 Domestic courts in the common law world draw on a variety of canons (basic rules or maxims) of interpretation in interpreting the meaning of legal rules or phrases in statutes. These include, for example, the rule that the court should interpret a statute according to its 'plain meaning' unless that meaning is ambiguous, in which case it may apply other canons of interpretation, such as examining the intent of the legislature. For a detailed exposition of the canons of legal interpretation in the common law, see generally Antonin Scalia and Bryan Garner, *Reading Law: The Interpretation of Legal Texts* (Eagan: West, 2012); Francis Bennion, *Understanding Common Law Interpretation: Drafting and Interpretation* (Oxford: Oxford University Press, 2009).

of reasoning employed within the legal community' as a whole in an effort to predict the outcome of future cases.[10]

Example

An example of all three of these techniques in action can be given from the realm of refugee law, which is itself a sub-set of international human rights law. Most jurisdictions in the common law world have incorporated verbatim the definition of refugee status provided for in the *Convention Relating to the Status of Refugees 1951* into their domestic law. That definition provides that a person may be considered as a refugee if he or she is able to show *inter alia* a well-founded fear of persecution on one or more of the following grounds: race, religion, nationality, membership of a particular social group or political opinion. Straight away, one may notice that the ground 'membership of a particular social group' is an amorphous term which does not lend itself to straightforward interpretation. When Ireland incorporated the definition of refugee status into its domestic law in the Refugee Act 1996, section (1) of that Act clarified that the term 'membership of a particular social group' included persons 'whose defining characteristic is their belonging to the male or female sex'. Accordingly, through a process of deductive reasoning, it could be easily inferred that a person who claimed refugee status because she feared being subjected to female genital mutilation (FGM) in her state of origin would qualify for refugee status in Ireland based on her fear of persecution because of her membership of a particular social group, i.e. her gender – as a woman who reasonably feared being subjected to FGM in her state of origin.

However, in other jurisdictions in which the social group category was not defined in legislation as in Ireland, such a claim would not necessarily be immediately deduced from the words of the legislation. Accordingly, the question of whether membership of a particular social group could include gender-based claims while assumed to be true in many quarters was still a matter of some speculation by others in the emerging field of refugee law in the 1980s.[11] Numerous articles were written by doctrinal scholars seeking to discern by analogical reasoning what factors courts and tribunals considered significant in deciding whether to recognize gender-based claims to refugee status as falling within the social group category. In the Canadian case of *AG (Canada) v Ward*, the Supreme Court of Canada conducted precisely such an exercise in the context of a very different set of facts to those concerning gender-based claims. Specifically, the Court was asked to review a judgment by a lower court denying refugee status to an Irish citizen who claimed refugee status *inter alia* on the basis of his fear of persecution by former associates

---

10 Ibid. 33.
11 See James Hathaway, *The Law of Refugee Status* (1st edn, Oxford: Butterworths, 1991) 162–163, in particular fn 192.

in a terrorist organisation of which he was formerly a member. In order to assess whether the applicant could be considered as a member of a particular social group, the Supreme Court considered numerous cases in which the social group category had previously been applied by Canadian courts and tribunals – including gender-based claims – before concluding that the term 'membership of a particular social group' includes persons who share a characteristic that is immutable or 'so fundamental to individual identity or conscience that it ought not to be required to be changed'. This is an example of *inductive reasoning* in which the Court extrapolated a general principle (or doctrine) that was common to the cases previously decided. This general principle has since been adopted and applied in several jurisdictions other than Canada and can now be considered a fundamental doctrine in the field of refugee law worldwide.

In sum, the primary characteristic of the doctrinal method is the search for coherence and clarity in all the legal materials that may have a bearing on the legal principle or dilemma under investigation.[12] Thus, it has been observed that the process of engaging in doctrinal research in an academic context involves essentially the deployment of the same skills of legal reasoning as those used by lawyers in the practising legal profession.[13] Whereas the lawyer will seek to identify the appropriate legal principle(s) or rule(s) to apply to a particular factual situation, the academic scholar's aim is usually to discern what legal rules or principles might be applicable to a wide range of hypothetical situations. As such, he or she is more likely to 'undertake a more in-depth analysis which is capable of informing the deliberations of practitioners and judges in future cases'.[14] The strong association between this methodology and the practising legal profession is probably the reason why many doctrinal scholars will describe themselves as 'academic lawyers',[15] since they usually identify more with 'the community of lawyers than with the community of scholars'.[16]

Over and above this most basic manifestation, doctrinal scholarship usually moves beyond pure exposition of the law (of the like found in 'black letter' text books) to adopting a critical stance on the law, highlighting inconsistencies in

---

12 'The finding of coherence in the given materials is seen as an important, if not *the most* important aspect of this type of scholarly work': Jan Smits, 'Redefining Normative Legal Science: Towards an Argumentative Discipline' in Fons Coomans, Fred Grünfeld and Menno T. Kamminga, *Methods of Human Rights Research* (Cambridge: Intersentia, 2009) 46.

13 Chynoweth (n 6) 32.

14 Ibid. 46.

15 Mathias M. Siems and Daithí Mac Síthigh, 'Mapping Legal Research' (2012) 71 *Cambridge Law Journal* 651, 653–654.

16 Posner (n 4) 1122; see also Smits, who argues that there is an 'intense inner relationship between legal scholars and legal practice: scholars accept a large part of what the legislators and the courts produce, while legal practice can profit from the criticism and further systematization of the law by academia': Smits (n 12) 46.

judicial decisions and possibly advocating reform or reinterpretation. As Hutchinson notes, most 'good' quality doctrinal research encompasses more than 'description, analysis, and critique, and invariably suggests ways the law could be amended or the philosophy, processes or administration of the law could be improved'.[17] In so doing, such reform-oriented doctrinal research can be described as being intrinsically normative, describing as it does not only what the law *is* in the view of its exponent but advocating what the law *ought to be*, or what the 'preferred' or 'better' view might be.[18] This additional dimension of doctrinal scholarship is one of the reasons why Van Hoecke describes it as an 'empirical-hermeneutic' as well as a normative discipline in which the researcher not only ascertains and discovers facts, but also makes normative choices about the relevance of legal texts and takes normative positions on values and interests.[19]

3 Critiques of the doctrinal method

Notwithstanding its well-established status as a dominant mode of legal research, the doctrinal method has been the subject of sustained critique, particularly in recent years.[20] At the root of this critique is the view that doctrinal analysis by its very nature is of limited value given its insular and self-referential nature. Because traditional doctrinal analysis works on the premise that law can only be understood from a close, 'objective' reading of authoritative texts, traditional doctrinal scholars implicitly view law as an autonomous system which can only be understood from within the system itself. The doctrinal method is thus described – sometimes in pejorative tones – as an 'internal method' in which as Westerman argues 'the legal system itself is not only the subject of inquiry, but its categories and concepts form the framework' and conceptual tools for the research.[21] This narrow epistemological assumption has accordingly been criticised not only for being inadequate to the task of explaining, much less understanding law, but also as having a potentially

17 Terry Hutchinson, 'The Doctrinal Method: Incorporating Interdisciplinary Methods in Reforming the Law' (2015) 3 *Erasmus Law Review* 130, 132.
18 Martha Minnow, 'Archetypal Legal Scholarship: A Field Guide' (2013) 63 *Journal of Legal Education* available at <http://www.swlaw.edu/pdfs/jle/jle631minow.pdf> accessed 7 February 2017.
19 Mark Van Hoecke, 'Legal Doctrine: Which Method(s) for What Kind of Discipline?' in Mark Van Hoecke (ed.), *Methodologies of Legal Research* (Oxford: Hart, 2013) 4, 10.
20 See generally Terry Hutchinson, 'Doctrinal Research: Researching the Jury' in Dawn Watkins and Mandy Burton (eds), *Research Methods in Law* (Abingdon: Routledge, 2013) pp. 15–17; Reza Banakar, 'Review Essay: Having One's Cake and Eating It: The Paradox of Contextualisation in Socio-Legal Research' (2011) *International Journal of Law in Context*, 487–489.
21 Pauline Westerman, 'Open or Autonomous: The Debate on Legal Methodology as a Reflection of the Debate on Law' in Hoecke, *Methodologies* (n 19) 86.

'disabling' effect on students.[22] By working within a narrow field of professional knowledge, practitioners of the doctrinal method can become shut-out from other questions that need to be answered in order to reach a clear understanding of law.

Another complexion to this essential criticism is the sceptical view expressed by detractors of the doctrinal method that its deployment in interpreting and analysing legal texts can ever be regarded as neutral, objective and value-free. As Bradney has argued 'doctrinal work has always been infused with intellectual presumptions and assumptions that have dominated the doctrinal argument even though the doctrinal argument has concealed their existence. Doctrinal method has never had the purity its partisans ascribed to it.'[23] This criticism is especially pertinent to the point at which doctrinal analysts engage in normative analysis. The risk being alluded to here is that by engaging in normative analysis without recognising or indeed acknowledging the ideological assumptions on which it is based, the analysis is likely to be shallow and unconvincing. Likewise, McCrudden points out that even the choices made by the doctrinal researcher as regards the appropriate sources of legal analysis is often contested,[24] with such choices inevitably influencing the range of interpretive and normative positions arrived at.

Undoubtedly, these critiques of the doctrinal method have contributed to the shift of thought in recent decades as to the appropriate methods of legal research. Scholars have been inspired and encouraged to eschew the purely doctrinal method in favour of other experiential methodologies examined in detail elsewhere in this collection. Smits characterises this shift as one by which the 'internal perspective towards law is increasingly replaced by an external one'.[25] Rather than focusing on legal texts as the means to explain and understand law, scholars have turned to other disciplines in the humanities to illuminate our understanding of law, as well as to the social sciences and to empirical methods of investigation to understand how it operates in wider society.[26] While this turn towards extra-legal disciplines signals an appetite to explore research questions that the doctrinal method simply cannot answer, it does not necessarily lead to the nuclear conclusion drawn by some commentators that doctrinal analysis is now entering its 'final death throes'.[27] A more realistic appraisal recognises the reciprocal value of each of these approaches in

---

22 See generally Anthony Bradney, 'Law as a Parasitic Discipline' (1998) 25 *Journal of Law and Society*, 71–84.

23 Ibid. 72.

24 Christopher McCrudden, 'Legal Research and the Social Sciences' (2006) 33 *Law Quarterly Review*, 635.

25 Smits (n 12) 47.

26 'The esteem of critical legal studies, behavioural and empirical analysis of law, law and economics and other "law and. . ." approaches are now much higher than traditional doctrinal analysis. In short, external legal research is in': Smits (n 12) 47.

27 Bradney (n 22) 71.

unpacking the meaning, function and operation of law. As Schwarz points out, both internal and external method have a role to play in current legal scholarship and neither is generally used in isolation from the other.[28] Doctrinal analysis of the content of law is often a 'first step' in an empirical project,[29] with evidence showing that extra-legal methods are being used 'to enrich the analysis of doctrine, not acting as a substitute for it'.[30]

4 Applying the doctrinal method in the international human rights context

In a recent empirical study, Eva Brems discovered that academic scholars who engage in legal human rights research seldom reflect on the method that they are using at the outset of their research projects.[31] The data which she generated from a small pool of 28 academics also revealed that despite this lack of methodological reflection, most participants indicated that they exclusively used 'desktop research'; seven stated they had no experience of interdisciplinary research; six reported drawing to a limited extent on material from other disciplines and integrating it in their own writing; six reported using a multidisciplinary approach (with two indicating it was challenging); and ten reported participating in an inter-disciplinary project with colleagues from other disciplines.[32] The vast proportion of participants also reported that their work was essentially normative in that they make statements about what should be the correct interpretation of a human rights norm.[33] Brems's findings largely mirror the trends highlighted above in academic legal scholarship generally. They demonstrate that doctrinal research is very much alive in the field of international human rights scholarship and that it is being deployed either exclusively, or increasingly in combination with other methods. Nonetheless, relatively few scholars appear to reflect or explain why they use it and how they go about it. This lacuna is ripe for explication since the field of international human rights law presents numerous challenges for the doctrinal legal scholar over and above those arising in domestic law generally. The following sections focus on a range of considerations and challenges that should be taken into account when embarking on research into international human rights law based on the doctrinal method.

28 Richard Schwarz, 'Internal and External Method in the Study of Law' (1992) 11 *Law and Philosophy*, 179, 194.
29 Hutchinson, 'Doctrinal Method' (n 17) 17.
30 Robert Ellickson, 'Trends in Legal Scholarship: A Statistical Study' (2000) 29 *Journal of Legal Studies*, 517, 524; see also Schwarz (n 28) 198; McCrudden (n 24) 650.
31 Eva Brems, 'Methods in Legal Human Rights Research' in Coomans, Grünfeld and Kamminga (n 12) 77, 90.
32 Ibid. 85–86.
33 Ibid. 86.

4a *The nature of the field of inquiry*

The first factor that should ideally be contemplated by the doctrinal researcher in the field of international human rights concerns the nature of the body of law under consideration. International human rights law is a relatively young body of law, the foundations of which emerged in reaction to the atrocities committed during the Second World War. It consists of a range of conventions, procedures and monitoring bodies which individually and collectively provide a means of holding governments accountable at the international level for the treatment of their citizens.[34] At the same time, it is important at the outset to grasp the inherent limitations of this body of law. First, it is a body of law, which as a subset of international law, is based on the consent of states. Accordingly, it is important to acknowledge that while much of the substantive law has been left wide open for interpretation, attempts to forge a consensus on the interpretation of numerous concepts of human rights law have been plagued by divergent conceptions of human rights as between nation states and rights' advocates as well as amongst different cultural communities. The increasing 'privatisation' of human rights abuses, whereby the actors are not necessarily rogue governments, but private parties or groups of individuals has simultaneously posed new challenges and contestation as to the reach of substantive law.[35] Further, the procedures on which much of the substantive law depends for implementation are often very weak. This contextual reality should always be considered at the outset of a project. As Forsythe reminds us, it is important, therefore, for legal researchers to adopt a critical stance[36] as to the nature of the body of law as an essentially decentralised system, in which legal obligation is not necessarily clear-cut and in contrast to domestic law, by no means easily enforced.

4b *Finding and choosing the appropriate sources*

Closely related to the previous consideration lies the challenge of finding and choosing the appropriate sources of international human rights law necessary to analyse a particular issue. As noted at the outset, the hallmarks of the doctrinal method involve the close analysis of authoritative texts intrinsic to the field of law being examined. In domestic law, this normally entails in the first instance identifying relevant constitutional and/or statutory provisions,

---

34 'The concept of accountability provides the overarching rationale for the establishment of an international human rights regime': Philip Alston, 'Richard Lillich Memorial Lecture: Promoting the Accountability of Members of the New UN Human Rights Council' (2005) 15 *Journal of Transnational Law & Policy*, 49, 50.

35 See generally, Andrew Clapham, *Human Rights Obligations of Non-State Actors* (Oxford: Oxford University Press, 2006).

36 David Forsythe, 'Human Rights Studies: On the Dangers of Legalistic Assumptions' in Coomans, Grünfeld and Kamminga (n 12) 59, 62.

as well as appellate case law and secondary literature (i.e. legal texts and academic articles) which may have a bearing on the legal problem or issue in question. Not only are the latter sources usually readily available to the legal researcher on modern legal databases, but it is usually reasonably clear *what* sources are applicable and *where* they may be accessed. For example, if the research concerns an issue of domestic human rights law, such as the applicability of the ECHR Act in Ireland or the HRA in the UK, the researcher can be relatively confident of the range of materials that ought to be consulted and where to find them, either in published form or by a thorough and expert search of online sources with the assistance if needs be of skilled librarians.[37] Such material would normally include, for example, the statutory provisions themselves, relevant judgments of the domestic courts and of the European Court of Human Rights, as well as pre-existing and relevant academic commentary. Undoubtedly, the decision to incorporate *further* sources, beyond domestic case law and statutes, as McCrudden has noted, can be highly contentious.[38] Certainly, if the gaze of the researcher turns to the wider international stage, for example, by considering for comparative purposes, interpretations of similar legal problems/issues by other international bodies, straight away he or she is thrust into a minefield of practical and conceptual problems. Firstly, there is the practical difficulty of *finding* relevant material. The issue of accessing the jurisprudence of the UN human rights treaty bodies, for example, has long since been a significant problem for researchers in the human rights field, albeit that significant efforts have been made in recent years to ameliorate the difficulties arising.[39] If the researcher wishes to consider the Concluding Observations of one or more of the treaty bodies on a particular issue relevant to a particular state, and/or the views of one of the UN Special Procedures Mandate Holders, or indeed those of the Human Rights Council, he or she may find it challenging to access appropriate material without a sufficiently knowledgeable grasp of how to search UN websites.

Over and above this practical difficulty, however, is the issue of the legal value and authority of these latter sources. Whereas the judgments of the regional human rights courts are binding on respondent states, the pronouncements of UN human rights treaty bodies are not technically legally binding. Views inevitably differ, therefore, as to the attention that should be given to the latter sources in a doctrinal legal analysis. Whereas the Concluding Observations and 'views' of the UN human rights treaty bodies on individual complaints may be regarded as 'authoritative' and persuasive statements of principle, and hence worthy of inclusion and respect in any pertinent legal

---

37 Stephanie Davidson, 'Way Beyond Legal Research: Understanding the Research Habits of Legal Scholars' (2010) 102 *Law Library Journal* 561, 566–567.
38 McCrudden (n 24) 635.
39 See UNHCHR, 'Report on Strengthening the United Nations Human Rights Treaty System' (2012) 71, para 4.3.3.

analysis,[40] many have highlighted flaws in the quality of reasoning, accuracy of treaty body outputs[41] and even the very legitimacy of these outputs.[42] In this respect, the doctrinal analyst must tread a fine line in evaluating and representing the significance of treaty bodies views – i.e. whether they indicate a rule of *lex lata* or *lex ferenda*. In other words, whereas traditional doctrinal analysis of case law and academic commentary in fields of domestic law involves the researcher in assessing the weight and cogency of *reasons* given by judges or fellow academics for reaching particular conclusions, research in the field of international human rights law requires the researcher to further grapple with, and ultimately rate the very authority of those sources.

Trickier still will be the attempt to ascertain whether a rule or principle of international human rights law has the status of customary international law. If this can be credibly established, it will mean that the rule will be legally binding on all states, regardless of treaty commitments or lack thereof. The task of identifying a principle of customary international law, however, is highly demanding as it requires the researcher to establish that state practice[43]

---

40 See, for example, the statement of the Human Rights Committee which monitors implementation of the International Covenant on Civil and Political Rights as regards the authority of its views on individual petitions: 'While the function of the Human Rights Committee in considering individual communications is not, as such, that of a judicial body, the views issued by the Committee under the Optional Protocol exhibit some important characteristics of a judicial decision. They are arrived at in a judicial spirit, including the impartiality and independence of Committee members, the considered interpretation of the language of the Covenant, and the determinative character of the decisions': UN Human Rights Committee 'General Comment 33 on the Obligations of States Parties Under the Optional Protocol to the International Covenant on Civil and Political Rights' (5 November 2008) UN doc CCPR/C/GC/33 para 11; see also Dominic McGoldrick, *The Human Rights Committee: Its Role in the Development of the International Covenant on Civil and Political Rights* (Oxford: Oxford University Press, 1991) 151; The ICCPR has been described as 'the pre-eminent interpreter of the ICCPR which is itself legally binding' and whose decisions are 'therefore strong indicators of legal obligations, so rejection of those decisions is good evidence of a State's bad faith attitude towards its ICCPR obligations': Sarah Joseph and Melissa Castan, *The International Covenant on Civil and Political Rights: Cases, Materials and* Commentary (Oxford: Oxford University Press, 2004) p. 24; see also Christian Tomuschat, 'Evolving Procedural Rules: The United Nations Human Rights Committee's First Two Years of Dealing with Individual Communications' (1980) 1 *Human Rights Law Journal*, 249, 255; 'The concluding observations of the treaty bodies have been characterized as an 'opportunity for delivery of an authoritative overview of the state of human rights in a country and for the delivery of forms of advice which can stimulate systemic improvements'. Micahel O'Flaherty, 'The Concluding Observations of United Nations Human Rights Treaty Bodies' (2006) 6 *Human Rights Law Review*, 27.

41 See for example Dennis: '. . .it is not at all clear that the international human rights treaty bodies have the expertise capacity to resolve complex questions of treaty interpretation': Michael Dennis, 'Non-Applicability of Civil and Political Rights Treaties Extraterritorially During Times of International Armed Conflict' (2007) 40 *Israel Law Review*, 453, 459.

42 See generally Suzanne Egan, *The UN Human Rights Treaty System: Law and Procedure* (London: Bloomsbury, 2011) 5.

43 Villiger defines state practice as 'any act, articulation or other behaviour of a State, as long as the behaviour in question discloses the State's conscious attitude with respect to its

indicating the existence of a rule ('custom') is consistent as between states; and second, that there is a belief on the part of states adhering to the practice that the practice is in some sense obligatory (*opinio juris*).[44] Sufficient state practice is assumed to exist where there is evidence of sufficient state practice, consensus in academic literature or in decisions of international tribunals.[45] Clearly this may be contentious and occasionally the doctrinal analyst may be accused of simply assuming the existence of a rule without providing the empirical evidence necessary to establish its existence.[46]

4c Applying the relevant canons of interpretation

As noted above, in order to engage in doctrinal research in fields of domestic law, the doctrinal researcher must be *au fait* with the accepted canons of interpretation and patterns of reasoning normally applied by domestic courts. In a similar way, the doctrinal analyst of international human rights law must be prepared to grapple with the methods and canons of interpretation deployed by relevant international human rights bodies in interpreting their parent treaties.[47] The task of interpretation, however, and the related effort to predict

recognition of a customary rule'. Mark Villiger, *Customary International Law and Treaties* (Leiden: Martinus Nijhoff, 1985) 4. On the difficulties in identifying 'state practice', see Jörg Kammerhofer, 'Uncertainty in the Formal Sources of International Law: Customary International Law and Some of its Problems' (2004) *European Journal of International Law*, 523.

44 *North Sea Continental Shelf Cases*, ICJ Reports (1969) para 74.

45 Ian Brownlie, *The Rule of Law in International Affairs* (Leiden: Martinus Nijhoff, 1998) 21.

46 See, for example, the critique made by Kay Hailbronner of Professor Guy Goodwin-Gill's doctrinal argument to the effect that the principle of *non-refoulement* in Article 33(1) of the Convention Relating to the Status of Refugees (which prohibits states parties from returning a refugee to any country in which her life or freedom is threatened on account of her race, religion, nationality, particular social group or political opinion) had by 1986 attained the status of customary international law: Guy Goodwin-Gill, 'Non-Refoulement and the New Asylum-Seekers' (1986) 26 *Virginia Journal International Law*, 897; Kay Hailbronner, 'Non-Refoulement and Humanitarian Refugees: Customary International Law or Wishful Legal Thinking?' (1986) 26 *Virginia Journal of International Law*, 857; for further commentary on the difference of opinion expressed by the latter two scholars, see Francesco Messineo, 'Non-Refoulement Obligations in Public International Law: Towards a New Protection Status?' in Satvinder S. Juss (ed.), *The Ashgate Research Companion To Migration Law, Theory And Policy* (Aldershot: Ashgate, 2013) 129–155.

47 While is not necessary to examine in this context, it is interesting to note that the question of the extent to which international human rights may be considered a 'specialised regime' of international law such as would entitle human rights bodies to invoke special interpretive rules beyond the Vienna Convention on the Law of Treaties is (ironically) a question that is not free from controversy amongst doctrinal scholars. See generally Başak Çali, 'Treaty Interpretation, 21 Specialized Rules of Treaty Interpretation: Human Rights' in Duncan B Hollis (ed), *The Oxford Guide to Treaties* (Oxford: Oxford University Press, 2012) p. 525; Malgosia Fizmaurice, 'Interpretation of Human Rights Treaties' in

outcomes of cases is a complex one, given the particular characteristics inherent in international human rights treaties. These include the fact that human rights treaties do not contain reciprocal obligations as between states (like most international treaties) but rather create obligations on all states vis-à-vis individuals; and second, human rights treaties are usually very general in their wording. Consequently, the scope of particular rights and the extent of state obligation in respect of them are frequently by no means clear from the texts of the treaties and often lend themselves to very subjective interpretations.

Thus, in approaching the task of interpretation it appears that all human rights bodies have recognised the applicability of the rules of treaty interpretation contained in Articles 31 and 32 of the *Vienna Convention on the Law of Treaties*, 1969.[48] Each subscribe to the principle expressed in Article 31 that a treaty must be interpreted in 'good faith in accordance with the ordinary meaning to be given to the terms of the treaty in their context and in the light of its object and purpose'.[49] This provision has spawned a range of expansive interpretive techniques, in particular the adoption by all such bodies to varying degrees of a robust teleological approach to interpretation,[50] dynamic or evolutive interpretation,[51] as well as comparative approaches in interpreting the scope and application of particular rights.[52] The European Court of Human Rights has further developed its specific 'margin of appreciation' doctrine in determining the scope of rights in the European Convention on Human

Dinah Sheldon (ed.), *The Oxford Handbook of International Human Rights Law* (Oxford: Oxford University Press, 2013) 739.

48 Vienna Convention on the Law of Treaties (23 May 1969) 1155 UNTS 331 (hereafter VCLT).

49 Article 32 VCLT provides further that supplementary means of interpretation (including the drafting history of the treaty and the circumstances of its conclusion) may be used to confirm an interpretation reached by the application of Article 31, or to determine the meaning when the interpretation according to Article 31: (a) leaves the meaning ambiguous or obscure; or (b) leads to a result which is manifestly absurd or unreasonable.

50 Thus, the European Court of Human Rights regularly emphasizes the importance of making the rights contained in the ECHR 'practical and effective' and in some instances has identified rights and 'positive obligations' of states not specifically contained in the Convention. See for example, *Artico v Italy* (1980) 3 EHRR 1 para 33; The African Commission on Human and People's Rights has done so by identifying certain 'unenumerated' rights in the African Charter of Human and Peoples Rights. See *Social and Economic Rights Action Centre (SERAC) and Another v Nigeria*, African Commission on Human and Peoples' Rights, Comm Nos 155/96 (2001); while the Inter-American Court of Human Rights expresses the principle in perhaps the strongest of terms in its *pro homine* approach, according to which it favours an interpretation of the text that favours the individual: *Tradesmen v Colombia* (5 July 2004) IACtHR (Ser. C) No 109 para 173.

51 The Court first applied this technique in the case of *Tyrer v United Kingdom* (1979) 2 EHRR 1 para 31; see further *Vo v France* (2005) 40 EHRR 12 para 82; *Mamatkulov and Askarov v Turkey* (2005) 41 EHRR 25 para 121.

52 See *Demir and Baykara v Turkey* (2009) 48 EHRR 54 para 85.

Rights or restricting their enjoyment in particular circumstances.[53] The application of each of these interpretive techniques, alone or in combination, by particular human rights bodies provides a challenging context and a rich source of critique in many instances for the doctrinal analyst.

4d Acknowledging the theoretical perspective

The critique raised earlier to the effect that doctrinal scholars sometimes fail to acknowledge the theoretical, ideological or value-perspective on which their analysis is based applies *a fortiori* to doctrinal scholarship in the field of international human rights. Peters has convincingly argued that 'all academic activity is inescapably political' and a 'complete value-free academic activity appears impossible because any kind of statement and any interpretation are pre-structured by the speaker's *Vorverständnis*' (i.e. prior-understanding).[54] Brems's empirical study on the methodological approaches of a discrete group of human rights scholars appears to bear out this critique insofar as many of the participants admitted that they 'generally work on the tacit assumption that their research should contribute to a better protection and promotion of human rights.'[55] Just as states are inclined to interpret legal rules in a narrow way in order to suit their own interests, it is hardly surprising that the natural tendency of most international human rights scholars will be to interpret the law in a way that best promotes the interests of the individual. However, the danger of not acknowledging this conscious (or perhaps sometimes unconscious) bias is that it may serve to threaten the quality of the reasoning and hence the value of the research. As Antonio Cassese maintains '[w]hat matters . . .is that he or she [the scholar] should make it explicit and clear that the choice between two conflicting values is grounded in a personal slant or bias, and not in any "objective" legal precedence of one value over the other'.[56]

5 Doctrinal research in practice

Having outlined the nature of the doctrinal research method and the particular challenges involved in applying it in the international human rights field, it may be helpful for the reader to consider some specific examples of the method

53 There is extensive commentary on the margin of appreciation doctrine in academic literature. For a good overview and reference to other literature, see Council of Europe, 'The Margin of Appreciation' <http://www.coe.int/t/dghl/cooperation/lisbonnetwork/themis/echr/paper2_en.asp> accessed 7 February 2017.
54 Mary Peters, 'Realizing Utopia as a Scholarly Endeavour' (2013) 24 *European Journal of International Law*, 533, 542.
55 Brems (n 31) 24–26.
56 Antonio Cassese, *Five Masters of International Law: Conversations with R-J Dupuy, E Jiménez de Aréchaga, R Jennings, L Henkin and O Schachter* (Oxford: Hart, 2011) p. 259 cited in Peters (n 54) 542.

in action in this context. The three pieces considered in this section are examples of the doctrinal method in action, each focusing to varying degrees on the legal principle established in the seminal case of *Soering v United Kingdom*.[57] Adjudicated on by the European Court of Human Rights (ECtHRts) in 1989, the case involved a German national who was being detained in Britain, pending extradition to the US where he faced capital murder charges in the State of Virginia. The essence of his claim, which was accepted by the Court, was that if the UK were to extradite him to the US, it would be acting in violation of Article 3 of the European Convention on Human Rights by exposing him to 'inhuman or degrading treatment' within the meaning of Article 3. The 'inhuman or degrading treatment' at issue in this case was the 'death row phenomenon' in operation in the State of Virginia in which he might have been detained for some 6–8 years. In the course of a wide-ranging judgment, the Court ruled that:

> [t]he decision by a Contracting State to extradite a fugitive may give rise to an issue under Article 3 (art. 3), and hence engage the responsibility of that State under the Convention, where substantial grounds have been shown for believing that the person concerned, if extradited, faces a real risk of being subjected to torture or to inhuman or degrading treatment or punishment in the requesting country.[58]

Reading 1

R.B. Lillich (1991) 'The Soering Case', *American Journal of International Law*, 85: 128–149.

This first piece by Lillich is a classic example of a case-note on the *Soering* case which typically involves a doctrinal analysis of a significant judgment from a particular court, including its likely implications for the future. In this example, Lillich first explains the facts that gave rise to the *Soering* case, before setting forth its journey from the domestic courts to the ECtHRts. A crucial stepping stone in this journey at that time was the requirement that an individual complaint under the ECHR must first be made to the (now defunct) European Commission on Human Rights. During its lifetime, the role of the Commission was to screen complaints for their admissibility under the Convention's admissibility criteria and if admissible, to render a legal opinion on the merits of the case before the case could be referred to the ECtHRts for a legally binding judgment. Lillich's case-note thus begins by outlining the legal reasoning of the Commission which clearly influenced the reasoning of the Court in its assessment of the appropriate legal principle to apply to the

57 (1989) 11 EHRR 439.
58 Ibid. para 91.

facts before it. His outline of the Court's reasoning also makes reference to the legal arguments of the parties before the Court, which he himself acknowledges 'helps to parse a court's judgment'.[59] These techniques thus help the reader to understand how the Court arrived at its ground-breaking statement of principle and how it differed from the Commission in applying that principle to the facts before it.

In evaluating the Court's judgment, Lillich highlights some possible implications of the Court's judgment for the wider application of the Convention, including the likelihood that the principle would be applied to all forms of expulsion, as well as in respect of other articles of the Convention, such as the fair trial guarantee in Article 6, as well as in respect of Articles 2, 4, 5 and 7 ECHR.[60] He also considers its wider ramifications in respect of extradition law generally and ratification by the US of other international human rights treaties.[61] Readers should note another typical trait of doctrinal analysis drawn on by Lillich whereby he uses extensive footnotes not just for citation purposes, but to point the reader to further sources as well as interesting information to supplement the core narrative. The true value of Lillich's thorough-going analysis for practitioners as well as academics alike is amply demonstrated by the fact that many of his predictions as regards the likely trajectory of the *Soering* judgment were confirmed in later judgments of the ECtHRts.[62]

Reading 2

> Irish Human Rights Commission (IHRC) (2007) 'Extraordinary Rendition: A Review of Ireland's Human Rights Obligations', IHRC Review Report. Dublin: IHRC. <http://www.ihrec.ie/publications/list/ihrc_rendition_report_final> accessed 7 February 2017.

While not an academic piece *per se*, this Review produced by the Irish Human Rights Commission (IHRC) of Ireland's human rights obligations in respect of the practice of 'extraordinary rendition' provides a useful example of how the theoretical/ideological perspective adopted by the doctrinal analyst can have a huge impact on the ensuing analysis. By way of context, it is important to point out that the IHRC was, at the time that the Review was published, the statutory body established by the Irish government with a mandate *inter alia* to keep under review the adequacy and effectiveness of law and practice in Ireland relating to human rights and to make recommendations to

59 Ibid. 140.
60 Ibid. 142–143.
61 Ibid. 145–147.
62 See for example, *Cruz Varas v Sweden* (1992) 14 EHRR 1; *Chahal v United Kingdom* (1996) 23 EHRR 413; *Ocalan v Turkey* (2005) 41 EHRR 45; *El-Masri v Former Yugoslav Republic of Macedonia* (2013) 57 EHRR 25.

government in relation to measures that can be taken to strengthen and protect human rights in the state.[63] The impetus for the Review was the emergence
of extensive reports by NGOs and inter-governmental bodies that Shannon
airport in the west of Ireland had been used for re-fuelling purposes by CIA
airplanes engaged in extraordinary rendition. Before publishing its Review
report in 2007, the Commission had engaged in an extensive dialogue on
the matter, both in written correspondence and in a formal meeting with
officials of the Irish government, details of which are reproduced in a series
of Appendices attached to the Review. Bearing in mind the perspectives of
each of the 'parties' to this dialogue, therefore, it is instructive for the reader
to compare how the legal conclusions differ between them based on their
interpretations of the relevant law.

While the Commission interprets the case law of the UN treaty bodies in
respect of the guarantee to prevent torture and other ill-treatment, and that of
the ECHR (including the judgment in *Soering*) expansively through a lens
that undoubtedly emphasizes the protection of individual rights; the responses from the Irish government, on the other hand, emphasize the limits on
the scope of the state's positive obligations reflected in the case law while
simultaneously denying the application of the case law to the facts. Further,
while the IHRC reinforces its view of the implications of the case law with
references to the views of the UN Special Rapporteur on Torture and Other
Cruel, Inhuman and Degrading Treatment or Punishment as well as that of
the Council of Europe's High Commissioner for Human Rights, their views
on the matter are never mentioned in the government's response. While the
perspectives of each of the IHRC and the government in this instance are
clearly implicit in each of their mandates, the piece is a sobering reminder to
the academic researcher of the need to declare his or her particular theoretical
perspective in order to enhance the credibility of the analysis arrived at.

Reading 3

> M. Jackson (2016) 'Freeing Soering: The ECHR, State Complicity in
> Torture, and Jurisdiction', *European Journal of International Law*, 27(3):
> 817.

This final article by Jackson is an example *par excellence* of pure doctrinal
analysis in the field of international human rights law which incorporates all
of the specific qualities identified earlier in Section 4 of this chapter. In the
Introduction to the article, the author notes the emergence of a phenomenon
whereby states parties to the ECHR have been implicated in the torture of
individuals by a foreign state, often in circumstances where the torture takes
place *outside* the territory of the ECHR state. In Section 2(A) and (B), the

---

63 Irish Human Rights Commission Act (2000), Section 2.

author points to a potential gap in 'orthodox' rules of international law and indeed in current understanding of what falls within the meaning of a state's 'jurisdiction' under Article 1 ECHR that might lead to the conclusion that a violation of the Convention could not be established vis-à-vis the ECHR state in those precise circumstances. The rest of the article interrogates that assumption and essentially asks: is the apparent assumption of the existing law necessarily correct? Or could there be an alternative interpretation of existing law that would cover the type of situation identified?

In Section 2(C), the author reveals the theoretical basis and strong policy reasons on which his analysis is based, i.e. that there are strong moral as well as legal reasons why states should be held responsible for complicity in torture regardless of where the torture actually takes place and that the apparent 'gap' in the law is an 'unprincipled' one. This theoretical position clearly informs the central argument which Jackson goes on to make throughout Section 3 as to why the rule in the seminal case of *Soering v United Kingdom* should be 're-imagined'. As Jackson notes, the principle in that case has since been 'challenged, reaffirmed, and refined' and applied to all expulsion cases. Jackson's key argument, however, is that the principle in *Soering* is not necessarily restricted to cases of expulsion (as might be the traditional understanding of the ruling in the case expounded above by Lillich) but that it *can* and *should* be understood more broadly as a broader *'preventive complicity rule'* which prohibits ECHR contracting states from facilitating a foreign state in engaging in ill-treatment. What is important is not *where* the torture takes place, but rather the degree to which the ECHR state can be considered as complicit in the principal wrong, i.e. the torture or ill-treatment. The author supports this nuanced interpretation of the *Soering* judgment by reference to a number of strands of reasoning in the case law of the ECtHRts, including its constant references to the 'absolute' nature of the prohibition on torture in Article 3 ECHR as well as its deployment of the teleological interpretive technique.

In short, Jackson's doctrinal analysis of current ECHR case law (incorporating analogical and inductive reasoning), based on a clearly articulated theoretical premise, presents a finely-tuned normative argument as to why the law can and should be interpreted to cover cases of extra-territorial complicity on the part of ECHR states. As such, the article can be characterised as a convincing attempt on the part of the author to identify a general *doctrine* of preventive complicity in the jurisprudence of the ECtHRts. In this respect, Jackson's analysis moves beyond that of the IHRC in the previous example by discerning an overarching doctrine applicable to a range of possible scenarios involving state complicity in torture.

6 Conclusion

The above analysis has sought to demystify the process of doctrinal research and to highlight some of the particular considerations which should be borne in mind when conducting doctrinal research in the international human rights sphere. In doing so, it has noted how the doctrinal method is one of the oldest research methodologies known to legal scholarship and one that is very much associated with the practising legal profession. With the upsurge in recent decades of other research methodologies, generating new modes of knowledge and understanding, doctrinal scholarship has been to some extent rather unfairly disparaged in some quarters as an inadequate research methodology for the purposes of academic scholarship. All seasoned researchers, however, know that different research questions call for different research methods.[64] The doctrinal method is clearly a valuable research technique in elucidating and critiquing the content and normative reach of law. When skilfully executed, its value lies in illuminating and critiquing legal reasoning, highlighting trends and predicting the implications of particular case law. Increasingly, doctrinal research acts as a complement to empirical research by explaining the normative assumptions on which an empirical project is based. This is particularly true in the case of international human rights scholarship in which doctrinal scholarship and social science methods very often go hand in hand in explaining the substance of human rights and the extent to which such rights are being adequately protected.

---

64 This point is eloquently made as regards the inter-play between doctrinal methods and social science methods in the field of international human rights by Hans-Otto Sano and Hatla Thelle, 'The Need for Evidence-Based Human Rights Research' in Coomans, Grünfeld and Kamminga (n 12) 93; see also Todd Landman, 'Social Science Methods and Human Rights' in Coomans, Grünfeld and Kamminga (n 12) 28.

4 Legal theory as a research methodology

Lee McConnell

1 Introduction

Researchers at all levels, from undergraduate students to those holding permanent academic posts, often feel overwhelmed as they begin to engage with legal theory. Common questions that readers will probably have asked themselves include: in which theoretical tradition is my work based? Which theory should I select in order to best advance this particular line of argument? Can I use multiple theories in the same project, and are they compatible? Which opposing theoretical perspectives do I need to respond to, and to what degree? Isn't my work already complicated enough without recourse to theory? Why should I engage with theory at all, surely it is practice that really matters? Researchers may also feel pressured to 'elbow' theory into their projects as an afterthought, following recommendations by their supervisors or colleagues. Others may feel concerned at the thought of opening a 'Pandora's box' of theoretical criticism to which they feel ill-equipped to respond, particularly if working towards a doctorate or submitting a paper to a research journal. Anxieties of this sort are experienced almost universally, and this response is understandable given the vast canon of theoretical perspectives that can be drawn upon when conducting research into human rights.

The aim of this chapter is to dispel some of these recurring concerns. It begins with some observations concerning legal theories, research questions and research methods, and the extent to which they can be seen as being relational. It then proceeds to provide a basic overview of some (but by no means all) of the theoretical perspectives that are commonly drawn upon when conducting legal research. It will draw specific examples of good practice from existing scholarship, and outline common critiques. Readers are encouraged to engage with each of the texts discussed, and to read them in conjunction with the commentary in this chapter. While all of the texts are at least indirectly relevant to human rights at the international level, it is not important that the reader has specific knowledge or is engaged in research that pertains directly to the topic addressed. Rather, readers should view this as an exercise in reading for the sake of methodology.[1] Read in this way, these works should enable readers to get a feel for the theories that might best suit their projects, and will encourage a process of self-assessment that may help bring to light the unconscious theoretical suppositions that are already embedded within their work. Reflection of this kind may also motivate readers to consider the extent to which their theoretical assumptions are 'interested', and whose interests they serve.

Few can claim to be experts in all facets of legal theory. For the purposes of this chapter, it is unimportant whether you are new to the field of jurisprudence, or have existing expertise. What is important is that readers understand that an awareness of legal theory can enhance the coherence of their arguments relating to human rights law, and can serve as a springboard to more incisive insights, connections and critiques. In addition, it is hoped that the chapter will help to expose readers' assumptions relating to the nature of law and legal reasoning that may otherwise be left uncritically accepted.

2 The relationship between theories, research questions and methods

As with many other approaches contemplated in this book, legal theory rarely operates in a vacuum. Indeed, it may be used in conjunction with empirical, comparative, and doctrinal approaches. Nonetheless, theory has significant practical consequences for every research project, whether one is conscious of them or not.[2] This is because a researcher's own theoretical assumptions concerning the nature of law will necessarily underlie the research questions they feel are exciting, relevant, and worthy of exploration, and thus, will have a direct bearing on the type of research pursued. For instance, if one is interested in analysing human rights compliance in light of the relatively weak nature of the enforcement mechanisms in place at the international level, it might be pertinent to consider theories relating to the role of coercive sanctions in the identification and validity of law.[3] This may be contrasted with approaches highlighting alternative factors inducing human rights compliance, which may stress the role of due process in enhancing the legitimacy of the law in the eyes of the relevant addressees,[4] or the influence of other forms of regulatory/governance regimes that sit outside traditional legal

1 Robert Cryer, Tamara Hervey and Bal Sokhi-Bulley, *Research Methodologies in EU and International Law* (Oxford: Hart, 2012) p. 5.
2 Andrea Bianchi, *International Law Theories* (Oxford: Oxford University Press, 2016) p. 3.
3 John Austin, *The Province of Jurisprudence Determined* (2nd edn, London: John Murray, 1832) p. 177.
4 Thomas Franck, *Fairness in International Law and Institutions* (Oxford: Oxford University Press, 1998).

frameworks.[5] These theories might then be tested, analysed or evaluated by reference to some form of empirical, comparative, or case study analysis, and vice versa. Deeper still, research projects of this type also raise potential issues concerning the relationship between legal validity and efficacy[6]; whether law is an affair of 'rules' enshrined within formal sources that are capable of constraining their addressees,[7] or whether it is entirely contingent on political and economic power and interests.[8] Such projects also allow scholars to consider whether a formal distinction between law and non-law can be realistically maintained.[9]

Thus, even the most basic research question will rely on a complex web of theoretical engagements. The depth with which these factors need to be acknowledged will depend on the precise nature of the research project, but an awareness of these features will doubtless prove beneficial in fostering the production of self-aware, reflective scholarship. This relationship between theoretical framings and research questions has been affirmed by scholars such as Cryer, Hervey and Sokhi-Bulley:

> Every legal research project begins from a theoretical basis or bases, whether such bases are articulated or not. The theoretical basis of a project will inform how law is conceptualised in the project, which in turn will determine what kinds of research questions are deemed meaningful or useful, what data is examined and how it is analysed (the method) . . . 'Method' has empirical and sociological connotations – that is, is the method a qualitative or quantitative analysis? Is it comparative? What methods of data collection are used – literature review, documentary analysis, observation, case studies, interviews? For us, 'methodology' has theoretical connotations . . . Methodology guides our thinking or questioning of, or within, that field or both.[10]

---

5 Kenneth W. Abbott and Duncan Snidal, 'Hard and Soft Law in International Governance' (2002) 54 *International Organisation*, 421; Rugider Wolfrum and Volker Röben (eds), *Legitimacy in International Law* (New York: Springer, 2008).

6 Hans Kelsen, *General Theory of Law and State* (Andres Wedberg tr.) (first published 1945, Cambridge, MA: Harvard University Press, 1949) p. 122.

7 Jean d'Aspremont, *Formalism and the Sources of International Law: A Theory of the Ascertainment of Legal Rules* (Oxford: Oxford University Press, 2012); H.L.A. Hart, *The Concept of Law* (first published 1961, 2nd edn, Oxford: Clarendon Press, 1997) p. 123.

8 Martti Koskenniemi, 'Carl Schmitt, Hans Morgenthau, and the Image of Law in International Relations' in Michael Byers (ed.), *The Role of Law in International Politics: Essays in International Relations and International Law* (Oxford: Oxford University Press, 2001) pp. 17–34; Jack L. Goldsmith and Eric A. Posner, *The Limits of International Law* (Oxford: Oxford University Press, 2005).

9 Jean d'Aspremont, 'Softness in International law: A Self-Serving Quest for New Legal Materials' (2008) 19 *European Journal of International Law*, 1075.

10 Cryer, Hervey and Sokhi-Bulley (n 1) 5.

A similar approach is taken by d'Aspremont, who suggests that no genuine distinction can be made between legal methodology and legal theory: 'legal theories are better construed as methodological packages . . . understood as a set of cognitive tools, techniques of argumentation, evaluative criteria and communicative protocols meant to secure persuasiveness within a certain audience adhering to a certain concept of law'.[11] This is a factor that is often overlooked by those engaged in legal research.

The framing of a particular research question is likely to be informed by the past experience of the researcher, and will depend on 'the kinds of questions that researchers are taught or conditioned to regard as worthwhile'.[12] There is nothing wrong with this position in principle, but some recognition of the reflexive relationship between methodology and the questions researchers seek to answer is 'an important first step to methodological and scholarly rigour'.[13] In a sense, the theoretical bases of a particular research project can be discovered through a process of reverse-engineering; through careful consideration of the key research question(s) posed by a piece of work. Different questions will engender different assumptions concerning what 'law' is as an object of study, as well as normative questions concerning the content of law or the nature of the social operation of law. Thus a reflection on the goals of one's research can prove enlightening.

> How are we to assess which method is "better"? For that we need some standard of evaluation, some way of determining which theory does a "better" job. And to answer that question, we need to ask, "A better job at *what?* What is the point of theorising about the law?" After all, we will not be able to identify a "method" of jurisprudence, unless we know what the method is being used for. One cannot decide which analytical tools are best employed until one is clear about the function and goal for which that tool is to be used. An initial step in bringing some clarity to the field of jurisprudence, therefore, is for theorists to be clear about the purpose of their analyses and to articulate the implications of that purpose for legal theory's methodology.[14]

11 Jean d'Aspremont, *Epistemic Forces in International Law* (Cheltenham: Edward Elgar Publishing, 2015) p. 178.
12 David Feldman, 'The Nature of Legal Scholarship' (1989) 52 *Modern Law Review*, 499–500.
13 Elizabeth Fisher, Bettina Lange, Eloise Scotford and Cinnamon Carlarne, 'Maturity and Methodology: Starting a Debate about Environmental Law Scholarship' (2009) 21 *Journal of Environmental Law*, 213, 241.
14 While Rappaport is principally concerned with the use of legal theory to answer normative questions, this point transcends the ascription of a particular purpose to jurisprudential thought: Aaron Rappaport, 'The Logic of Legal Theory: Reflections on the Purpose and Methodology of Jurisprudence' (2004) 73 *Mississippi Law Journal*, 559, 563.

A close examination of this kind may help to reveal the methods best suited to answering a particular research question, and even prompt new insights into the issue addressed that would otherwise have been obscured by the researcher's doctrinal predilections.

When selecting the theoretical lens that is best suited for a particular research project, it is necessary

> to define the theoretical agenda by considering the nature of the controversy besetting the practice of law for which we seek a theoretical solution . . . it is the neglect of this very issue that is responsible for the wasted years of jurisprudence.[15]

In other words, it is the nature of the problem to which the researcher is seeking an answer that is determinative of the appropriate theory (or theories). Viewed in this way, there is no need to assert the primacy or validity of one particular methodology over another[16]; all that is important is that it is defensible in the context of the aims of the research. Some might feel a sense of unease at the recognition of the inherent contingency in the adoption of theory in a piece of research. Yet, enquiry into the law and reflection on controversies arising from legal processes is clearly valuable, even absent the ability to articulate a definitive, self-contained account of the nature of law.[17] That is not to say that certain theories will not be more widely accepted or esteemed than others, and that these social factors will not be relevant and influential to researchers. Indeed, it is these considerations relating to the function or purpose of the research, as well as social factors relating to the popularity or acceptability of a theory, that provide researchers with methodological choices at all.[18]

The relationship between theories, research questions and methods having been sketched, the remainder of this chapter provides a broad overview of some of the theoretical traditions that are often applied to human rights law. As with other chapters in this book, examples will be drawn from scholarship demonstrating direct engagement with each theoretical framing in the context of international human rights. Clearly, it would be impossible to provide more than a cursory overview of each theoretical approach, and the accounts provided below are undoubtedly reductive in character. For this reason, the reader is encouraged to locate and engage directly with the sources discussed, as well as the wider reading suggested for each approach, and the more general material cited throughout addressing the nature of theoretical methodologies.

---

15 Andrew Halpin, 'The Methodology of Jurisprudence: Thirty Years Off the Point' (2006) 19 *Canadian Journal of Law & Jurisprudence*, 67, 87.
16 D'Aspremont, *Epistemic Forces* (n 11) 179–180.
17 Halpin (n 15) 92.
18 D'Aspremont, *Epistemic Forces* (n 11) 182.

A note on labels and categorisation is necessary before proceeding. Readers must be made aware that although each approach has been detailed under a separate heading, this is purely a device employed to make navigation of the text more accessible, and does not mean to imply that each tradition is discrete. Taking feminism as just one example, variants of this approach have direct links to liberal, critical and postmodern traditions, among others. Theory is very difficult to silo, and for this reason, readers are likely to notice substantial overlaps as they conduct wider reading. Similarly, the headings under which the theoretical approaches have been organised do not necessarily represent the sole descriptor for a particular perspective, nor are they to be taken as at all determinative of a particular scholar's work. As with other works of this kind, the adopted headings 'are merely a way of grouping people together in a manner which makes introductions such as those we are making manageable'.[19] Many of the scholars discussed could be brought under a myriad of alternative and even opposing headings, detailed engagement with which has not been possible owing to space constraints in this collection.

3 Natural law

Natural law is by far the oldest jurisprudential tradition. H.L.A. Hart classically defined the naturalist method as acknowledging that there are 'certain principles of human conduct, awaiting discovery by human reason, with which man made law must conform if it is to be valid'.[20] In other words, there are a number of immutable standards with which law must correspond, or at least, be compatible, and these standards provide law with its authority. To varying degrees, the substantive content of law will be affected by these standards, which may be moral, ethical, theological or secular in nature, depending on the particular strain of naturalism adopted.

For much of its history, natural law featured prominently in explanations for the validity of international law.[21] Even Hugo Grotius, often described as one of the fathers of legal positivism at the international level, maintained a dualistic method that 'depended on the assumption that there are higher norms of justice and morality'.[22] While the natural law tradition undoubtedly suffered significant setbacks in terms of its popular appeal from the eighteenth-century Enlightenment onwards, where scholars were keen to establish international law as a 'science' and rid the discipline of its apparently subjective

19 Cryer, Hervey and Sokhi-Bulley (n 1) 14.
20 Hart (n 7) 186.
21 For a detailed overview, see: Stephen C Neff, *Justice Among Nations* (London: Harvard University Press, 2014) pp. 5–136.
22 Thomas Mautner, 'Grotius and the Sceptics' (2005) 66 *Journal of the History of Ideas*, 577–578; Hendrik van Eikema Hommes, 'Grotius on Natural and International Law' (1983) 30 *Netherlands International Law Review*, 61; Hersch Lauterpacht, 'The Grotian Tradition in International Law' (1946) 23 *British Yearbook of International Law*, 1.

and indeterminate character,[23] natural law doctrines continue to feature heavily in international legal discourse. This is particularly evident in relation to human rights law, a field that gained prominence in the immediate aftermath of the Second World War, and reflected the recognition of potential dangers stemming from the strict moral relativism adopted in positivist explanations of legal validity.[24] Take, for example, the condemnation by the United Nations (UN) General Assembly of genocide, a crime that 'shocks the conscience of mankind . . . and is contrary to moral law and to the spirit and aims of the United Nations'.[25] Two years later, the adoption of the Universal Declaration on Human Rights (UDHR) emphasised 'faith in fundamental human rights, in the dignity and worth of the human person and in the equal rights of men and women'.[26] Thereafter, the substantive codification of human rights through positive law gained momentum.

It is useful at this stage to consider the following passage from Stephen Hall's article 'The Persistent Spectre: Natural Law, International Legal Order and the Limits of Legal Positivism'. For Hall, positive law is incapable of providing a complete picture of international legal reality, and has adversely affected the theory and practice of human rights law. He argues that positive law cannot be seen as the ultimate source of human rights. Rather, it merely codifies pre-existing, natural principles. Thus, the piece provides a naturalist theoretical framing, emphasising the *a priori* nature of human rights. For Hall, some recognition and reacquaintance with the 'perennial jurisprudence of natural law' in light of the 'rotting timbers of legal positivism' will be of significant benefit to the discipline.[27]

> Our natural rights . . . are fundamental components of the common good. They may be conveniently mediated by treaties and custom, but they are not *conferred* by positive law. Natural rights form part of the broad limits within which we are free to fashion positive laws. In a culture which has largely forgotten the perennial jurisprudence of the natural law and in which Enlightenment naturalism has been discredited, human rights must lead an insecure life as the hostage of positivism in its various manifestations. Notwithstanding the ambition of some social philosophies to promote government as the sole or principal dispenser or guardian of important social goods, States . . . are not the source of our natural

---

23 Jochen von Berstorff, 'German Intellectual Historical Origins of International Legal Positivism' in Jörg Kammerhofer and Jean d'Aspremont, *International Legal Positivism in a Postmodern World* (Cambridge, Cambridge University Press, 2014) p. 50.

24 Raymond Wacks, *Understanding Jurisprudence* (4th edn, Oxford, Oxford University Press, 2015) p. 28.

25 UNGA Res 96(I), 'The Crime of Genocide', 11 December 1946, UN Doc A/64/Add.1.

26 Universal Declaration of Human Rights (10 December 1948) UNGA Res. 217 A (III).

27 Stephen Hall, 'The Persistent Spectre: Natural Law, International Legal Order and the Limits of Legal Positivism' 12 (2001) *European Journal of International Law*, 269, 306.

rights. State sovereigns can facilitate the exercise of our natural rights, but cannot grant them. Similarly, States are physically capable of hindering or preventing the enjoyment of natural rights, but cannot withhold them.[28]

Other developments, such as the codification of the concept of *jus cogens* norms within the Vienna Convention on the Law of Treaties (VCLT) also invoke aspects of the natural law method.[29] Indeed, widespread recognition of the *jus cogens* character of certain human rights, including freedom from torture and inhuman treatment or punishment, further demonstrates the tension between positivism and perennial naturalism described by Hall. Andrea Bianchi highlights this link in his article 'Human Rights and the Magic of *Jus Cogens*':

> René Dupuy, at the time a member of the Holy See's delegation to the Vienna Conference, accurately noted that the inclusion of Article 53 in the VCLT sanctioned the positivisation of natural law. In other words, to have codified in a treaty a normative category with an open-ended character, the content of which could only become intelligible by reference to some natural law postulates, was tantamount to dignifying the latter's otherwise uncertain foundation by granting it the status of positive law. By opening her box, Pandora let uncontrollable forces into the word, which have profoundly affected the structure and functioning of international law.[30]

Finally, the notion of 'inherent dignity' features prominently in human rights discourse, a factor charted by McCrudden. While not overtly naturalist, and wary of attempts to move beyond any 'minimum notion of human dignity' in the human rights context, the article clearly engages with and critiques elements of natural law methodology, and the role it plays in human rights adjudication.

> I am *not* arguing . . . that there is no coherent extra-legal conception of dignity which could form the basis of a common transnational legal approach. The problem is rather the opposite: as the historical examination of the development of dignity indicated, there are several conceptions of dignity that one can choose from, but one cannot coherently hold all of these conceptions at the same time. Dignity appears to become other

---

28 Ibid. 301–302; cf Samantha Besson, 'Human Rights: Ethical, Political . . . or Legal?' in Donald Earl Childress, *The Role of Ethics in International Law* (Cambridge, Cambridge University Press, 2012) p. 211.

29 For reflections on the methodology underlying *jus cogens* norms see: Mary Ellen O'Connell, 'Jus Cogens: International Law's Higher Ethical Norms' in Childress (n 28) 93–97.

30 Andrea Bianchi, 'Human Rights and the Magic of *Jus Cogens*' (2008) 19 *European Journal of International Law*, 491–493.

than impossibly vague only when it is tethered to a coherent community of interpretation. It could be, therefore, that the interpretation of dignity within Catholic social doctrine, or within a social democratic framework, or within an Islamic framework, or within the Jewish tradition, or based on Kant, might fulfil this role. But none of these currently provides a consensus conception of the legal use of dignity, and I am sceptical whether any of these could really provide a secure foundation for its judicial application in the future. When any one of these conceptions is adopted, dignity loses its attractiveness as a basis for generating consensus with those who do not share that tradition.[31]

It is not suggested that the above theorists subscribe to natural law theory in all aspects. Bianchi in particular is engaged in an evaluative contextualisation of the operation of natural law concepts in international law. Nonetheless, the topics addressed by this research engage directly with the naturalist methodological tradition. Hall highlights the potential benefits that might stem by embracing legal recourse to natural law doctrine, whereas Bianchi and McCrudden are far more cautious. Indeed, the latter scholars make express recourse to the potential pitfalls of the method, such as the difficulty in establishing the precise nature of the apparently immutable principles said to underscore the method, the indeterminacy and subjectivity that can bleed into the law by engagement with principles that lie beyond positive determination, and the difficulties in reconciling local or regional conceptions of supposedly universal values. It is impossible here to engage in a detailed discussion of these common critiques, but the continued invocation of natural law doctrines in the context of human rights sustains the relevance of this theory in legal scholarship.

4 Positivism

In contrast to natural law, legal positivism is a theoretical tradition that sees no necessary connection between the validity of law and its compatibility with moral, ethical or theological principles. While law may often enshrine standards that we consider to be of a moral or ethical nature, this is not the reason for the validity of those laws. Instead, the validity of law lies elsewhere. For the classical positivists of the late-eighteenth and early-nineteenth century, the validity of international law lay in the consent of territorial states, expressed via the ratification of treaties or through their participation in the formulation of customary international law.[32] Viewed in this way, the validity

---

31 Christopher McCrudden, 'Human Dignity and Judicial Interpretation of Human Rights' (2008) 19 *European Journal of International Law*, 656, 723–724.

32 Roland Portmann, *Legal Personality in International Law* (Cambridge, Cambridge University Press, 2010) p. 61; Martti Koskenniemi, *The Gentle Civiliser of Nations: The Rise and Fall of International Law 1870–1960* (Cambridge, Cambridge University Press, 2002) p. 204.

of law arises via adherence to predetermined procedures in the creation of formally recognised sources of law. Thus, positivists are principally concerned with the *identification* and *description* of law and legal processes – their theory is not contingent upon normative arguments as to what the substantive content of law ought to be. Any research project that operates on the assumption that there are formally identifiable, 'pedigree' sources of law, and that engages in a detailed doctrinal analysis of these sources, will engage positivist methodology.[33]

The proliferation of 'soft law' and governance regimes falling outside of formal legal sources, which are often aimed at achieving recognition and observance of human rights by particular sectors of society or by non-State actors, throws up a number of issues from the perspective of legal positivism. Scholars such as d'Aspremont have sought to develop a modernised account of the positivist objection to soft law instruments of this kind (soft *instrumentum*). Yet, as we have already seen, even formal sources of human rights law might lead to the inclusion of indeterminate concepts such as 'dignity'. In this respect, d'Aspremont is also able to analyse 'soft' nature of formal sources of international law or as he terms it 'soft *negotium*'.

> [N]umerous treaties nowadays enshrine such a soft *negotium*. One of the most obvious examples is provided by the 1995 Council of Europe Framework convention on the protection of national minorities, which deliberately falls short of defining the concept of minorities, leaving it to the parties to determine whether there are national minorities on their territory. Such (parts of) conventions and the (scope of) application is to be determined by the parties are said to be 'potestative'. They have no normative character, as they fail to provide any directive as to which behaviour the parties should adopt irrespective of their own will . . . [T]he use of the expression 'soft law' to designate these norms which are not cast in normative terms naturally presupposes, of course, that the existence of specific obligations is neither a constitutive element of any legal act nor a condition of the validity of any legal act. Because these acts are legal acts which are entirely valid, they can, even from the positivist vantage point . . . be considered to be law. The absence of normative character, however, requires that their legal character be qualified. The adjective 'soft' may play such a qualifying role.[34]

While the above description of legal positivism may lead the reader to conclude that it is a rather dry, static and conservative methodology, this is

---

33 For a detailed overview of positivist methodology in international law, see: Mónica García-Salmones Rovira, *The Project of Positivism in International Law* (Oxford, Oxford University Press, 2013).

34 D'Aspremont, 'Softness' (n 9) 1085–1086.

not the case. Indeed d'Aspremont's exposition on soft law permits him to analyse the motivations behind proponents of the movement, who are essentially
seeking to artificially 'enlarge the object of their science and consider international law as anything with an international dimension'.[35] Thus, while legal
positivism is, at its core, a descriptive methodology concerned with identifying
and explaining the nature of law, there is no reason why this cannot serve as a
foundation to explore normative arguments relating to the development of
law and legal scholarship.[36]

   This is an approach I have attempted to adopt in my own research, centring
on the extension of directly binding international human rights obligations
to multinational corporations. This work adopts Hans Kelsen's *Pure Theory of
Law*,[37] a modern positivist model that is highly critical of dominant, consent-
based positivism, which has led to a conflation between the subjects of international human rights laws and the creators of those obligations. This doctrine
has restricted the extension of obligations to actors that are not able to formally consent to treaty law, or to engage in the formulation of customary
international law. Kelsenian positivism permits human rights law to break
from this contractarian rationale:

> [The Pure Theory of Law] is premised on a strict methodological separa-
> tion between 'is' and 'ought'. It views legal orders as hierarchal systems of
> 'norms'. A norm describes a behaviour that *ought* to occur, as entirely
> distinct from the actual exercise or fulfilment of the act prescribed. Thus,
> while a legal rule might provide that 'all murders are to be punished', this
> rule says nothing about whether all murderers are actually caught,
> convicted and sanctioned. Legal norms are simply prescriptive statements;
> their validity is not contingent upon facts . . . [T]his method distinguishes
> itself from contractarian explanations of validity advanced in dominant
> positive scholarship. Such an approach would violate the *is/ought* dicho-
> tomy by utilising an *is* (the factually conceived State) to explain the
> validity of an *ought* (legal norms). A State is not an area of territory, a
> government, a permanent population, or an amalgam of these properties.
> It is the *rule* defining a State's territory that is relevant to the study of law,
> rather than the actual territory. According to this view, States are like all
> legal persons; they are personified bundles of rights and duties ultimately
> addressing individuals . . . Legal persons are merely devices employed to
> describe legal phenomena, in particular the referral or imputation of

35 Ibid. 1088.
36 Halpin (n 15) 92.
37 Hans Kelsen, *The Pure Theory of Law* (Max Knight tr.) (2nd edn, Berkeley, CA: University
of California Press, 1970).

norms regulating human behaviour to an 'order' or 'corporation'. This includes, but is not necessarily limited to, States.[38]

The consequences of Kelsen's positivist account of international legal personality serve as a springboard to discuss matters of shared responsibility for breaches of human rights obligations by States and non-State actors, the spatial delimitation of human rights obligations, and enforcement mechanisms at the international level. Taken in this way, positivism can be viewed as a potentially progressive force, capable of expanding the addressees of human rights beyond the traditionally recognised subjects of international law.

As a final observation, classical positivist descriptions of the character of law have proven problematic when exported to the international level. John Austin's characterisation of law as a system of sovereign commands backed by coercive sanctions caused him to doubt the legal quality of international law,[39] given its decentralised law-making processes and weak enforcement mechanisms. While Hart resolutely dismissed the necessity of coercive sanctions to the characterisation of law,[40] others (including Kelsen) have maintained the necessity of the doctrine, pointing to the ability of members of the international community to engage in war, reprisals and issue sanctions in relation to particular wrongful acts.[41] This in turn has produced controversies surrounding the coherence of Kelsen's theory, in particular, whether the use of an apparently empirical factor such as coercion violates his adherence to the separation of *is* and *ought*. Scholars such as Kammerhofer have questioned the necessity of Kelsen's characterisation of legal systems as coercive orders, and developed an approach premised on a stricter adherence to Kelsen's own methodological parameters.[42] Yet, the apparent disengagement with social reality by positivist models of this kind, which largely sever any connection between the production of valid law and individual instances of enforcement or compliance, open the method to significant realist criticism.[43] After all, one may sensibly question, what use are valid human rights laws absent widespread enforcement? Is the positivist depiction of law as a set of norms exerting a binding force on its subjects accurate, or is compliance wholly dependent on extra-legal factors such as economics and power politics? Have the material

---

38 Lee McConnell, 'Assessing the Feasibility of a Business and Human Rights Treaty' (2017) 66 *International and Comparative Law Quarterly*, 143, 148–149.

39 Austin (n 3).

40 Hart (n 7) 26–49.

41 Kelsen, *General Theory* (n 6) 328.

42 Jörg Kammerhofer, 'Kelsen – Which Kelsen? A Reapplication of the Pure Theory to International Law' (2009) 22 *Leiden Journal of International Law*, 225, 240–241.

43 Hans Morgenthau, 'Positivism, Functionalism and International Law' (1940) *American Journal of International Law*, 260, 275; Koskenniemi, 'Carl Schmitt, Hans Morgenthau, and the Image of Law in International Relations' (n 8); cf Alexander Somek, 'Kelsen Lives' (2007) 18 *European Journal of International Law*, 409.

social and economic conditions giving rise to positive law as we today experience it embedded a particular ideology into the deep structure of law, and does this insight undermine law as a vehicle for progressive reform?[44] While it is not possible to drill down into these critiques here, readers should bear these perspectives in mind, and contemplate their potency in relation to positivist methodologies.

5 Liberalism

The term 'liberal' is commonly appended in the description of a variety of fields, including law, politics, sociology and economics.[45] While this factor complicates the articulation of a precise statement on what liberal theory is, it is possible to point to some characteristics that are broadly shared among these fields. The most prominent feature of liberal theory is its emphasis on individuals, including their equality, liberty and autonomy.[46] Liberal theories often stress the role of the individual in providing legitimacy to political orders via democratic participation, and the adoption of rights in safeguarding individual freedom and equality from the exercise of arbitrary power.[47]

The *a priori* significance of the individual in legal and political philosophy can be observed in the works of social contract theorists such as Hobbes and Locke, who emphasised the natural condition of humankind as autonomous individuals living in a state of nature until, by their own consent, those individuals chose to form a civilised society governed by political and legal conventions to which they agreed.[48] The presumptive significance of the autonomous individual and the role this concept plays in validating and shaping society is readily apparent in this theoretical tradition. The assertion of seemingly innate individualistic rights to life, liberty and property are also observable in Locke's work, notions which would later be codified in more or less express terms in the American Declaration of Independence and later the UDHR.[49] As is now clear, liberal narratives have been extremely influential in the realisation of human rights at both the domestic and international levels. When engaging in any form of rights analysis, readers should keep in mind

---

44 China Miéville, *Between Equal Rights: A Marxist Theory of International Law* (Leiden: Brill, 2005); Robert Knox, Marxism, International Law, and Political Strategy (2009) 22 *Leiden Journal of International Law*, 413.

45 John Charvet and Elisa Kaczynska-Nay, *The Liberal Project and Human Rights: The Theory and Practice of a New World Order* (Cambridge: Cambridge University Press, 2008) pp. 3–5.

46 Nicola Lacey, 'Feminist Legal Theory and the Rights of Women' in Karen Knop (ed.), *Gender and Human Rights* (Oxford: Oxford University Press, 2004) p. 19.

47 Henry Steiner and Philip Alston, *International Human Rights in Context* (Oxford: Clarendon, 1996) pp.187–190.

48 John Locke, *Second Treatise on Government* (1690) Ch II, §15; Thomas Hobbes (Richard Tuck, ed.), *Leviathan* (Cambridge: Cambridge University Press, 1991) p. 91.

49 Ilias Bantekas and Lutz Oette, *International Human Rights Law and Practice* (Cambridge: Cambridge University Press, 2013) p. 34.

the debts this legal tradition owes to liberal thought, and the potential links to natural law jurisprudence that may be drawn.[50]

It would therefore seem unsurprising that more contemporary theorists operating on variants of social contract theory would engender similar liberal presumptions. The scholarship of John Rawls provides such an example. His work *A Theory of Justice*[51] entails the use of a thought experiment where individuals are situated in an 'original position', free from knowledge of their social, cultural and economic interests – a sort of variant on the 'state of nature' of Hobbes and Locke. From this basis, Rawls seeks to establish a set of agreeable principles which would provide a foundation for social cooperation between those who share those beliefs. Another influential piece by Rawls is *The Law of Peoples*,[52] in which he recognises the pluralism inherent in the political, economic and cultural values of different states, and with this in mind, attempts to articulate a liberal basis for a peaceful international order in which societies can flourish. Not all societies will align entirely with this liberal model, but 'decent peoples' will at the very least abstain from aggressive foreign policy, and ensure some form of representative government and respect for basic human rights.[53] This conclusion reveals the Kantian influence in contemporary liberal thought, which considers 'just' states to be those that are 'organised internally in accordance with the fundamental natural law principle of equal freedom [which] must be expressed in the political realm through republican institutions'.[54] Kant postulated that a just international society 'formed by an alliance of separate free nations, united by their moral commitment to individual freedom' could then follow.[55]

A useful overview of Rawls' scholarship, alongside that of other liberal scholars such as Fernando Tesón[56] and Anne-Marie Slaughter,[57] is provided in Gerry Simpson's article 'Two Liberalisms'.[58] In this piece, Simpson highlights the tension between 'classical liberalism' emphasising the values of tolerance, diversity and equality, and what he terms 'liberal anti-pluralism',

50 Susan Breau, *The Responsibility to Protect in International Law* (Abingdon: Routledge, 2016) 44.
51 John Rawls, *A Theory of Justice* (first published 1971, Oxford: Oxford University Press, 1999).
52 John Rawls, *The Law of Peoples* (Boston: Harvard University Press, 2003).
53 Charles R Beitz, 'Rawl's Law of Peoples' (2002) 110 *Ethics*, 669, 674.
54 Charvet and Kaczynska-Nay (n 45) 71.
55 Fernando Tesón, 'Kantian International Liberalism' in David R Mapel and Terry Nardin (eds), *International Society* (Princeton, NJ: Princeton University Press, 1998) p. 103; Patrick Capps, 'The Kantian Project in Modern International Legal Theory' (2001) 12 *European Journal of International Law*, 1003.
56 Tesón (n 55).
57 Anne-Marie Slaughter, 'International Law in a World of Liberal States' (1995) 6 *European Journal of International Law*, 503.
58 Gerry Simpson, 'Two Liberalisms' (2001) 12 *European Journal of International Law*, 537.

where amenability to liberal values is used to determine the standing of a state in the international community.

> To illustrate the difference between these two liberalisms consider John Rawls. Rawls, in his recent book on international law . . . might be characterised as an old liberal in style and a new liberal in substance. His tone is full of the sort of equivocation often found in liberal scholarship . . . On the other hand, Rawls' distinction between 'decent' and 'outlaw' peoples places him in the camp of the new liberals. In substance, Rawls' *The Law of Peoples* is a philosophical justification for one form of liberal anti-pluralism or the liberal intolerance of intolerant governments. This in turn, can be distinguished from Rawls' liberal pluralism found in the sketch of international law in *A Theory of Justice*, where an international original position produces the norms of classical, [UN] Charter liberalism, most notably an equality of nations, 'analogous to the equal rights of citizens in a constitutional regime'.[59]

Here, Simpson is able to engage in a detailed analysis of the purported aims of the liberal tradition, and at the same time highlight potential critiques that may emerge in relation to their contemporary, transnational application. Liberal scholarship has also unsurprisingly been subject to criticism from feminist and other critical approaches (discussed below) in privileging Western, capitalist values at the international level, and maintaining a public/private divide that is characteristic of liberal legalism.

6 Cosmopolitanism

Readers may find it useful to compare the liberal influences in human rights law sketched above with cosmopolitan theory. For Pogge, cosmopolitan theories share three common positions:

> First, *individualism*: the ultimate units of concern are *human beings* or *persons*, rather than say, family lines, tribes, ethnic, cultural, or religious communities, nations, or States. The latter may be units of concern only indirectly, in virtue of their individual members or citizens. Second, *universality*: the status of ultimate unit of concern attaches to *every* living human *equally* . . . Third, *generality*: this special status has a global force. Persons are ultimate units of concern for *everyone* – not only for their compatriots, fellow religionists, or such like.[60]

---

59 Ibid. 540.
60 Thomas Pogge, 'Cosmopolitanism and Sovereignty' in Chris Brown (ed.), *Political Restructuring in Europe: Ethical Perspectives* (Abingdon: Routledge, 1995) pp. 89–90.

Like liberalism, cosmopolitan theories also emphasise the *a priori* importance of autonomous individuals and are indebted to Kant's *Perpetual Peace*,[61] but they are in other ways distinct. It is possible for theorists to embrace cosmopolitanism while at the same time rejecting liberalism by choosing to embrace, for example, authoritarian or theocratic political philosophies.[62] Equally, it is possible for liberals to eschew cosmopolitanism. For instance, Rawls's account in *The Law of Peoples* expressly argues against the universal application of liberal principles to every society, on the basis that it would constitute an act of intolerance toward 'decent non-liberal societies'.[63] We have already seen how scholars in the liberal tradition could be accused of engendering a double standard on this position, in that his approach effectively produces a system of ranking 'decent' and 'outlaw' societies on the basis of their alignment with liberal principles.[64]

This tension between tolerance, diversity, universality and immutability is apparent within scholarly discussions of cosmopolitanism and human rights.[65] Whether universal rights should be minimal in their content to account for global cultural diversity, or whether this robs legal rights of their moral and legal worth has been a matter of significant debate.[66] Sweet has analysed this matter in the context of the European human rights system, which has given rise to what he terms a Kantian 'cosmopolitan legal order' that seeks to ensure universal observance of human rights standards in the region. This legal order necessarily produces effects in relation to the plurality of domestic constitutional arrangements of State parties to the European Convention on Human Rights. In this regard, Sweet argues that the European Court of Human Rights (ECtHR) has adopted an approach that 'has transcended rights minimalism while maintaining a meaningful commitment to principles of national diversity and regime subsidiarity'.[67]

> While I have focused on the European case, the theoretical materials developed in the paper have general relevance to global constitutionalism,

---

61 Martha C. Nussbaum, 'Kant and Cosmopolitanism' in Garrett W. Brown and David Held (eds), *The Cosmopolitan Reader* (Cambridge: Polity Press, 2010) pp. 28–29.

62 Simon Caney, *Justice Beyond Borders: A Global Political Theory* (Oxford: Oxford University Press, 2005) p. 5.

63 Rawls, *The Law of Peoples* (n 52) pp. 82–83; Simon Caney, 'Cosmopolitanism and the Law of Peoples' (2002) 10 *Journal of Political Philosophy*, 98–99.

64 For a direct illustration of this tension, see: Rawls, *The Law of Peoples* (n 52) pp. 80–83.

65 Anthony J. Langlois, 'Human Rights and Cosmopolitan Liberalism' (2010) 10 *Critical Review of International Social and Political Philosophy*, 29.

66 For a variety of views, see Alessandro Ferrara, 'Two Notions of Humanity and the Judgment Argument for Human Rights' (2003) 31 *Political Theory*, 392; Rawls, *The Law of Peoples* (n 52); Seyla Benhabib, 'Claiming Rights Across Borders: International Human Rights and Democratic Sovereignty' (2009) 103 *American Political Science Review*, 691; Thomas Pogge, 'The International Significance of Human Rights' (2000) 4 *Journal of Ethics*, 45.

67 Alec Stone Sweet, 'A Cosmopolitan Legal Order: Constitutional Pluralism and Rights Adjudication in Europe' (2012) 1 *Global Constitutionalism*, 53–54.

in particular, to cosmopolitan variants. I sought to define a [cosmopolitan legal order] and related concepts to make them useful for thinking about how new judicial orders might emerge and evolve under conditions of rights-based, constitutional pluralism . . . In my view, a stable cosmopolitan legal system is only likely to emerge within a zone of liberalism, that is, within an interstate territory where the conditions for 'perpetual peace' have been met. In addition, national legal systems must be reconfigured so as to permit judges to render cosmopolitan justice . . . If the protection of fundamental rights is a core value of pan-European constitutionalism, then the [cosmopolitan legal order] is good for Europeans. Of course, the principles associated with parliamentary democracy are also core values. The evolution of rights pluralism, however, has undermined the models that officials and scholars have long used to describe, and normatively circumscribe, how State organs, including parliament and the courts, function . . . It may be that such notions are in the process of being adapted to cosmopolitan precepts and realities. But it also may be that the discursive battles between the values of rights cosmopolitanism and those of classic statist conceptions of the legal system have barely begun.[68]

In later parts of the article, the international effects of the cosmopolitan vision of human rights embedded within the European human rights regime are analysed in relation to the jurisprudence of the ECtHR concerning extraterritorial jurisdiction. Readers may find it useful to consider the potential magnification of this tension when cosmopolitan legal regimes are taken out of their regional setting and exported to international level. It might also be worthwhile considering the interaction between cosmopolitan theories and the emerging tradition of 'global constitutionalism' to which Sweet alludes.[69] Conversely, research projects might adopt the cosmopolitan argument in order to advocate the universal application of human rights standards to individuals within a particular bounded political community (e.g. a territorial state).[70] Such an approach might emphasise the cosmopolitan entitlements owed to all individuals and seek to challenge, on that basis, the domestic legal inequalities afflicting refugees, asylum seekers or similar groups that have been marginalised or 'othered' as a result of social or economic policy within a particular polity.

68 Ibid. 83–84.
69 Anne Peters, 'The Merits of Global Constitutionalism' (2009) 16 *Indiana Journal of Global Legal Studies*, 397; cf David Kennedy, 'The Mystery of Global Governance' in Jeffrey L. Dunoff and Joel P. Trachtman (eds), *Ruling the Wold: Constitutionalism, International Law and Global Governance* (Oxford: Oxford University Press, 2009) p. 37.
70 Seyla Benhabib, *Another Cosmopolitanism* (Oxford: Oxford University Press, 2006).

7 Feminism

It must be stated at the outset that, as with many of the other theories outlined in this chapter, there is no single archetypal feminist perspective on the nature of law. While feminist theories are often grouped into various waves or traditions, often including liberal, cultural, radical and postmodern perspectives, there are many internal variations within each approach. Unsurprisingly, liberal feminists proceed from a theoretical basis that emphasises the primacy of the autonomous individual, often asserting 'sameness' of men and women as individual human beings, and demanding equal legal rights to those currently held by men.[71] Other schools are generally more suspicious of the liberal equality narrative, questioning whether the pursuit of equality with a male archetype can sufficiently safeguard the particular harms and values of women,[72] and seeking to 'deconstruct the naturalistic, gender-blind discourse of law'.[73] Such perspectives often highlight the underlying effects of legal liberalism, such as its maintenance of a public/private divide, and a rights discourse that privileges the civil and political harms traditionally experienced by men, but trivialises or ignores harms experienced by women in the private sphere.[74]

Lacey provides a useful overview of the history of feminist legal theory, and sets out some general observations on the relationship between feminist theory and methodology:

> [An] important feature of feminist legal theory has to do with its methodology. We often think of legal theories as dividing roughly into the internal and the external—theoretical approaches which seek to rationalize and explicate the nature of law and legal method from the point of view of legal reasoning or legal practice itself, contrasting with theoretical approaches which self-consciously stand outside legal practices, subjecting them to an analysis from the point of view of a particular social scientific method or from distinctive normative points of view. We can see, however, that a large section of feminist theory in fact occupies a third perspective, which might be called interpretive. In other words, feminist legal theories do not merely seek to rationalize legal practices; nor, conversely, do they

---

71 Martha C. Nussbaum, *Sex and Social Justice* (Oxford: Oxford University Press 1999).
72 Patricia A. Cain, 'Feminism and the Limits of Equality' (1990) 24 *Georgia Law Review*, 803.
73 Carol Smart, *Feminism and the Power of Law* (Abingdon: Routledge, 1989) p. 88.
74 Christine Chinkin, 'A Critique of the Public/Private Dimension' (1999) 10 *European Journal of International Law*, 387; Gayle Binion, 'Human Rights: A Feminist Perspective' (1995) 17 *Human Rights Quarterly*, 509; Ursula A. O'Hare, 'Realising Human Rights for Women' (1999) 21 *Human Rights Quarterly*, 364, 368; Pamela Goldberg and Nancy Kelly, 'International Human Rights and Violence against Women' (1993) 6 *Harvard Human Rights Journal*, 195; Rhonda Copelon, 'Recognising the Egregious in the Everyday: Domestic Violence as Torture' (1994) 25 *Columbia Human Rights Law* Review, 291.

typically engage in entirely external critique and prescription. Rather, they aspire to produce a critical interpretation of legal practices: an account which at once takes seriously the legal point of view yet which subjects that point of view to critical scrutiny on the basis of both its own professed values and a range of other ethical and political commitments. For this reason among others (notably the political antecedents of the social movements which generated feminist scholarship) feminist legal scholarship is characterized by a particularly intimate linkage between theory and practice.[75]

Other observations on the feminist method have been drawn by Fellmeth, who identifies two primary techniques in feminist scholarship. The first involves questioning how legal processes fail to account for women's perspectives, seeking to 'expose hidden assumptions and biases in seemingly neutral legal rules, as well as the real world impact of those rules on women'.[76] Thus, the seemingly neutral individualist discourse of most human rights can be subject to critique; are rights that presume women to be *separate, autonomous* individuals helpful to women as a group, or do they overlook the fact that women are materially, politically and biologically *connected* to other human life?[77] The value of this method is recognised among a number of feminist schools, though it may be subject to critique from postmodern feminists, in that it arguably *essentialises* 'women' as a category. In other words, it presumes that laws affect all women in the same way, as a uniform, homogenous group.[78] The second technique is termed 'feminist practical reasoning', which advocates a focus on the real world experiences of women, and demonstrates a general scepticism towards bright-line rules and abstract theories which are 'characteristic of male-dominated economics, sociology, or political science [which] often generalise about social conditions or effects, ignoring gender-based disparities'.[79] Following these observations, Fellmeth offers some useful illustrations of different feminist responses to international human rights law which will likely be of interest to readers. These include analyses of the masculine nature of rights discourse, the maintenance of a public/private divide in international law, procedural inequality in international institutions, gender bias in the substantive content of human rights and humanitarian law, and issues of non-enforcement of women's human rights.

Another useful text that readers should engage with is Charlesworth, Chinkin and Wright's 'Feminist Approaches to International Law', a piece

---

75 Lacey (n 46) 16–17.
76 Aaron Xavier Fellmeth, 'Feminism and International Law: Theory, Methodology and Substantive Reform' (2000) 22 *Human Rights Quarterly*, 658, 666.
77 Robin West, 'Jurisprudence and Gender' (1998) 55 *University of Chicago Law Review*, 1.
78 For an outline of the methodology of this critique, see: Angela P. Harris, 'Race and Essentialism in Feminist Legal Theory' (1990) 42 *Stanford Law Review*, 581, 585–586.
79 Fellmeth (n 76).

which brought feminist analysis of international law into the mainstream.[80] The article's introduction expressly echoes many of the methodological features outlined above:

> In the first section, we examine the problems of developing an international feminist perspective. We then outline the male organisation and normative structure of the international legal system. We go on to apply feminist analyses developed in the context of domestic law to various international legal principles. Our approach requires looking behind the abstract entities of States to the actual impact of rules on women within States. We argue that both the structures of international lawmaking and the content of the rules of international law privilege men; if women's interests are acknowledged at all, they are marginalised. International law is a thoroughly gendered system. By challenging the nature and operation of international law in context, feminist legal theory can contribute to the progressive development of international law. A feminist account of international law suggests that we inhabit a world in which men of all nations have used the Statist system to establish economic and nationalist priorities to serve male elites, while basic human, social and economic needs are not met . . . By taking women seriously and describing the silences and fundamentally skewed nature of international law, feminist theory can identify possibilities for change.[81]

Again, readers should retrieve and consider these texts in full in order to gain insight into the substantive theoretical content and effects of feminist scholarship in the field of human rights law. It is impossible to provide a full enumeration of feminist theory here, yet it is hoped that in 'reading for methodology', the broad links between feminist theory and the other approaches contemplated above (and indeed below) are starting to become apparent.

8 Critical approaches

The term 'critical' is often used as an umbrella term to describe a number of interrelated theoretical perspectives. Again, it is not possible to advance beyond a broad overview of these theoretical approaches, but it is perhaps useful to sketch some observations on their methods. First, there is the Critical Theory associated with the Frankfurt School, which is influenced by the thought of Kant, Hegel, Marx, Weber, Freud and Lukács, and seeks to provide

---

80 Cryer, Hervey and Sokhi-Bulley (n 1) 64.
81 Hilary Charlesworth, Christine Chinkin and Shelley Wright, 'Feminist Approaches to International Law' (1991) 86 *American Journal of International Law*, 614.

an interdisciplinary analysis of contemporary late-capitalist societies.[82] A key theme of this scholarship is its emphasis on reflexivity – in particular, reflection on the social and historical context in which research methodologies are employed in order to recognise the hidden values that are communicated through apparently neutral or disinterested processes. Consider the observations of Horkheimer and Adorno in relation to the scientific method that developed during the Enlightenment, where a subject (scientist) seeks knowledge of its object (the natural world).[83] For Horkheimer and Adorno this form of reason is not, as it is often presented, a neutral method for the production of knowledge by a subject that is detached and disinterested from its object of knowledge. Rather, this method is built on a subject-object relationship, where the scientist seeks to achieve domination and manipulation of its object of study. Applied to human and social relations, humans are treated as objects of domination.[84] Thus, this form of methodology, which Horkheimer and Adorno term 'instrumental reason', reifies manipulation and domination.

This notion of exposing reified values in 'neutral' methodological processes has been influential in Critical Legal Studies (CLS) scholarship.[85] Thus, while the legal positivist theories outlined above may be regarded by their proponents as providing a descriptive enumeration of law (their object of study), and may base themselves on a strict separation between facts and values, CLS scholars might argue that such a perspective privileges the values of political elites that have wielded the power to shape the law to reflect their interests. In the words of Robert Gordon,

> [Legal discourses] are among the discourses that help us to make sense of the world, that fabricate what we interpret as reality. They construct roles for us like "Owner" and "Employee" and tell us how to behave in those roles . . . They wall us off from one another by constituting us as separate individuals given rights to protect our isolation, but then prescribe formal channels (such as contracts, partnerships, corporations) through which we can reconnect. They split up the world into categories that filter our experience – sorting out the arms we must accept as the hand of fate, or as our own fault, from the outrageous injustices we may resist as wrongfully forced upon us.[86]

82 David Held, *Introduction to Critical Theory: Horkheimer to Habermas* (Cambridge: Polity Press, 2004) pp. 1–18.

83 Max Horkheimer and Theodor Adorno, *Dialectic of Enlightenment* (John Cummin tr.) (London: Verso, 1997).

84 Robert Sinnerbrink, *Understanding Hegelianism* (Abingdon: Routledge, 2007) pp. 89–92; Held (n 82) 148–157.

85 Jeffery A. Standen, 'Critical Legal Studies as an Anti-Positivist Phenomenon' (1986) 72 *Virginia Law Review*, 983, 992–996.

86 Robert W. Gordon, 'Law and Ideology' (1988) 3 *Tikkun*, 14–15.

Here, the role of positivist legal theories in entrenching dominant political values (including the individualist rights-focus of legal liberalism) and the links between CLS and the feminist critiques outlined above should be clear to readers. The debt the human rights project owes to liberal legal doctrines, and the ideological consequences this engenders, has been analysed in depth by Duncan Kennedy and David Kennedy.[87] A useful overview and critical appraisal of the links between CLS and feminist jurisprudence in relation to rights discourse is drawn in Schneider's 'Dialectic of Rights and Politics' and West's 'Jurisprudence and Gender'.[88]

Retuning briefly to the Critical Theory of the Frankfurt School, theorists such as Jürgen Habermas have criticised the observations of the first-wave scholars outlined above. Habermas takes issue with Horkheimer and Adorno's assertion that 'instrumental reason' based on subject-object relations is a methodology that is characteristic of social modernity. Instead, he posits that knowledge production can take place in an intersubjective (subject-subject) fashion, through discursive processes. For Habermas, 'discourse' entails a situation in which participants are able to argue on an equal basis, free from coercion or external influences other than the force of the best argument.[89] This approach has contributed to the establishment of discursive demo-cratic theories and been applied to law-making at the international level.[90] Involvement in discursive law-making processes can be taken as legitimating legal norms by way of 'rational self-legislation'. In short, the addressees of norms are also taken to be their authors.[91] Engagement with these insights are visible in Miller's scholarship, which considers the status of transnational corporations (TNCs) in international human rights law, and the extent to which such actors may be engaged in discursive processes in elaborating human rights norms, alongside other international actors such as states and NGOs.

> Habermas's discursive democracy typically characterises the conditions for just relations between individuals; leading to the creation of gover-ning institutions and the norms those institutions apply. But, with some adaptation that embraces social identity theory, it may be possible to extend discursive democracy to interactions between collectives like TNCs, NGOs and states. Thus, the interactions between collectives

---

87 Duncan Kennedy, 'The Critique of Rights in Critical Legal Studies' in Wendy Brown and Janet Halley (eds) *Left Legalism/Left Critique* (Durham and London: Duke University Press, 2002) p. 179; David Kennedy, *The Dark Sides of Virtue: Reassessing International Humanitarianism* (Princeton: Princeton University Press, 2004) p. 18.

88 Elizabeth M. Schneider, 'The Dialectic of Rights and Politics: Perspectives from the Women's Movement' (1986) 61 *New York University Law Review*, 589; West (n 77).

89 Jürgen Habermas, *Theory of Communicative Action* Vol. 1 (Boston: Beacon Press, 1984) p. 25.

90 Steven Wheatley, *The Democratic Legitimacy of International Law* (Oxford: Hart, 2010).

91 Jürgen Habermas, *Between Facts and Norms* (Boston: MIT Press, 1996) p. 120.

would be held to the standard of Habermas's discursive democracy, consisting of a complementary relationship between political actors . . . This would be a relationship characterised by discourse and guided by a consensual ideal of the common good that comes to define the norms of justice. This application of Habermas's discourse theory to collectives is an innovation I have urged elsewhere with regard to indigenous peoples self-determination claims against states.[92]

Miller ultimately concludes that the tripartite structure of the International Labour Organisation, which engages states, workers' organisations and NGOs, echoes Habermas's discursive vision, and could enhance the legitimacy of efforts to regulate the adverse consequences emanating from the activities of TNCs.

The traditions of postmodernism and poststructuralism have also proven influential to CLS scholars. These approaches often challenge modernist tendencies to promulgate objectively valid 'grand narratives' which purport to offer structured, logical and coherent explanations of law and social phenomena. The grand narratives pervade modern accounts of legal phenomena and are visible in the Kelsenian account of law as a uniform hierarchical system of norms, Bentham's utilitarianism, the liberal social contract tradition, Rawls's theory of justice, Marxist social and political theory and beyond. Totalizing theories of this kind are characteristic of post-Enlightenment thought, an age of reason and progress in which the rational subject was seen to have triumphed over previously prevailing theological accounts of social phenomena.[93] Instead, a new faith in reason and mankind's capacity to explain the world as a coherent whole conforming to an overarching theory was privileged. Postmodern theorists seek to destabilise this neat worldview that prescribes a single ordering principle with which society must conform:

> In methodological terms, postmodernism seeks to 'deconstruct' the 'meta-narratives' by which those with power seek to prescribe or 'write' the conditions by which the rest of us should lead our lives. In its place, it advocates a politics of radical contingency, founded on respect for 'difference,' from one situation to another and from one individual to another.[94]

Postmodern theorists often borrow from the works of philosophers such as Michel Foucault, who substituted the Enlightenment's narrative of 'progress

92 Russell Miller, 'Paradoxes of Personality: Transnational Corporations, Non-Governmental Organisations and Human Rights' in Russell Miller and Rebecca Bratspies (eds), *Progress in International Law* (Leiden: Martinus Nijhoff, 2008).
93 James E. Penner and Emmanuel Melissaris, *McCoubrey & White's Textbook on Jurisprudence* (5th edn, Oxford: Oxford University Press, 2012) p. 241.
94 Ian Ward, *Introduction to Critical Legal Theory* (Abingdon: Routledge, 2004) p. 155.

and emancipation' as a means of understanding law and legal processes, for an analysis based on the arrangement of power relations:

> Humanity does not gradually progress from combat to combat until it arrives at universal reciprocity, where the rule of law finally replaces warfare; humanity installs each of its violences in a system of rules and thus proceeds from domination to domination.[95]

This tendency is visible in David Kennedy's rejection of genealogical narrative or progress presented by mainstream positivist accounts of international law. Kennedy criticises the identification of the 'fathers' of international law and their framing as primitive precursors of the present. Such a view aims to reaffirm

> public international law's paradigmatic historical narrative. We have progressed, so the story goes, from a few original truths scattered in a void, through the rationalization of philosophy, to the development of modern institutional machinery. We can see here our first glimpse of the basic dynamic narrative of public international law – a narrative as familiar to lawyers (who know it as the movement from jurisdiction through the merits to remedies) as to Christians (who know it as the movement from fall – through covenant – to salvation and redemption).[96]

Readers can also observe the poststructuralist insights apparent in the work of Hammer,[97] who advances an expressly Foucauldian perspective on international law, and Martti Koskenniemi,[98] whose work demonstrates influences from Jacques Derrida.[99]

Derrida famously developed the notion of 'deconstruction',[100] a philosophical strategy or technique that may be employed to question the determinacy and coherence of legal texts that is often purported by mainstream positivist theorists.[101]

---

95 Michel Foucault, 'Neitzsche, Genealogy and History' in *Hommage a Jean Hyppolite* (Paris: Presses Universitaires de France, 1971) p. 151.
96 David Kennedy, 'A New Stream of International Law Scholarship' (1988) 7 *Wisconsin International Law Journal*, 1, 15–16.
97 Leonard M. Hammer, *A Foucauldian Approach to International Law* (Aldershot: Ashgate, 2007).
98 Martti Koskenniemi, *From Apology to Utopia: The Structure of International Legal Argument* (first published 1989, Cambridge: Cambridge University Press, 2005).
99 Nicholas Onuf, *International Legal Theory: Essays and Engagements 1966–2006* (Abingdon: Routledge, 2008) pp. 278–279.
100 For an accessible overview: see Jonathan Culler, *On Deconstruction: Theory and Criticism after Structuralism* (Abingdon: Routledge, 2008).
101 This is particularly apparent of works in the Hartian tradition: d'Aspremont, *Formalism* (n 6).

Deconstructive readings of texts attempt to draw out the limitations of language, to indicate that a text may not represent all that it appears to, or that there may be dynamics operating within a text that are at odds with what it *prima facie* seems to state. For example, there may be subtle but crucial shifts in the meanings that underlie certain words (or 'signs') used. Thus in the legal context, deconstruction will aim to identify blind spots, hidden rhetoric and multiple meanings within texts; it will lead on to question accepted, mainstream liberal legal concepts by highlighting their unstable, contingent nature.[102]

Deconstruction is often applied in the context of the binary oppositions with which legal doctrine is replete. Some obvious examples include the divisions between public/private, subject/object, naturalist/positivist, State/non-State, is/ought. By engaging in a temporary reversal of the terms in a particular dichotomy, thus privileging the concept that is usually treated as subordinate, deconstruction can reveal mutual reliance of one term on the other, and highlight the illusory, socially constructed and ideological (rather than objective and naturally occurring) nature of the division.

The above themes are present in the work of David Kennedy, both in his rejection of progress narratives presented by modern historiographical accounts of international law, and in his discussion of the rhetorical function played by such accounts and the binary oppositions to which they give rise:

> Mine is a relational and rhetorical image of a 'law' and a 'society' – invoked by a language which establishes them as positing their originality, their priority, their presence. My sense is that this rhetorical project – in many ways *the* rhetorical project of public international scholarship – accounts for the doctrinal structures of 'public' and 'private' or 'objective' and 'subjective' which we find recurring throughout international public law doctrine and the recurrent scholarly contrasts we find between theory and practice. In this alternative picture, law is nothing but an attempt to project a stable relationship between spheres it creates to divide. As a result, the relationship between these zones is much looser than we usually think.[103]

In the context of human rights, readers may find it useful to consider Moosavian's 'Deconstructing "Public Interest" in the Article 8 vs Article 10 Balancing Exercise', which offers a concise and lucid introduction to the deconstructive technique employed by some poststructuralist scholars in the context of the rights to privacy and freedom of expression.[104]

---

102 Rebecca Moosavian, 'Deconstructing "Public Interest" in the Article 8 vs Article 10 Balancing Exercise' (2014) 6 *Journal of Media Law*, 234, 237.
103 Kennedy, 'A New Stream' (n 96) 8.
104 Moosavian (n 102).

The critical, reflective approaches to legal theory briefly sketched in the final two sections of this chapter serve as a useful end point. While discussion of each of the individual theoretical traditions is far too brief to fully account for their theoretical complexities, it is hoped that taken in aggregate, these sketches will serve as a useful starting point that will lead to the formulation of more coherent research methodologies. Even if readers are not compelled by the insights discussed in these final sections, their contemplation should at least serve as a useful exercise in beginning to question the unarticulated theoretical assumptions that are at play in their own understandings of legal doctrine. It is hoped that this discussion will help readers to recognise, account for and respond to these suppositions in their particular research projects, and that this will in turn encourage innovation and scholarly rigour in human rights research.

Further reading

General

Andrea Bianchi, *International Law Theories: An Inquiry in to Different Ways of Thinking* (Oxford: Oxford University Press, 2016).
Robert Cryer, Tamara Hervey and Bal Sokhi-Bulley, *Research Methodologies in EU and International Law* (Oxford: Hart, 2012).
Michael D.A. Freeman, *Lloyd's Introduction to Jurisprudence* (9th edn, London: Sweet and Maxwell, 2014).
Florian Hoffmann and Anne Orford (eds) *The Oxford Handbook of the Theory of International Law* (Oxford: Oxford University Press, 2016).
Steven Ratner and Anne-Marie Slaughter (eds) *The Methods of International Law* (Washington, DC: American Society of International Law, 2004).
Ian Scobbie, 'A View from Delft: Some Thoughts about Thinking About International Law' in Malcolm Evans (ed), *International Law* (4th edn, Oxford: Oxford University Press, 2014).

Naturalism

Geoff Gordon, 'Natural Law in International Legal Theory – Linear and Dialectical Presentations' in Florian Hoffmann and Anne Orford (eds) *The Oxford Handbook of the Theory of International Law* (Oxford: Oxford University Press, 2016).
Stephen Hall, 'The Persistent Spectre: Natural Law, International legal Order and the Limits of Legal Positivism' (2001) 12 *European Journal of International Law*, 269.
Hersch Lauterpacht, 'The Grotian Tradition in International Law' (1946) 23 *British Yearbook of International Law*, 1.

Positivism

Jean d'Aspremont, *Formalism and the Sources of International law* (Oxford: Oxford University Press, 2012).

Jörg Kammerhofer, 'International Legal Positivism' in Florian Hoffmann and Anne Orford (eds) *The Oxford Handbook of the Theory of International Law* (Oxford: Oxford University Press, 2016).

Jörg Kammerhofer and Jean d'Aspremont (eds) *International Legal Positivism in a Postmodern World* (Cambridge: Cambridge University Press, 2014).

Bruno Simma and Andreas L Paulus, 'The Responsibility of Individuals for Human Rights Abuses in Internal Conflict: A Positivist View' (1999) 93 *American Journal of International Law*, 302.

Liberalism

Thomas Franck, *Fairness in International Law and Institutions* (Oxford: Oxford University Press, 1998).

Thomas Franck, *The Power of Legitimacy among Nations* (Oxford: Oxford University Press, 1990).

Daniel Joyce, 'Liberal Internationalism' in Florian Hoffmann and Anne Orford (eds) *The Oxford Handbook of the Theory of International Law* (Oxford: Oxford University Press, 2016).

Anne-Marie Slaughter, 'A Liberal Theory of International Law' (2000) 94 *American Society of International Law Proceedings*, 240.

Anne-Marie Slaughter, 'International Law in a World of Liberal States' (1995) 6 *European Journal of International Law*, 503.

Cosmopolitanism

Anthony Appiah, *Cosmopolitanism: Ethics in a World of Strangers* (London: Penguin, 2007).

Seyla Benhabib, *Another Cosmopolitanism* (Oxford: Oxford University Press, 2008).

Simon Caney, *Justice Beyond Borders: A Global Political Theory* (Oxford: Oxford University Press, 2005).

Patrick Capps, *Human Dignity and the Foundations of International Law* (Oxford: Hart, 2009).

Wouter Werner and Geoff Gordon, 'Kant, Cosmopolitanism and International Law' in Florian Hoffmann and Anne Orford (eds) *The Oxford Handbook of the Theory of International Law* (Oxford: Oxford University Press, 2016).

Feminism

Doris Bus and Manji Ambreena (eds), *International Law: Modern Feminist Approaches* (Oxford: Hart, 2005).

Hilary Charlesworth, 'Feminist Methods in International Law' (1999) 93 *American Journal of International Law*, 379.

Karen Knop, *Gender and Human Rights* (Oxford: Oxford University Press, 2004).

Sari Kouvo and Zoe Pearson (eds), *Feminist Perspectives on Contemporary International Law: Between Resistance and Compliance?* (Oxford: Hart, 2011).

Dianne Otto, 'Feminist Approaches to International Law' in Anne Orford and Florian Hoffmann (eds), *Oxford Handbook of International Legal Theory* (Oxford: Oxford University Press, 2016).

Critical approaches

Deborah Z. Cass, 'Navigating the Newstream: Recent Critical Scholarship in International Law' (1996) 65 *Nordic Journal of International Law*, 341.

Leonard M. Hammer, *A Foucauldian Approach to International Law* (Aldershot: Ashgate, 2007).

David Kennedy, 'A New Stream of International Legal Scholarship' (1988–1989) 7 *Wisconsin International Law Journal*, 1.

Martti Koskenniemi, *From Apology to Utopia: The Structure of International Legal Argument* (Cambridge: Cambridge University Press, 2006).

China Miéville, *Between Equal Rights: A Marxist Theory of International Law* (Leiden: Brill, 2005)

Nigel Purvis, 'Critical Legal Studies in Public International Law' (1991) 32 *Harvard Journal of International Law*, 81.

5 Qualitative methods

Rhona Smith and Lorna Smith

1 Introduction

Human rights are for the benefit of all people, so finding out how human rights work in practice inevitably can benefit from asking those people most affected. Gathering information from people can help explain why policies and laws work or fail; if you ask the policy and lawmakers, an understanding of what the law/policy was meant to do, and any constraints, can be garnered.

Everyone is entitled to all universal human rights. Rights holders are all individuals or groups of individuals; duty bearers are primarily states and, therefore, members of government broadly construed. Accordingly, it is unsurprising that researching human rights may involve trying to gain a better understanding of the human dimension – what is the impact of a particular law? Why do police interrogate detainees in a particular manner? How do children best learn about human rights? What motivates people smugglers? Which government strategies are designed to combat violence against women? What challenges do a community face practising their particular culture? What is life like for a person with disabilities in a particular situation? How much consideration is given to human rights when a legislature is reviewing a potential new law? Interacting directly with people helps deepen understanding of behaviours and practices and therefore fosters a better understanding of human rights. Qualitative approaches can contribute through the gathering of information on the views, opinions and experiences of those directly involved. Interviews, focus groups and surveys can provide insights into lived experiences of human rights implementation and indeed violations, as well as illuminating findings in quantitative, more statistical, data.

2 What is a qualitative method?

Qualitative data aim to identify explanations of behaviour. Most qualitative researchers deploy a phenomenological or interpretivist approach aimed at understanding social phenomena from the perspective of the actor concerned. How land grabbing affects a particular community would be an example. Such findings inevitably can be subjective as they are based on the data from a specific situation and reflect the views of the participants, but the findings can sometimes validly be used to extrapolate trends or more general understandings. 'Go to the people' is the subheading of the first chapter of one introductory textbook.[1]

Whilst quantitative data approaches primarily reduce data to numbers and facilitate statistical analysis, qualitative data are primarily text based. The source is either original text (diaries, archived material, transcribed interviews, filled in questionnaires and so on), or written records of phenomena (descriptions of observed behaviour, descriptions of photographs or films). Qualitative research is more concerned with words than numbers and the approach may involve interpreting, as well as reporting and recording, words. Furthermore, as will be seen, key words or phrases can be coded and therefore, in effect, reduced to numbers.

Qualitative methods may also be used by positivists investigating specific facts – a textual analysis of laws is an obvious example – but in human rights research there is undoubtedly more emphasis on phenomenological perspectives as researchers try to understand the impact of laws and treaties and the effect of rights holders or duty bearers. This can entail theoretical perspectives such as feminist research and critical ethnography which analyse reality from the perspective of marginalised, oppressed or powerless people. Different vantage points are therefore given space and offer different understandings of human rights in reality. Qualitative research is also common in applied fields such as education[2] or indigenous studies.

Qualitative research covers a broad methodology which encompasses many different research methods. Qualitative methods can be particularly useful at obtaining cultural specific information about the values, interests, behaviours and opinions of groups in society. In international human rights, that has particular relevance. Intangible factors such as social norms, gender roles and socio-economic factors can also be better understood through qualitative research. Inevitably this means the research is inductive – the researcher does not know what s/he is going to find until the research is underway. Initial perceptions may prove erroneous and the research direction may change as a result. This is inevitable, as it is not always feasible to know what a person thinks or feels or how a person is affected by something until one asks them. The research process can be particularly illuminating. It provides the human side of an issue, so is ideally suited to human rights research and, depending on the pitching of the findings, can also be in keeping with a human rights based approach to research.

---

1 Steven Taylor and Robert Bogdan, *Introduction to Qualitative Research Methods: a Guidebook and Resource*, 3rd edn. (New York: John Wiley, 1998) p. 3, repeated in the final concluding remarks, p. 261.

2 See for example, William Wiersma, *Research Methods in Education, an Introduction*, 7th edn. (Massachussetts: Pearson, 2000) Chapter 8.

Qualitative approaches can be more flexible and iterative than quantitative approaches, in that they are more spontaneous, easier to respond to changes in questions and offer more interaction between the researcher and the subject. The most common methods are perhaps participant observation (anthropological), in-depth interviews, open-ended survey questions, focus groups and action research. The subset of action research is also relevant as the researcher and affected individuals collaborate in diagnosing and then developing a solution for a particular problem or issue. These are often practical solutions, therefore when trying to identify how to prevent malnutrition through failed crops, the need to develop the capacity to rotate crops and enrich the soil evolved as a solution.[3] Action research is also common in the field of education.[4]

Qualitative analysis can also be undertaken using pre-prepared texts – judgments,[5] treaties, UN treaty body reports, diaries, or even transcribed historical (often archived) material,[6] are examples. Selecting the appropriate method is partly dictated by the research question/s, partly by the context (including resources) and partly a matter of personal choice or experience.

Four popular sources of qualitative data, often used by human rights researchers, will now be outlined: interviews, surveys, focus groups and case studies.

For all qualitative approaches, advance preparation and planning can pre-empt problems later in the process. Piloting a questionnaire on a small test group can 'test the water' to ensure that the questions are understood by the target group and the data you are likely to receive is appropriate for the type of analysis you wish to do. Similarly, a sample test run of planned coding will ensure a better understanding of whether the coding design will successfully roll out to the whole data set.

2a Interviews

Interviews can take place under differing levels of formality, depending on context.[7] In essence, an interview is a conversation with a purpose. Taylor and

---

3 Jacques Somda, Robert Zougmore, Issa Sawadogo, Babou Andre, Bationo, Saaka Buah and Tougiani Abasse, 'Adaptation Processes in Agriculture and Food Security: Insights from Evaluating Behavioral Changes in West Africa' in J.I. Uitto, J. Puri and R.D. van den Berg (eds), *Evaluating Climate Change Action for Sustainable Development* (Los Angeles: Sage, 2017).
4 Mary Mcateer, *Action Research in Education* (Los Angeles: Sage, 2013); Lin Norton, *Action Research in Teaching and Learning: A Practical Guide to Conducting Pedagogical Research in Universities* (Abingdon: Routledge, 2008).
5 Hélène Tyrrell, *UK Human Rights Law and the Influence of Foreign Jurisprudence* (Oxford: Hart Publishing, 2017).
6 Heather Roberts, 'Women Judges, "Maiden Speeches," and the High Court of Australia', in Beverley Baines, Daphne Barak-Erez and Tsvi Kahana (eds), *Feminist Constitutionalism: Global Perspectives* (New York: Cambridge University Press, 2012) p. 113.
7 For a review of a range of relevant considerations, see Rosalind Edwards and Janet Holland, *What is Qualitative Interviewing?* (London: Bloomsbury, 2013).

Bogdan note that 'the hallmark of indepth qualitative interviewing is learning how people ... view, define and experience the world'.[8] The relationship between interviewer and interviewee varies, with the balance able to shift in favour of either party depending on the nature and extent of the interview. As a partial caveat, when deciding on a qualified interviewer for human rights violations, human rights expertise and knowledge of the specific affected group can be important. Precise training is recommended before interviewing victims of violations.[9] The Office of the High Commissioner for Human Rights recommends having two human rights officers present during interviews: one to maintain eye contact and ask questions, the other to discreetly take notes, identify gaps and note further questions.[10]

Interviews are usually conducted on an individual basis, either in person or by telephone. It is not unknown for an interviewee to request a copy of the questions in advance, especially if they are government/duty bearers or other senior officials. It can help the interview to run efficiently if questions are provided beforehand. It can, however, make for an artificial interview if the answers are pre-prepared. It is more likely that the interviewer would have a set of topics to be explored that are then tailored to suit each interviewee. The interviewer can also adapt to answers that are provided for previous questions when shaping the subsequent questions. Kvale et al. detail conceptualising the research interview, planning it, carrying it out, transcribing and analysing the resultant data.[11]

There are obvious cultural and contextual considerations when interviewing somone regarding alleged human rights violations, or simply ensuring a human rights based approach to the interview. These include ensuring the interviewers respect the culture of the interviewee. This can mean considering issues such as the gender of the interviewee and the gender of the interviewers, choice of clothing, language issues and so on. Sometimes barriers arise – for example, interviewing a woman on intimate partner violence when cultural norms require a male relative to be present when the woman is meeting with an unknown interviewer can present obvious challenges. Consideration may also have to be given to ensuring confidentiality – this is difficult in some field situations when the entire community is interested in what is happening and even local police or authorities may also turn up.

Interviews can be oral or written (e.g. a questionnaire). They can be structured, in-depth or semi structured. In a structured interview, the interviewer already has the specific questions s/he wants answered. These are asked to

8 Taylor and Bogdan (n 1) 101.
9 See Rhona Smith, Chapter 1.
10 OHCHR, *Manual on Human Rights Monitoring*, Chapter 11 Interviewing, revised edn. (Geneva: OHCHR, 2011), available from ohchr.org in updated chapters at 10.
11 Steiner Kvale and Svend Brinkmann, *Interviews: Learning the Craft of Qualitative Research Interviewing*, 2nd edn. (London: Sage Publications, 2009).

the interviewee and the answers recorded. In-depth interviews do not aim to compare, but to explore the individual. For semi-structured interviews, the interviewer retains a greater degree of flexibility. A broad plan is prepared in advance, but there is scope for the interviewer to explore on tangents and delve into related issues as well as focussing on the principal topic. Obviously if there is a structured interview, then the answers of different respondents can be directly compared; in semi structured interviews, this is not always so easy as the different questions may have elicited different responses from each respondent.

Feminist researchers often use semi-structured interviews to ensure the voice of women can be reflected accurately. East Timorese women were interviewed by researchers, for example, to better understand the experiences of East Timorese asylum seekers living in Australia.[12] Researchers working with other 'marginalised' groups do likewise. Such a flexible approach enables the researcher to 'go with the flow' of the interview and probe deeper into areas of particular interest.

Should you be interviewing for the first time then it is highly recommended that you practice the skills required for carrying it out. Practice listening to an interview during a current affairs programme and try to record the relevant points from the interviewee. Taking notes during an interview reduces eye contact with the interviewee but does provide valid information recorded in real time that can be used during the interview itself as well as afterwards. Probably the best way to start is with open-ended descriptive questions.

- Could you tell me about a typical day?
- I'd like to know more about that experience, can you tell me what happened?
- I'm interested in how you ended up here, can you tell me how you got here?

Probing questions can then elicit more detail and provide clarity. Often details need to be clarified, and it must be remembered that different scenarios/words/ concepts can mean different things to different people. This can result in difficulties with, in effect, details and meaning 'lost in translation' even if the researcher and subject are speaking the same language. When translators or interpreters are used and/or when one or other party is working in a second or third language, the potential for miscommunication grows. Potential power imbalances are also an issue when undertaking interviews in the field. A victim of torture may feel that an interview is a scenario akin to interrogation, for example. There is also a real risk of retraumatisation, or stigmatisation of

12 Susan Rees, 'Refuge or Retrauma? The impact of asylum seeker status on the wellbeing of East Timorese women asylum seekers residing in the Australian community' (2003) 11 *Australasian Psychiatry Supplement*, 96–101.

an interviewee within the community.[13] Vulnerable individuals must have their rights safeguarded before, during and after the interview. This applies particularly to children and victims of human rights violations.

Other documentation can help when shaping questions – diaries, blogs, background research, reports. These can give a greater understanding of context for the research which can help in preparing questions to be asked – though, as noted above, the researcher must be prepared to have any pre-conceptions challenged by the answers given. Piloting the planned questions can allow the researcher to anticipate problem areas.

Consideration must also be given to how the interview is recorded – paper notes, electronic notes, a taped recording? Not every participant will be happy with recordings being made. Clear advice must be provided to the interviewee in terms of how the data will be collected, stored, analysed and used. They must be assured of confidentiality if not anonymity.[14] Ensure that they cannot be identified from your brief description of them, either in terms of their position/role in an organisation or identifying characteristics.

Interviews can be time consuming and logistics (cost, travel, personnel) can limit the number of people who can be interviewed. Sampling techniques are discussed below. To achieve a greater number of responses, surveys or questionnaires can be used.

2b Survey – open questions

Using open questions in a questionnaire allows participant numbers to increase. Postal questionnaires have a fairly low response rate of around 60 per cent and on-line surveys may not always be answered by the intended target audience.[15] As long as bias can be controlled for or accepted, then this allows the qualitative researcher to access the attitudes, beliefs and opinions of a large representative sample of the target population (e.g. send an on-line survey to all undergraduate law students in a department; or to registered members of a minority rights group nationwide, if such a database exists). There will be bias in terms of those who complete and submit their responses, but there should also be a wide spread of results. More data can be gained than with using individualised interviews, however the researcher is unable to clarify responses or seek further expansion on areas of particular interest. The respondent also cannot ask for clarification of questions and may not provide justification of a response.

13 Discussed below, 'ethics'.
14 Anonymity can rarely be ensured as the interviewer will normally know the identity of the person being interviewed and this data will be recorded. Confidentiality prevents the disclosure of any identifying information of the interviewee.
15 For a more detailed introduction to online interviewing, see Nalita James and High Busher, 'Online Interviewing' in David Silverman (ed.), *Qualitative Research*, 4th edn. (London: Sage, 2016) pp. 245–260.

Example of use

Closed question (quantitative):

Do you believe that capital punishment can be justified? Yes ☐ No ☐

Scale question (quantitative):

To what extent do you agree with the following statement where 1 is 'not at all' and 10 is 'completely': (Please circle your response)

'Capital punishment should be permitted in specific cases' 1 2 3 4 5 6 7 8 9 10

Open question:

What do you think about capital punishment?

Open questions are often used to add to the understanding gained from a quantitative approach. This is an example of mixed methods or triangulations, with the qualitative data adding to and possibly even clarifying or verifying the quantitative data.[16]

Piloting a survey in advance can help the researcher test the effectiveness of the questions and the likely answers. Then, to gain further depth of understanding, depending on the situation, volunteers may participate in a physical or virtual focus group.

2c Focus groups

Focus groups generally permit free-flowing conversation. The researcher works with a group of people, essentially in open-ended discussions. The researcher must act as a facilitator and ensure that everyone who wants to contribute to the discussion can, as well as monitoring the pace and structure/order of the discussions. Focus groups are commonly used, including in education and market research, to gain an understanding of the general situation of a particular group. They became common in the 1990s.[17] Participants may be selected because of their particular interests or involvement (e.g. in a study on the realisation of the rights of persons with disabilities, the focus group brings together people in a particular village who have been actively campaigning on disability rights). There can be a group interview with several topics discussed, or a more focussed structure. An example of the latter would be bringing together respondents to a survey in order to explore some of their responses in more detail.

---

16 Discussed further below.
17 Sue Wilkinson, 'Analysing Focus Group Data' in Silverman (n 15).

Through the group interaction, a different understanding can emerge than were the participants to be interviewed individually. Views expressed may be qualified as the participants listen to each other's views. Moderating focus groups can be tricky, especially when participants may talk over each other, or when one or more participants dominate (or do not participate). Given the time and effort involved in setting up focus groups, it is not as easy to 'wipe' a poor attempt as it is with single interviews; a focus group will potentially represent a much larger contribution to the data for the research project.

The number of focus groups needed to gather sufficient data depends on the context and scope of the research question. If the focus group is the main source of data then several groups may be required. Most researchers agree that when little new data emerges from a focus group, saturation is reached and the maximum data collection achieved. Of course, just as with interviews, focus group data need to be recorded and analysed. It can be more time consuming and tricky to transcribe focus group content rather than single interviews due to the number of contributors. A primary consideration is whether or not separate contributors require to be identified differently within the transcript. Should this be required then the transcription becomes necessarily more complex, time-consuming, and costly. These additional layers of complexity are rarely necessary within the more typical market-research type of environment, however it may be required where an individual's voice needs to be heard in context within the group.

Inevitably attention must be given to the selection of participants. Focus groups are sometimes considered empowering for the participants and have gained support amongst child and feminist researchers. However, there is a potential latent bias in a sample based solely on self-selection. There are also questions to be addressed as to how representative that group may be of the general population. This is perhaps particularly so if the focus group is conducted online – more people can be involved and geographical challenges are obviated, but equally the group may lack coherence and interaction may be compromised, particularly if the 'discussion' is fully online and not con-temporaneous.[18] Moreover, an online forum would require competence in IT which can create age or cultural bias in the sample.

2d Case studies

Case studies produce incredibly rich, in-depth sources of data, however, they are the most time-consuming and labour intensive. Data are rarely com-parable across case studies, which can reduce their value unless exploring a unique phenomenon, individual or small group. However, the volume of

---

18 In online discussion fora, people can leave views for others to comment then return later and add or refine views. The discussion is not 'live' in the sense that face-to-face groups are talking together.

detail available and the body of knowledge that can be built can be particularly useful in developing an understanding of, for example, causes of specific human rights abuses.[19]

A case study is particularly useful if the potential information gained can justify the time and labour intensity of the method.

Case studies can be longitudinal or retrospective, depending on when the case presents itself. Information can be sought about the individual or group from the point they come to the attention of researchers, and then studied for a period of time, or once a case is known, their past can be explored to identify all relevant information that led to their coming to the attention of researchers.

Longitudinal case studies will not have a clear timescale. The body of evidence that builds a case study can use multiple research methods such as experiment, interview and observation, alongside conventional background information provided through, for example, medical, academic, employment and criminal records. Groups can be studied intensively using a combination of externally sourced resources such as educational attainment, demographic spread, class, literacy levels, mortality rates, and contact with the group itself. Longitudinal case studies often take place over a period of several years or decades. This involves significant resources and careful record-keeping. There are many quantitative longitudinal human rights studies, the annual UNICEF State of the World's Children,[20] the World Bank Development Indicators,[21] or the UNDP Human Rights Development Index[22] are three examples. These statistical analyses facilitate an overview of changes in time and feed in to longitudinal action plans such as those associated with the UN sustainable development goals. Qualitative studies add depth to these statistics. Poverty impact can be measured by qualitative data – asking a group for their definition and measurement indicators of poverty at the ages of 15, 25, 35 and 45 years could lead to an understanding of what a particular group of people consider the most important indicators of success and an adequate standard of living.

19 For example, see Verite, 'A Verité Assessment of Recruitment Practices and Migrant Labor Conditions in Nestlé's Thai Shrimp Supply Chain: An Examination of Forced Labor and other Human Rights Risks Endemic to the Thai Seafood Sector,' 2015, https://www.verite.org/wp-content/uploads/2016/11/NestleReport-ThaiShrimp_prepared-by-Verite.pdf, accessed 7 February 2017.

20 UNICEF, State of the World's Children, https://www.unicef.org/sowc, accessed 7 February 2017. These reports are published annually with core data allowing for longitudinal analysis along with a thematic analysis.

21 World Development Indicators, annually updated, http://data.worldbank.org/data-catalog/world-development-indicators, accessed 7 February 2017. This database pulls together a range of international sources.

22 UNDP, *Human Rights Development Index*, http://hdr.undp.org/en/data, accessed 7 February 2017, which includes longitudinal data on indicators of development covering 1980–2015 and the conclusion of the millennium development goals (www.un.org/milllenniumgoals, accessed 7 February 2017).

Should a retrospective case study be carried out then the inherent bias is predominantly memory.[23] Human memories contain selective bias. Emotion and mood can affect recall, as can injury. Should an extreme event have happened to the participant then this can cause memory repression. Alternatively, 'flashbulb' memories can be remarkably detailed but limited in scope and duration. Consider moments in history such as JFK being assassinated, the dawn of the new millennium or the Twin Towers of New York falling. People can often recall in great detail where they were and what they were wearing/doing. It is unlikely that they hold such a clear and specific memory for the previous day or the following day. Personal emotional peak events such as marriage proposals, births and bereavements are often comprised of 'flashbulb' memories. Memories that are less clear are open to subjective bias and distortion. Most memories are reconstructions rather than accurate recollections, therefore revisiting an indistinct memory can change it without the person realising. The changed memory is then believed to be true. Leading questions and the unreliability of eyewitness testimony provide a strong argument against using memories as the dominant source of data within a retrospective case study. Just as legal evidence requires corroboration beyond a single eyewitness's testimony, so too does a case study. Corroboration can come from other parties such as family or friends, or more objective records.

3 Issues and challenges

As with all research methods, there are issues and challenges of which the qualitative researcher should be aware. This chapter will also look at sampling techniques, issues around recording and data reliability, then ethics. Ethics are of paramount importance in human rights based research.

3a Sampling

Webley notes that all researchers need to consider whom to interview, or what to observe or analyse and how many participants or data sources are necessary to elicit findings in which one may have confidence.[24] The research question will determine how much primary data will be required to elucidate a credible answer. Theories of sampling shape decisions on how many people data must be gathered from. Interviewing 40 people, for example, would not permit general conclusions to be extrapolated on a 5 million-person population.

---

23 See, for example, Alison Jobe, *The Causes and Consequences of Re-trafficking: Evidence from the IOM Human Trafficking Database* (Geneva: International Organisation for Migration, 2010), http://publications.iom.int/system/files/pdf/causes_of_retrafficking.pdf, accessed 7 February 2017.

24 Lisa Webley, 'Qualitative Approaches to Empirical Legal Research' in Peter Cane and Herbert Kritzer (eds), *The Oxford Handbook of Practical Legal Research* (Oxford: Oxford University Press, 2010) p. 933.

However, interviewing 40 people out of the 50 people possibly affected by a hydropower dam project in a small rural community could mean that generalised statements on the impact on the entire community of 50 are more credible. The choice of sample should be purposive – the researcher does not seek to sample participants on a haphazard basis; there should be an underlying reason to the selection. There are many different approaches to sampling. Extreme or deviant sampling is used when usual cases or instances are identified at the extreme end of a spectrum and these are targeted for investigation.[25] The opposite of this is typical case sampling whereby a participant is selected for being specifically the subject of interest. In human rights research, it is often necessary to be proactive when seeking out victims, witnesses and other relevant sources.

When selecting samples, care must be taken to recognise any bias. Theoretical saturation is difficult to achieve, thus there is inevitably some degree of narrowing down which may mean the sample is not genuinely representative of the initial wider target group. This is not a problem as long as the analysis and results are accurately recorded and careful consideration is given to whether wider claims can be supported by the evidence.

3b Adequate recording

As has been noted above, it is necessary to ensure that an accurate record is prepared for interviews, focus groups and observations. Ultimately this has to be in a form permitting analysis. Usually this means in writing, therefore transcription is often required – the recorded interview must be written up verbatim. Consideration must be given to how the detail is transcribed (hesitations, particular intonations and such like). These can be important at the analysis stage as, inevitably, it is not necessarily purely a textual analysis. Of course, if it is purely documentary analysis, then just the text of the documents is necessary.

Good recording is a crucial precursor to good analysis. Most analyses use an initial transcript. This can be obtained by taking notes in real time or by transcribing recorded interviews. Using a professional transcription service can save considerable time and also allow you to tailor the level of transcription you receive. There will be a direct trade-off with increased cost of resources and a potential time cost depending on how quickly a recording can be transcribed and returned to you. By transcribing the recordings yourself you will have the contexts and the specific terms used. Allow approximately 3 to 4 hours to transcribe 1 hour of interview in terms of spoken fluent language, and approximately 10 hours to transcribe a 1-hour interview with full detail including stresses, hesitations, tone, inhalations and length of pauses. If the

---

25 The spectrum could be identified through quantitative data collection – a survey for example. The extreme cases are then singled out for follow-up interviews.

interviewee laughs, is it a nervous laugh? A long laugh? Does it need to be recorded in terms of nature and extent? Does it need to be recorded at all?

During an interview or focus group, it can be useful to note particular responses or the reaction of the participants. If this is not possible, then soon after, it is advisable to note down your memories of the session, including issues such as the body language of the interviewees. This can help provide background context of the interview and assist in the understanding of the analysis. Your notes and recollections can also be used to cross check the records in transcription (for example, it may explain interruptions). For observation, again a record is required. If the observation is recorded on paper/computer, then consideration has to be given in advance as to what information is required. Some degree of coding is required insofar as abbreviations, shorthand or codes are inevitably required to allow a contemporaneous record to be maintained.

These considerations affect the quality of data you will then have available for your analysis. Should you transcribe yourself then you will already have started the analysis through choosing what you put into the transcription. This first level of analysis is critical. It is also important to revisit the original recordings once you progress through the analysis in order to maintain rigour and accuracy. Although thematic analysis takes you away from the actual words and into semantics, it can be easy to move away from what was originally meant.

Examples of transcription:

Interviewer A: "Could you tell me about your experience of seeking asylum here last year?"

Interviewee #14: "It's difficult to find the words. I don't remember everything. I remember being very cold and very scared."

Interviewer A: "When we spoke last week you said you had been tortured in your country of origin. You were upset and asked if we could talk about it this week instead. Can you tell me more about that experience now?"

Interviewee #14: "I don't know. I don't think so."

[Interviewee #14 becomes distressed. Interview terminated at 14:08]

Further considerations:

There can be subtle differences that affect meaning but are virtually impossible to differentiate. Do they affect your results?

"I don't know. I don't think so." Versus "I don't, no, I don't think so." Versus "Uh (1.5) ehm (.) ah don't (..) uhm (.) I don't (1.0) no/know [unclear which homonym is being said] (1.0) I don't think so (..)"

The whole tone is different from the more definite first version through to the final version showing hesitation. If this is a critical part of the interview then the interviewer should follow up the information.

3c *Reliability*

As with all empirical data, it is necessary to verify the accuracy of the data gathered. However, as the data may be based on subjective evaluations and lived experiences, accuracy is not necessarily easily cross-checked. If accuracy of the record is confirmed, can the results be considered reliable as a source? In other words, what is the quality of the data? Can the work be relied upon and have validity without the immediate context – for example, does work on how an elderly community copes with the rising price of fuel and food validly reflect the experience of all (or most) elderly people in the country? To determine that, it may be necessary to cross-check the results elsewhere in the country. Similarly, an investigation in the causes of violence against women and children may be global[26] in scope, but may not capture all the underlying causes as its validity may depend on who had access to the technology to respond to the questions posed.

There have been a lot of concerns expressed in the literature about the reliability of qualitative methods. Although the evidence may be accurate, it may lack credibility. To ensure the research has validity, it is necessary to check, usually through triangulation[27] or respondent validation. Confirming that the data are correct with the interviewees themselves can help, though obviously the interviewees may not like the overall findings. Validation can be sought from the community or organisation to ensure a degree of perspective when reviewing findings. Qualitative research is also deep and narrow, rather than broad. Interviewing a hundred people may be feasible; interviewing 5 million in a country is not. This means that consideration must be given to how far you can extrapolate the findings. Are they valid generally or just specific in respect of the group chosen? So, when considering human rights education and how students learn, a study of a single class may or may not reflect how all students learn.

Complete objectivity is difficult. Unconscious bias on the part of the interviewer may shape the findings, or indeed the conduct of the interview or focus group.[28] What is important is that the researcher has acted in good faith

---

26 Ban Ki-Moon, *In-depth study on all forms of violence against women, Report of the Secretary-General*, UN Doc A/61/122/Add.1, 6 July 2006.

27 For more on triangulation, see the final chapter on mixed methods.

28 Biases are influenced by background, cultural environment and personal experiences. They are termed unconscious because the researcher may not even be aware of these views and opinions, or their full impact and implications.

and declares any potential bias or influence s/he is aware of. Honesty and transparency are key. Research can be influenced externally but still retain rigour and balance to give it validity.

Quality is determined and evaluated with reference to a variety of factors including the sampling technique, the credibility of the findings, the diversity of context, the rigour of data collection, consideration of ethical issues, documentation and recording, and overall, how defensible the research and findings are.

3d Ethics

When real people are used, ethics become ever more prominent. Good research must be ethical. The rights and dignity of the participant must be respected. History attests to many shocking infringements of the rights of people, particularly in medical research.

Human rights research often involves particularly vulnerable people. Victims of human rights abuses and violent conflicts are often sought out to provide greater understanding of the impact of the abuse or the conflict. However, by definition, interviewing such victims raises the spectre of retraumatisation or stigmatisation and great care must be taken, especially if the interviewer is not fully trained in such techniques. There are too many examples of ill-advised interviews and distraught interviewees. However, good research in such sensitive fields can yield tremendous results – work on female victims of sexual violence during conflicts in Sierra Leone, for example,[29] helped develop the framework for rape being identified as a war crime.[30]

Whenever research involves real people, the wellbeing of those people has to be the primary consideration. There are sadly research experiments which exhibit a shocking disregard for the participants involved. In the early 1960s Stanley Milgram, working at Yale University, sought to better understand why people obey instructions even when such instructions are contrary to their own conscience.[31] On the face of it, such a research project could help

---

29 Louise Taylor, '"We'll Kill You If You Cry": Sexual Violence in the Sierra Leone Conflict,' New York: Human Rights Watch, 2003, https://www.hrw.org/report/2003/01/16/well-kill-you-if-you-cry/sexual-violence-sierra-leone-conflict, accessed 7 February 2017; Lynn Amowitz and others, 'Prevalence of War-Related Sexual Violence and Other Human Rights Abuses Among Internally Displaced Persons in Sierra Leone' (2002) 287(4) JAMA513-521, http://jamanetwork.com/journals/jama/fullarticle/194586, accessed 7 February 2017.

30 See Kunarac, Kovac and Vukovic (Foca) Case IT-96-23 and 23/1, ICTY (found guilty in 2001 of rape as a war crime and a crime against humanity), *The Prosecutor v. Jean-Pierre Bemba Gombo*, ICC-01/05-01/08 (found guilty in 2016 of rape as a crime against humanity and as a war crime); see also, SC Resolution 1820 (2008) on Women and Peace and Security.

31 A resource website on the experiment and modern revisits is http://www.age-of-the-sage. org/psychology/milgram_obedience_experiment.html#Stanley_Milgram_odedience_experiment_study, accessed 7 February 2017.

inform understanding of why police torture detainees, why extrajudicial killings, genocide and other gross breaches of human rights occur. The experiment involved 'teachers' administering ever greater electric shocks to 'learners' following each and every wrong answer. Unknown to the 'teachers', the 'learners' were actors and no actual shocks were administered. The 'teachers' gave ever greater shocks to the 'learners', up to a lethal 450 volts, despite the growing apparent distress of the 'learners'. The research was written up and published,[32] and indeed has been re-enacted repeatedly thereafter. Obedience was found to be extensive. However, public outcry at both the results and the traumatisation of participants meant the experiment was also seminal in leading to the regulation of research with live subjects in the United States of America.[33] The level of deception would fall foul of contemporary research ethics regulations in the US, and most countries with ethics regulations, today. Today, university, government, CSO/NGO and various institutional guidelines govern the ethics of research, whether academic or practical.

Informed consent is a mechanism for ensuring that participants in your research understand what they are agreeing to and agree to participate, even in light of possible consequences. Consent normally pre-supposes that the participants understand the purpose of the research, what is expected of them, the possible risks and management of those risks, understand that participation is voluntary and understand how confidentiality will be protected. Using a human rights based approach respects the rights of the interviewee, so an appropriate balance must be determined between the benefits of the research and the potential deleterious consequences to the victim, irrespective of any determination on the part of the victim to participate. The interviewer should also be appropriately trained and sensitive to the impact the interview is having and may have on the interviewee.

4 Analysis techniques

In law, classic content analysis is often used for examining texts – this can be done with case reports, for example. Webley notes that content analysis has wide application and can be descriptive.[34] However, it can also involve a degree of quantification of material – for example, coding references to human rights then reviewing all newspapers in a particular country between specific dates to determine the frequency with which human rights issues are reported on. Often such analysis is used on a large volume of material and it is possible that computer systems, such as NVivo, may be deployed to assist with the coding and analysis (although many researchers in law still code, annotate

---

32 Stanley Milgram, *Obedience to Authority, An Experimental View* (New York: Harper Collins, 1974/2006).
33 The Belmont report (https://www.hhs.gov/ohrp/regulations-and-policy/belmont-report/index.html, accessed 7 February 2017) led to the National Research Act 1974.
34 Lisa Webley (n 24) 941.

and analyse manually). As much qualitative data is from interviews or participant observation, the raw data can comprise a vast amount of unstructured
textual material. Robson argues for a flexible research design[35] to ensure that
appropriate data are gathered and that the research questions can be adequately
addressed. Nevertheless, the analysis should be rigorous and scientific.

For those with a legal background, some elements of qualitative work can
be normal. Cases, legislation, treaties, all doctrinal material are regularly analysed. Generally, analysis is simply a case of striving for an understanding of
the text.[36] However, such data can also be analysed qualitatively. For example,
all judgments of a particular court are selected. The researcher then chooses a
method of coding words in the judgments to enable an analysis of the influence
of human rights vocabulary in the final judgments of national courts. The
coding allows for a degree of quantitative analysis, but the researcher then
uses the full text to add depth to understanding, or even interviews with the
judges to further deepen the analysis (mixed methods).

In almost all qualitative research work, a great amount of data is collected. Even judicious use of sampling does not reduce the amount of data.
Further refinement is needed. The main methods of data analysis in qualitative
approaches include

- Thematic analysis
- Phenomenological analysis (including interpretative phenomenological
  analysis [IPA])

Once the language-based information has been collected, the analysis can
start. If the researcher has carried out the interview (or observation) first-hand
then s/he will already have an initial perception of the data. Where a team of
researchers are carrying out research then analysis can be conducted as a whole
team or in sub-groups. It can help to have objectivity for some aspects of
analysis while subjectivity and immersion in the subject material can bring a
different, yet just as valid, insight.

4a Thematic analysis

This, in effect, involves reading through transcripts several times to identify
emergent themes. There are various methods and systematic approaches which
can provide reliable scientific data through thematic analysis.

Narrative

Ethnographic approaches are focused on describing the values, beliefs and
practices of groups of people. They are largely descriptive. It may be relevant

---

35 Colin Robson, *Real World Research*, 3rd edn. (Chichester: John Wiley, 2011) p. 130.
36 See Suzanne Egan, Chapter 3.

to simply cite sections of narrative directly from your participant. This can be useful to allow their voice to be heard. It can be a powerful tool in terms of allowing insight into another person's perspective of the world, and meeting the requirements of a human rights based approach by enabling an under-standing of the rights holder's or duty bearer's perspective as a precursor to building awareness and/or capacity. The participant's real-world experience can provide data which require no further treatment. It will be a true picture of the individual's views.[37]

Thematic chart

This is a very basic form of analysis. It may form an early stage of analysis or it may be sufficient in itself to address your research question. A thematic chart reduces the body of data to a small manageable overview. It utilises minimal analysis but adopts the language of the respondent. It should sample from the whole body of data gathered. Specific quotes can be drawn from the text, and marked as quotes with standard quote marks and page numbers. It should reduce the entire body of work to a fraction while maintaining a sense of the whole. A 16-page transcript could, for example, be reduced to one page. This is useful to summarise documents, however, it does not involve analysis in the conventional sense of the word. For lawyers, this is something which is often used when dealing with volumes of textual materials – a (lengthy common law) case report or transcripts from a UN interactive dialogue or stakeholders' meeting, for example.

Memoing

This takes place as you read through a transcript. It comprises the little flashes of insight you have while you read through, and the researcher should make notes literally as these flashes of insight appear. Do not wait until you finish reading that section or that page. Write it as it comes. Many notes made during memoing will be discarded, but they all help form the whole analysis. They provide structure and context for remarks, and these can form the basis of the next level of analysis. Often, just a few words are jotted down, however memoing can run to paragraphs if an idea takes shape and develops. At this stage your ideas and impressions can be brought into the process. Having a holistic overview of, for example, all the transcripts, can help with the emergence of themes. Close cooperation and consultation between researchers is needed if different researchers are memoing different parts of the whole data set.

It can be good practice to have a 'scribble page' for notes and memoing, whether in hard copy or electronically. For example, using the 'track changes'

---

37 See D. della Porter and M. Keating (eds), *Approaches and Methodologies in the Social Sciences: A Pluralist Approach* (Cambridge: Cambridge University Press, 2008) p. 296.

function on an ordinary word document allows sections to be highlighted and notes to be recorded.

Thematic grouping

The next step in analysing qualitative data is to group together data presenting with common themes. Ensure, however, that you retain connection to the whole. By isolating parts of a transcript and focusing more intensively on them, you will have identified their importance. They remain part of the overall body of data, however, and should not be analysed in isolation from their source. It can be very easy to fall into the trap of picking out certain pertinent sections that support your work, or specifically address your research question, while ignoring the majority of the data that do not. The themes should reflect the whole in a holistic, meaningful way.

Grouping findings can take many forms, depending on what is suitable and appropriate for your data. As a simple guide, start by defining the dominant or critical themes that are emerging. Refine these with a second level of analysis, where your analysis starts to move your data away from their original form and the wording into a more abstract form. This level of abstraction is still close to the original, however the cognitive input from the researcher should be apparent. There should be evidence that the researcher is thinking about the different themes and their relationship to the original data. The new findings arising from this should still be strongly grounded in the original raw data.

A note of caution at this point: although qualitative analysis software exists, it tends to utilise coding and key words. It can be very effective in searching for key words but it does not replace a skilled researcher. Although you could use a computer to search for a key word in a hundred transcripts and it could do this much more quickly and accurately than a human eye, unless specifically programmed, a computer cannot pick up a synonym or mistyped word. Neither can a computer adapt to every colloquialism a participant may have used, or recognise incomplete words in a transcript. There is a view that using such software is more of an attempt to quantify than to fully embrace qualitative analysis, however it can be used alongside more in-depth qualitative analysis.[38]

4b Phenomenology

To look beyond the words that participants use and accessible themes that arise on reading through material is to enter the core of qualitative research.

---

38 For further critique of qualitative analysis software including NVivo, see John Gerring and Dino Christenson, *Applied Social Science Methodology: An Introductory Guide* (Cambridge: Cambridge University Press, 2017) p. 278.

Phenomenology seeks to understand the lived experience. It seeks meaning through experience, and seeks to explain that meaning in terms of the individual's lived experience. The analysis involves being able to transform someone's lived experience into a written form that we interpret, and from which we can extract meaning.

The importance of a researcher approaching their participant with an open mind cannot be overemphasised. Of central importance within phenomenological research is what the participant finds important (whether they realise it or not!) The skilled researcher will observe the way a participant responds to questions as well as the actual words spoken. In order to fully understand their lived experience, the researcher has to seek to understand the world from their participant's point of view. Every researcher will carry their own biases within them. By recognising them and leaving them at the door, so to speak, when you begin a phenomenological study then the researcher can allow their participant's views and values to be heard and understood.[39]

Consider the following extracts from imagined interviews with students who attended a community-based learning centre for classes including computing, foreign language/s and soft furnishings. The researcher was tasked with understanding the role of community-based education, an integral part of the right to education and lifelong learning initiatives. The community learning centre was small scale, and each learner there was interviewed several times over a period of months to explore their identity as a learner and their relationship with the centre.

Participant 1: Male, aged 52 years, attending computing classes after suffering a life-changing accident at work which forced him to leave his job

Researcher (R):	Can you tell me a little bit about your reason for coming to this centre?
Interviewee (I):	I saw the advert in the local paper and, em, I decided to come along and give it a shot
R:	What attracted your attention here?
I:	Em, Em, well it had a computing class and I didn't know anything about them. I can't walk anymore and the Job Centre said I should try a desk-based job. You need computing for that.
R:	How did you contact the centre?
I:	I phoned up and they said to come in for a chat. They didn't call it an interview, which helped.

---

39 See Kvale and Brinkmann (n 11) Chapter 2 for further examination of phenomenological interviews.

Participant 2: Female, aged 26 years, lone parent with two young children, attending soft furnishings class

R: Can you tell me a little bit about your reason for coming to this centre?

I: The youngest kid was starting nursery so I had time to come to classes. There's a nursery right next door so I can drop her off at her class then come in for my own class. They don't start until after the nursery so I'm not late.

R: Is the nursery part of the centre here?

I: No, I mean, it's in the same building but it's run separate. There's a Food Bank as well, but that's run by a charity.

R: What first caught your attention about the centre?

I: I had brought my wee girl along to the nursery for registration and there was someone from the centre here standing outside with leaflets asking if we were interested. I didn't think I was but they had tea and coffee inside and they were saying to the mums dropping off their children that they could just come in out the rain while the kids got settled. I went in and read the leaflet and they weren't pushy or anything. I didn't know what 'soft furnishings' meant so I just asked the lady and she said it was curtains and cushions and stuff. I always wanted to learn how to do that kind of stuff but I told her I wasn't very good and she said to come along and try if I wanted to. I mean, I'm on benefits so it didn't cost me anything. I've done loads. All you need to buy is the material and they provide everything else you need.

Participant 3: Female, aged 71 years, attending computing class

R: Can you tell me a little bit about your reason for coming to this centre?

I: My grandchildren live on the other side of the world and I don't get to see them. I heard someone talking about video calling people and being able to see who you speak to so I asked around and the librarian suggested I phone here. She gave me the number. I called them and they had a basic computing course aimed at older people. You should have seen my grandson's face when I first used a computer to talk to him!

Participant 1 views the centre through a deficit model. He is unable to continue in his former occupation, which had been as a skilled manual worker, so is actively looking for alternatives. He has had encouragement from the Job

Centre, which indicates that he is actively seeking work. He is motivated to develop new skills. Through further interviews, this functionalist view of the centre was explored further. He anticipated that the centre would be a stepping stone on to more advanced study and employment in the computing sector.

Participant 2 seems to have been attracted to the centre through interaction with a member of staff. She had not realised that she had needs that could be met there. Instead, she is developing a sense of identity as a learner through her class, almost with a sense of wonder. Her identity as a parent is strong, her awareness of financial poverty high, and the role of the centre in developing her as a skilled person is clear. Further interviews explored these aspects further, and recognised the importance of the proximity to the nursery as becoming less over time. This would allow her to develop her learner identity independently of the centre, and continue with learning in other environments, as long as her responsibilities as a parent could be accommodated around her studies. She mentions costs and her children a lot. This subtle emphasis strengthens her identity as a mother struggling to make ends meet. Learning expands her horizons and provides opportunities that she had not recognised before.

Participant 3 had a specific need to be met and was pro-active about seeking out information. She was using the centre for a specific purpose, which was met very quickly. However, she also became friends with other learners in the centre and they continued studying more as a social group than for specific learner goals. They felt strongly affiliated to the centre.

These three extracts show different motivations and expectations, however the centre in question was able to meet all their needs, whether the learner themselves recognised their particular need or not. The centre was accessible and identifiable. The initial contact secured their interest by providing justification for attending. The centre was fit for purpose – around a variety of such purposes. It also personalised the learners. The phenomenological approach explores the individual, personal experience of each learner, pulls all the qualitative information into a ball, then tugs out different threads and explores the meaning and different aspects of the participants' lived experience. The researcher can focus on proximity, purpose, personal validation and then the emotional attachment to the centre, to learning and to their changing identity. Looking at the ball of data from different perspectives allows the researcher to pick out the essence and discard the incidentals. It requires immersion in the ball of data, and a lack of preconceptions about what the results will be.

Due to the nature of phenomenological inquiry, different researchers can identify different aspects from the same data. A team approach can work well, with individual or pairs of researchers studying the transcript, then brainstorming their meanings from them. Through this, common themes and essences can emerge, strengthening the findings.

Interpretative phenomenological analysis brings in additional levels of interpretation providing more depth. Such a layering of complexity is very time consuming, though this level of complexity is not always necessary to understand the lived experience. The approach aims to offer a rich, in-depth insight into how a given person, in a given context, makes sense of a given phenomenon. Therefore, when used, it can provide valuable insights and understanding.[40] A seminal example is the work of Paul Flowers and colleagues on understanding the impact of an HIV positive diagnosis amongst gay men in Scotland using interviews with newly diagnosed men to identify recurrent themes, and to highlight the participants' experiences of struggling to live with their diagnoses.[41]

4c Grounded theory

Grounded theory is often associated with qualitative analysis.[42] In essence, rather than starting with a theory and gathering data to prove or disprove it (a more positivist law approach), the theory for the research emerges as the data is reviewed and potential patterns and themes emerge, the data is then re-reviewed and coded as categories of ideas come together.[43] The theory therefore comes from working the data. This approach enables the researcher to develop her or his understanding as the inquiry progresses. It is an inductive approach but also in effect a systematisation of the research process – fully ascribing to a grounded theory approach means adhering to the associated practices of data collection, analysis and theory generation. It is not without its critics, but does offer a robustly structured and recognised system of qualitative research.

5 Drawbacks and common pitfalls

First, with traditional legal content analysis of documentation, the principal risk is that aspects of context are lost. For this reason, it is common for legal researchers to analyse the texts being used then go back and consider the wider context – for example, the chronology of judgments if cases are being considered, or the political and cultural context contemporaneous to each document. This can enrich and add further depth to the analysis.

Second, it is impossible to over-emphasise the importance of ensuring appropriate informed consent for research on people – the researcher cannot

40 See Jonathan Smith, Paul Flowers and Michael Larkin, *Interpretative Phenomenological Analysis: Theory, Method and Research* (London: Sage, 2009).
41 Paul Flowers, Mark McGregor Davis, Michael Larkin, Stephanie Church and Claire Marriott, 'Understanding the impact of HIV diagnosis amongst gay men in Scotland: An interpretative phenomenological analysis' (2011) 26(10) *Psychology and Health*, 1378.
42 B. Glaser and A. Strauss, *The Discovery of Grounded Theory: Strategies for Qualitative Research* (New York: Aldine de Gruyter, 1967); A. Strauss and J. Corbin, 'Grounded Theory Methodology: An Overview', in N.K. Denzin and Y.S. Lincoln (eds), *Handbook of Qualitative Research* (London: Sage, 1994).
43 See Kathy Charmaz, *Constructing Grounded Theory: A Practical Guide through Qualitative Analysis* (London: Sage, 2006).

breach the rights of the subjects or participants, and must respect their dignity and, as appropriate, privacy. In many countries, and more specifically academic and government institutions, ethics boards are established to oversee, audit or approve of research on and with humans (or animals). For a human rights based approach to research, this is even more central. The rights of the participants must be fully respected by the researchers and care taken to minimise the risk of reprisals and other detrimental consequences. The risk of retraumatisation or stigmatisation of victims of human rights violations must not be ignored when undertaking human rights research.

Are interviewees happy for their identity to be known? This is not so common in human rights research, when government ministers and officials may wish not to be named or specifically identified and rights holders, especially if victims of violations may suffer reprisals if identified. However, if the responses are electronic (e.g. open text responses through an online survey) then it may be they are fully anonymised and cannot be traced, although that can also bring challenges of proving authenticity. Particular care must be taken when explaining confidentiality, with attention given to whether confidentiality can actually be maintained. Anonymity is not usually practicable as the interviewer may know the identity of the individual. Nevertheless, it is usually necessary to ensure that no-one can be identified from your description of them, either in terms of their role/position in an organisation or of their personal identifying characteristics.

Third is the challenge of generalising from qualitative research.[44] As noted above, qualitative research may be collected from a sample of the general population. It is therefore necessary to consider the extent to which the findings from the study have relevance beyond the sample. The question is therefore whether the findings can be applied to the parent population from which the sample was drawn (and how to define that parent population – e.g. all indigenous peoples or a specific group of indigenous peoples). Beyond that, can the findings be generalised to other settings (e.g. all people) and can the findings support the emergence of theoretical principles which can be applied more generally.

There are many good examples of qualitative methods being used for human rights and development programme reporting. These reports are usually available on the NGO or government website.

6 Conclusions

Qualitative methods undoubtedly offer an opportunity to understand more deeply the real lived experience of people in relationship to human rights.

---

44 See, for example, Jen Lewis and Jane Ritchie, 'Generalising from Qualitative Research' in Jane Ritchie and Jane Lewis (eds) *Qualitative Research Practice: a Guide for Social Science Students and Researchers*, (London: Sage, 2003) pp. 263–286.

Whether migrant workers, refugees, prisoners, indigenous people, children, women, or any other marginalised group, capturing first hand experiences gives the researcher greater understanding. The scope for introduced bias is high in qualitative methods, so care must be taken to remain aware of this during the process and, where necessary, to acknowledge it. Ethical considerations are also particularly prominent in qualitative work as care must be taken not to retraumatise the individuals being interviewed and, of course, to protect their identity.

Recommended reading list

Alan Bryman, *Quantity and Quality in Social Research* (Abingdon: Routledge, 1988).

Alan Bryman, *Social Research Methods*, 5th edn. (Oxford: Oxford University Press, 2016).

Donatella Della Porta and Michael Keating, *Approaches and Methodologies in the Social Sciences: A Pluralist Perspective* (Cambridge: Cambridge University Press, 2008).

John Gerring and Dino Christenson, *Applied Social Science Methodology: An Introductory Guide* (Cambridge: Cambridge University Press, 2017).

Steiner Kvale and Svend Brinkmann, *InterViews: Learning the Craft of Qualitative Research Interviewing*, 3rd edn. (London: Sage, 2014).

Gale Miller and Robert Dingwall (eds) *Context and Method in Qualitative Research* (London: Sage, 1997).

Colin Robson, *Real World Research*, 3rd edn. (London: Wiley, 2011).

David Silverman (ed.) *Qualitative Research* (London: Sage, 2016).

6   Quantitative analysis

Todd Landman

1 Introduction

Since the 1948 Universal Declaration of Human Rights, there has been a proliferation of human rights legal instruments, which have expanded both the breadth and depth of human rights that are legally articulated and which form the basis for: (1) domestic, transnational, and international advocacy; (2) observation, mapping, and descriptive analysis of human rights situations; and (3) fact-finding, transitional justice processes, and successful prosecution of those responsible for committing crimes against humanity, genocide, torture, and other forms of cruel, unusual, and inhumane treatment of individuals and groups. Parallel to these legal developments and outcomes, there has been burgeoning work from statisticians, social scientists, and computer scientists who have developed methods for: (1) counting violations, (2) measuring human rights conditions, (3) surveying attitudes and perceptions of human rights, (4) capturing human rights narratives and sentiments, and (5) building large-scale explanatory models that account for the variation in the promotion and protection of human rights.

These two developments began from very different starting points. The legal developments in human rights draw on a longer history of the struggle for citizenship rights that was universalised and galvanised in the aftermath of the Second World War, where the global community came together to articulate a set of human rights that are seen to be inherent and inalienable and which have been 'socially constructed' through a series of iterations led by human rights scholars, practitioners, and activists in ways that have increasingly fortified a set of global normative commitments.[1] The second set

---

1 Joe Foweraker and Todd Landman, *Citizenship Rights and Social Movements: A Comparative and Statistical Analysis* (Oxford: Oxford University Press, 1997); Joe Foweraker and Todd Landman 'Individual Rights and Social Movements: A Comparative and Statistical Inquiry' (1999) 29 *British Journal of Political Science*, 291; Todd Landman, *Protecting Human Rights: A Global Comparative Study* (Washington, DC: Georgetown University Press, 2005); Todd Landman, *Human Rights and Democracy: The Precarious Triumph of Ideals* (London: Bloomsbury, 2013).

of developments on the quantitative analysis of human rights were borne of the 'behavioural revolution' in the social sciences with an impulse to measure and operationalize social science concepts at the micro and macro levels of analysis. This work has become increasingly more advanced and mature, with cutting edge developments that include cross-national time-series analysis, regional and comparative analysis, social media and supervised machine learning analysis, and geospatial analysis of a wide range of human rights problems across the different categories and dimensions of human rights.[2]

Despite the two different geneses of the law of human rights and quantitative analysis of human rights, the two developments have become increasingly intertwined as the human rights legal community has been interested in the evidentiary value of quantitative human rights analysis, and the scholarly community has seen human rights as a research area that is susceptible to a wide range of quantitative analytical techniques. The initial unease in the human rights community over using sterile and scientific approaches to analyse human suffering has given way to a new demand for quantitative analysis and insight.[3] The initial unease among quantitative analysts over turning their toolkits and attention to largely moral and normative concerns has given way to a thriving research and practitioner community making great strides in developing quantitative methods that are appropriate for analysing human rights problems.[4]

This chapter provides an introduction to the quantitative analysis of human rights. It begins with providing a definition and outlining the different purposes of quantitative analysis as it is applied to human rights problems. It then outlines the different measures of human rights that have been developed and used in quantitative analysis of human rights. It then discusses the different types of quantitative analysis and concludes with a discussion of remaining lacunae and future developments in this exciting area of work. Throughout the discussion, the chapter remains committed to the idea that quantitative analysis is one of many ways of 'knowing the world' and acts as a useful complement to other forms of analysis equally interested in uncovering, explaining, and understanding the promotion and protection of human rights in the modern world.

---

2 Todd Landman and Edzia Carvalho, *Measuring Human Rights* (Abingdon: Routledge, 2009); Todd Landman and Larissa Kersten 'Measuring Human Rights,' in Michael Goodhart (ed.) *Human Rights: Politics and Practice*, 3rd edn. (New York: Oxford University Press, 2015) pp. 127–144.
3 Ibid.
4 Landman, *Protecting Human Rights* (n 1); Philip Alston and Sarah Knuckey (eds), *The Transformation of Human Rights Fact Finding* (Oxford: Oxford University Press, 2015); Todd Landman, 'Rigorous Morality: Norms, Values and the Comparative Politics of Human Rights' (2016) 38(1) *Human Rights Quarterly*, 1.

2 The purpose of quantitative analysis

Quantitative analysis is quite literally a form of analysis that starts with a simple question of 'how many of them are there?' For human rights, this 'how many' question can include (1) individual violations (single or multiple) suffered by individual people; (2) aggregations of violations experienced by groups of different people over time; (3) subjective scores of human rights performance, based on narrative accounts of human rights practices within countries; (4) perceptions, sentiments, and experiences of human rights across samples of mass publics; (5) socio-economic and administrative data collected by public and private organisations that relate directly or indirectly to the promotion and protection of human rights; (6) so-called 'big data' harvested from the public sphere in the form of social media, consumer behaviours, and data collected from analysis of mobile devices; (7) geo-spatial data collected through techniques of 'earth observation' using satellite images and remote sensing technologies.

These types of data are very different from one another and are used in very different ways by different analysts, but the fundamental goal of quantitative analysis is to make the most secure and unbiased inferences about the human rights question that is the subject of the analysis. An inference is a set of analytical statements that generalise from a specific sample of quantitative information that has been collected. In human rights work, as we shall see, the sample of information itself is hugely problematic, since it is typically biased, unrepresentative, and incomplete; problems which do not preclude carrying out quantitative analysis and or making inferences, but problems that if left unaddressed can reduce the security and reliability of the inferences that are made. For a community of scholars and practitioners interested in advancing human rights through quantitative inquiry, both the security and reliability of inferences about human rights problems in the world are the pillars for sound human rights advocacy.[5]

So, what are the kinds of inferences that can be made from the quantitative analysis of human rights? The following examples are drawn from the existing quantitative literature and published studies on human rights problems:

1. The estimated number of people killed in the conflict in Peru between 1980 and 2000 was between 61,007 and 77,552.[6]
2. Between March 2011 and April 2013, there were 92,901 unique killings reported in the Syrian Arab Republic.[7]

5 Landman, 'Rigorous Morality' (n 4).
6 Patrick Ball, Jana Asher, David Sulmont and Daniel Manrique, 'How Many Peruvians Have Died?' (Washington, DC: American Association for the Advancement of Science, 2003) <http://shr.aaas.org/hrdag/peru/aaas_peru_5.pdf> accessed 7 February 2017.
7 Megan Price, Jeff Klinger, Anas Qtiesh and Patrick Ball 'Updated Statistical Analysis of Documentation of Killings in the Syrian Arab Republic' (San Francisco: Human Rights Data Analysis Group, 2013).

3. There is a positive and significant relationship between democracy and human rights.[8]
4. The single biggest factor in accounting for the violation of civil and political rights is whether a country is experiencing civil war or not.[9]
5. Countries with better human rights records received more financial assistance from the World Bank, but once they had received the assistance, the human rights situation deteriorated.[10]
6. There is a positive and significant relationship between state ratification of human rights treaties and the protection of physical integrity rights.[11]
7. There is a positive and significant relationship between high levels of income and land inequality and the violation of physical integrity rights.[12]
8. There has been an improvement in the protection of civil and political rights over the last 30 years, even after taking into account a rising standard of accountability.[13]
9. Some countries over-perform and other countries under-perform in their fulfilment of economic and social rights.[14]

Across all these examples, the statements are made on the basis of a sample of information. In the Peruvian example, the statement is about an estimation of a number of deaths relating to civil conflict, which in the official report stated the estimation itself (69,280 people) and the 'margin of error' in that estimation (± 7000 people). The margin of error is a function of the method that was used to make the estimation from three different sources of information in which deaths were recorded, but between which there were varying degrees of overlap.[15] In the Syrian example, the total number of reported killings was

---

8 Steven C. Poe and C. Neal Tate, 'Repression of Human Rights to Personal Integrity in the 1980s: A Global Analysis' (1994) 88(3) *American Political Science Review*, 853.

9 Ibid.

10 Rodwan Abouharb and David Cingranelli, *Human Rights and Structural Adjustment* (Cambridge: Cambridge University Press, 2007).

11 Landman, *Protecting Human Right* (n 1); Beth Simmons, *Mobilizing for Human Rights: International Law in Domestic Politics* (Cambridge, Cambridge University Press, 2009); Christopher Fariss, 'The Changing Standard of Accountability and the Positive Relationship between Human Rights Treaty Ratification and Compliance' (2018) 48(1) *British Journal of Political Science* 239–271; Christopher Fariss, 'Are Things Really Getting Better? How to Validate Latent Variable Models of Human Rights' (2018) 48(1) *British Journal of Political Science*, 275–282.

12 Todd Landman and Marco Larizza, 'Inequality and Human Rights: Who Controls What When and How' (2009) 53(3) *International Studies Quarterly*, 715.

13 Christopher Fariss, 'Respect for Human Rights Has Improved Over Time: Modelling the Changing Standard of Accountability' (2014) 108(2) *American Political Science Review*, 297; Fariss, 'Are Things Really Getting Better?' (n 11); Fariss, 'The Changing Standard' (n 11).

14 Sakiko Fukuda-Parr, Terra Lawson-Remer and Susan Randolph, *Fulfilling Social and Economic Rights* (Oxford, Oxford University Press, 2015).

15 Ball, Asher, Sulmont and Manrique (n 6); Landman and Carvalho (n 2); Todd Landman and Anita Gohdes 'A Matter of Convenience: Challenges of Non-Random Data in Analyzing

the result of collecting and analysing data across eight different databases and only reports those killings for which there are actual names of the victims, which means it is an enumeration of the killings and not a total estimation of all killings during that period.[16] In the other examples, the statements are about general tendencies drawn from the sample of data used. The data samples are all from a large number of countries over periods of time ranging from 20 to 30 years. The statements are generalisations from these samples and as they use the term 'statistically significant', they would expect to find a similar set of relationships using a new sample of countries and over different periods of time.

These and other stylised statements are made possible through quantitative analysis, where the human rights research specifies a research question, develops a theory and a set of observable implications from that theory about what the research expects to find,[17] collects data on the human rights specified in the research question along with other additional data, and then analyses the data to see if and to what degree the observable implications of the theory are borne out by the data. The key to this kind of analysis is either the availability of data on human rights, or a method for the systematic collection and analysis of data on human rights. The field of quantitative human rights analysis has made great strides in providing new ways to collect and analyse an increasing number of categories and dimensions of human rights. Before discussing in more detail the different kinds of human rights data, let us first consider the different uses of quantitative analysis of human rights.

First, quantitative analysis and the use of human rights measures allow for contextual description and documentation, which provide the raw information for the monitoring carried out primarily by non-governmental organizations, as well as for developing and deriving standardized measures of human rights typically used by human rights scholars. Second, it can help efforts at classification, which allow for the differentiation of rights violations across their different categories and dimensions, and for grouping states and regimes into different categories, such as authoritarian, personal dictatorship, fragile states, unconsolidated or weak democracies, and one-party dominant regimes. Third, it can be used for monitoring the degree to which states respect, protect, and fulfil the various rights set out in the different treaties to which they may be a party. Fourth, it can be used for mapping and pattern recognition, which provide time-series and spatial information on the broad patterns of violations within and across different countries, as well as within different groups of

Human Rights Violations during Conflicts in Peru and Sierra Leone' in Taylor Seybolt, Jay Aronson and Baruch Fishoff (eds), *Counting Civilian Casualties* (Oxford, Oxford University Press, 2013).

16 Price, Klinger, Qtiesh, and Ball (n 7).

17 Gary King, Robert O Keohane and Sidney Verba, *Designing Social Inquiry: Scientific Inference in Qualitative Research* (Princeton: Princeton University Press, 1994).

countries.[18] Fifth, it is used for secondary analysis, including hypothesis-testing, prediction, and impact assessment, the inferences from which can be fed into the policy-making process.[19] Finally, it can be used for advocacy at the domestic and international level by showing the improvement or deterioration in rights practices around the world, the patterns of violation that form part of official truth commissions, such as those in South Africa, Peru, Sierra Leone, and East Timor;[20] special tribunals, such as those for Rwanda (ICTR) and the Former Yugoslavia (ICTY); and domestic trials, such as the 2013 trial of General Efrain Rios Montt in Guatemala for genocide and crimes against humanity.[21] The accumulation of information on human rights protection in the world and the results of systematic analysis can serve as the basis for the continued development of human rights policy, advocacy, and education.[22]

3 Measuring human rights

Quantitative analysis of human rights relies on six main types of measures that have been developed over many years, that serve as direct measures of human rights or as significant proxy measures for different dimensions of human rights. Events-based data count and chart the reported acts of violation committed against groups and individuals. Standards-based data establish how often and to what degree violations occur and then translate such judgments into quantitative indicators that are designed to achieve commensurability by coding narrative information on human rights conditions into a standardised scale. Survey-based data use random samples of country populations to ask a series of standard questions on the perception of rights protection and/or experiences with human rights violations. Increasingly, socio-economic and administrative statistics have been used to measure, in more indirect fashion, states' efforts to respect, protect, and fulfil human rights. The era of big data also includes a look at human rights and measures relevant to human rights, as new techniques are being developed to harvest information in the public domain from social media and other sources to provide insights into human

18 Todd Landman, David Kernohan and Anita Gohdes, 'Relativising Human Rights' (2012) 11(4) *Journal of Human Rights*, 460; Fukuda-Parr, Lawson-Remer and Randolph (n 14).
19 Todd Landman, 'Review Article: The Political Science of Human Rights' (2005) 35(3) *British Journal of Political Science*, 549; Todd Landman, *Studying Human Rights* (Abingdon: Routledge, 2006); Landman and Carvalho (n 2); Landman and Kersten (n 2).
20 See Landman and Carvalho (n 2).
21 Landman, 'Rigorous Morality' (n 4).
22 Barnett R. Rubin and Paula R. Newberg, 'Statistical Analysis for Implementing Human Rights Policy' in Paula R. Newberg (ed.) *The Politics of Human Rights* (New York: New York Press, 1980) 268; Richard P. Claude and Thomas B. Jabine, 'Exploring Human Rights Issues with Statistics' in Thomas B. Jabine and Richard P. Claude (eds), *Human Rights and Statistics: Getting the Record Straight* (Philadelphia: University of Pennsylvania Press, 1992) 5–34; Landman, 'Rigorous Morality' (n 4); Landman and Carvalho (n 2); Landman and Kersten (n 2).

rights problems. Finally, some efforts at measurement have combined different types of data to measure human rights or compare human perceptions to human rights performance of different countries.[23] These different kinds of measures are considered in turn.

3a Events data

Events-based data answer the important questions of what happened, when it happened, and who was involved, and then report descriptive and numerical summaries of the events. Counting such events and violations involves identifying the various acts of commission and omission that constitute or lead to human rights violations, such as extra-judicial killings, arbitrary arrest, or torture. Such data tend to be disaggregated to the level of the violation itself, which may have related data units such as the perpetrator, the victim, and the witness.[24] Data projects over the years that adopt this framework and set of measures have been used by a large number of truth commissions (e.g. South Africa, Haiti, El Salvador, Guatemala, Peru, Sierra Leone, and East Timor), international tribunals (e.g. the International Tribunal for the Former Yugoslavia, ITCY), and domestic trials (e.g. the trial against General Efrain Rios Montt for genocide and crimes against humanity in Guatemala). Across these different official bodies, formal legal mandates were established for the kind of human rights violations that should be counted, and events-based data were used to show the full nature and extent of violence, including differences in treatment across groups, the geographical dimensions of the violence, and the ratio of killings between one group and another. Events data and the quantitative analysis that underpins it sit alongside other kinds of evidence to build comprehensive portraits of contested periods of conflict and legal arguments to convict suspected perpetrators of human rights abuse.

3b Standards

Standards-based measures of human rights are one level removed from event counting and violation reporting and merely apply an ordinal scale to qualitative information, where the resulting scale is derived from determining whether the reported human rights situation reaches particular threshold

---

23 For example, see Christopher J. Anderson, Aida Paskeviciute, Maria Elena Sandovici and Yuliya V. Tverdova, 'In the Eye of the Beholder? The Foundations of Subjective Human Rights Conditions in East-Central Europe' (2005) 38 *Comparative Political Studies*, 771; James Ron, Shannon Golden, David Crow and Archana Pandya, *Taking Root: Public Opinion and Human Rights in the Global South* (Oxford, Oxford University Press, 2017).

24 Patrick Ball, Herbert Spirer and Louise Spirer, 'Making the Case: Investigating Large Scale Human Rights Violations Using Information Systems and Data Analysis' (Washington, DC: American Association for the Advancement of Science, 2000); Landman, *Studying Human Rights* (n 19) 82–83; Seybolt, Aronson and Fishoff (n 15).

conditions. The most prominent examples include the Freedom House scales of civil and political liberties,[25] the 'political terror scale',[26] a scale of torture,[27] and a series of 17 different rights measures collected by Cingranelli and Richards.[28] The scales use narrative information on the human rights situations in countries reported in the US State Department Country Reports and the Amnesty International Country Reports, and then apply a standard scale that reflects the severity of the violation of different categories of human rights. These scales are standardised and yield an absolute overall score for a country that can then be used for comparative quantitative analysis for many countries in the world over time. Subsequent analyses of these scales have explored ways of combining them into an index of human rights,[29] a relative measure of human rights that reflects underlying socio-economic conditions,[30] and an adjusted measure to reflect a rising global standard of accountability.[31]

3c *Surveys*

Survey data have been used less in social scientific research on human rights than either events-based or standards-based measures. They have usually featured more often in research on the support for democracy,[32] trust and social

---

25 Raymond D. Gastil, *Freedom in the World: Political Rights and Civil Liberties 1978* (Boston: GK Hall, 1978); Raymond D. Gastil, *Freedom in the World: Political Rights and Civil Liberties 1980* (Westport, CT: Greenwood Press, 1981); Raymond D. Gastil, *Freedom in the World: Political Rights and Civil Liberties 1986–1987* (New York: Freedom House, 1988); Raymond D. Gastil, 'The Comparative Survey of Freedom: Experiences and Suggestions' (1990) 25 *Studies in Comparative International Development*, 25; Freedom House <www.freedomhouse. org> accessed 7 February 2017.

26 Christopher Mitchell, Michael Stohl, David Carleton and George Lopez 'State Terrorism: Issues of Concept and Measurement' in Michael Stohl and George Lopez (eds) *Government Violence and Repression: An Agenda for Research* (New York: Greenwood Press, 1986); Poe and Tate (n 8); Mark Gibney and Michael Stohl, 'Human Rights and US Refugee Policy' in Mark Gibney (ed.), *Open Borders? Closed Societies? The Ethical and Political Issues* (Westport, CT: Greenwood Press, 1988); The Political Terror Scale <www.politicalterrorscale.org> accessed 7 February 2017.

27 Oona Hathaway, 'Do Treaties Make a Difference? Human Rights Treaties and the Problem of Compliance' (2002) 111 *Yale Law Journal*, 1932; Oona Hathaway, 'The Cost of Commitment' (2003) 55 *Stanford Law Review*, 1821; Oona Hathaway, 'Why Do Countries Commit to Human Rights Treaties?' (2007) 51(4) *Journal of Conflict Resolution*, 588.

28 CIRI Human Rights Data Project, <www.humanrightsdata.com> accessed 7 February 2017.

29 Landman and Larizza (n 12).

30 Landman, Kernohan and Gohdes (n 18).

31 Fariss, 'Respect for Human Rights' (n 13); Fariss, 'Are Things Really Getting Better?' (n 11); Fariss, 'The Changing Standard' (n 11).

32 Max Kaase and Kenneth Newton, *Beliefs in Government* (New York, Oxford University Press, 1995).

capital,[33] patterns of corruption,[34] or as components of larger indices of 'post-material' values and political culture.[35] But increasingly, household surveys have been used to provide measures for popular attitudes about rights and to uncover direct and indirect experiences of human rights violations. The approach in using surveys is to use a random sample of the population to which one seeks to make inferences, and then use structured, or semi-structured survey instruments to ask people questions about human rights. These questions can probe general attitudes towards human rights, the type of issue areas that people think involve human rights, the degree to which people support the idea of human rights, and the degree to which people think human rights are respected within their countries. Surveys can also be used on particular communities of people, such as displaced people and refugees, victims of sexual violence, or other marginalised groups around the world. The questions on human rights can be complemented with questions on social demographic information, such as age, income, education, gender, location, religious affiliation, religiosity, occupation, etc. Together, such data sets can then be used to look at the sorts of factors that have an impact on popular attitudes to human rights (see below).

3d Administrative and socio-economic data

Administrative and socio-economic statistics produced by national statistical offices or recognized international governmental organizations have been increasingly seen as useful sources of data for the indirect measure of human rights, or as indicators for rights-based approaches to different sectors, such as justice, health, education, and welfare. Government statistical agencies and inter-governmental organizations produce a variety of socio-economic statistics that can be used to approximate measures of human rights. For example, academic and policy research has used aggregate measures of development as proxy measures for the progressive realization of social and economic rights. Such aggregate measures include the Physical Quality of Life Index (PQLI), the Human Development Index (HDI) and the Social and Economic Rights Fulfilment Index (SERF Index). In these examples, sets of official statistics

33 Paul Whiteley, 'The Origins of Social Capital' in Jan Van Deth, Marco Maraffi, Kenneth Newton and Paul Whiteley (eds), *Social Capital and European Democracy* (London: Routledge, 1999); Paul Whiteley, 'Economic Growth and Social Capital' (2000) 48 *Political Studies*, 443.

34 Transparency International, <www.transparency.org> accessed 7 February 2017.

35 Ronald Inglehart, *Modernization and Postmodernization* (Princeton: Princeton University Press, 1997); Ronald Inglehart and Pippa Norris, *Rising Tide: Gender Equality and Cultural Change Around the World* (New York: Cambridge University Press, 2003); Ronald Inglehart, *Culture and Social Change: Findings from the Value Surveys* (Leiden: Brill, 2003); Christian Welzel and Ronald Inglehart, 'Agency, Values, and Well-Being: A Human Development Model' (2010) 97(1) *Social Indicators Research*, 43.

that relate to particular categories and dimensions of human rights can be used to approximate the degree to which certain human rights are being fulfilled. The Social and Economic Rights Fulfilment Index uses data relevant to the right to food, the right to education, the right to health, the right to housing, and the right to work. These different elements are then used to calculate the degree to which countries are achieving benchmark levels of obligation relative to their level of economic development.[36]

3e 'New' and 'big' data on human rights

Alongside the continued development and refinement of these existing measurement strategies, there are new trends in data collection that make use of the 'democratization of technology' that has taken place more or less during the first decade of the twenty-first century. The rise of social media, and the increasing availability of smartphones and other mobile devices has led to a revolution in the ability of individual people to have a voice in ways that were hitherto not possible. User-generated content on the internet, in the form of 'tweets', YouTube videos, SMS alert networks, and other platforms of information dissemination, have created a volume of information on country conditions that is beginning to transform the ability of quantitative analysts to study human rights. The information that is now available is 'double edged': on the one hand, it provides the ability for grassroots reporting and narrative accounts of real time events as they unfold, and on the other hand, it provides 'meta data' on the events themselves, as smart technology often contains automatic functions that include the date, time and location that something has happened (typically through embedded 'global positioning system' technology, or GPS). These forms of data can be quite large, but they are still plagued by all the same issues such as bias, representativeness, internal validity (do they measure what they are supposed to measure?), and external validity (can someone else replicate their production and analysis?).

Despite these potential problems, which are true of any kind of data, the combination of real-time data and meta data allows for the collection, fusion, and visualization of human rights events across space and time (known as geo-spatial analysis), often at the 'street corner' level of accuracy. The collection of these kinds of data occurs in two ways: (1) 'crowd sourcing' through special-ized data collection 'portals' such as the platform made available through Ushahidi,[37] or (2) collection of data from already existing 'open data' sources, such as Facebook, Twitter, news media, and NGO reporting, among others. In their raw form, the data are not particularly useful, but, through fusing different sources into well-structured databases, they can be used for human rights assessments of countries alongside other more traditional forms of data.

36 See Fukuda-Parr, Lawson-Remer and Randolph (n 14); Landman and Kersten (n 2).
37 Ushahidi <www.ushahidi.com> accessed 7 February 2017.

Moreover, since the meta data may contain additional information about date, time, and location of events, it is possible to map violations on publicly available mapping programmes, such as Google Maps. In addition, analysts are also exploring ways to harness satellite technology for collecting information on humanitarian crises, border conflicts, and large scale human rights violations, as well as contemporary forms of slavery.[38]

4 Types of quantitative analysis

Having outlined a wide range of different measures of human rights, it is now possible to discuss the different ways in which quantitative analysis uses these measures, and the kinds of statements that are made possible through different kinds of analysis. These different types of analyses range from the very straightforward and simple to the advanced and complex, where the underlying structure to the data, the types of sources, and the ways in which the data will be used all matter for the kinds of inferences that can be drawn about human rights. The choice of the type of analysis that is used is a function of the research questions posed and the purpose of the analysis that is set out in the first place. For example, many projects start with the simple question 'how many are there?' Or 'what has been the trend in cruel, inhuman and degrading punishment in country X?' Or 'how many people died between date T_1 and date T_2?' These kinds of questions are known as descriptive in nature, since they are a straight reporting of a trend or number of something relating to human rights. They might also include questions like 'what is the average number of people summarily executed per year?' Or 'what is the average number of people on death row across the states of the United States of America?'

Table 1 reports the findings from the Peruvian Truth and Reconciliation Commission (CVR) on how many people died during the conflict between 1980 and 2000. The table reports the total estimated killings (how many were there?) and the number of people likely to have been killed by the army, the Sendero Luminoso revolutionary group, and others (i.e. who did what to whom?). The results in the table are the outcome of 18 months of data collection, 17,000 statements taken by the Truth and Reconciliation Commission, additional data sources that helped triangulate the statement data, and further analysis of census data and trends in the population by region of the country. The table thus summarises a vast amount of work in a straightforward and easy to understand format. The figures reported also include the range of possible values for each category since the numbers are an estimation of the total number of people killed, where the estimated number is expressed as a range from the lower boundary to the upper boundary of that estimation

38 Ball, Spirer and Spirer (n 24); Ball, Asher, Sulmont and Manrique (n 6); Alston and Knuckey (n 4).

Table 6.1 Statistical estimation of the number of people killed in Peru, 1980–2000 (Multiple Systems Estimation, MSE)

		Main perpetrators in the conflict			
		Shining Path	*The state*	*Others*	*Total*
Full range of estimated killings	Maximum	37,840	23,893	20,076	77,552
	Estimate	31,331	20,458	15,967	**69,280**
	Minimum	24,823	17,023	11,858	61,007

Source: Adapted from Ball, Asher, Sulmont and Manrique (2003: 7); http://shr.aaas.org/hrdag/peru/aaas_peru_5.pdf.

based on the degree of overlap of the different sources of data that were used and where the true value lies somewhere between those two boundaries.[39]

In another example that uses the same method for counting human rights violations or concepts relating to human rights, Bales et al. estimated the total number of contemporary slaves in the UK.[40] For them, a slave is someone who is working in a role that is paid or unpaid, but in a role from which they have no freedom to leave. Using six different sources of data on slavery in the UK, their analysis finds that the total number of estimated slaves in the UK is 11,418, where the lower limit of that range is 9,982 and the upper limit to that range is 13,181.[41] This kind of work can have a great impact on policy makers and practitioners. In the Peruvian case, the Truth Commission findings showed that many more people had been killed than first imagined; that the army was far more responsible for killings than first imagined; and that there were differences in the patterns in killings between the coastal regions around the capital Lima and the mountainous regions such as Ayacucho. In the UK slavery example, this was the first most scientific estimate that had ever been provided to the Home Office on this social phenomenon, which then allowed the UK government to think about how to tackle the problem. Counting slaves in this way for the first time allowed something to be done about the problem.

So called 'second-order' questions focus on simple relationships between human rights data and other data and require what is called bivariate analysis, since the analysis seeks to uncover the possible relationship between two variables. There are numerous examples of bivariate relationships in human rights research, such as economic development and the protection of civil

---

39 Ball, Asher, Sulmont and Manrique (n 15).
40 Kevin Bales, Olivia Hesketh and Bernard Silverman, 'Modern Slavery in the UK: How Many Victims?' (2015) 12(3) *Significance*, 16.
41 Ibid.; see Table 2 below.

political rights,[42] civil war and personal integrity rights,[43] treaty ratification and human rights,[44] foreign direct investment and human rights,[45] and many others. To illustrate a bivariate relationship, Figure 1 is a scatterplot of the relationship between income inequality and human rights. The x-axis plots a standardised measure of income distribution, where a higher score denotes a more unequal distribution of income. The y-axis plots a human rights factor score, which combines different standards-based measures of human rights into a single index, where higher scores denote a better protection of human rights. The line sloping downward to the right shows that countries with more unequal distributions of income also have worse records of protecting human rights. The analysis that sits behind this scatterplot also determined that the relationship is statistically significant, which means that if a different sample of countries was used for a different year, the relationship would still be the same, i.e. a negative relationship between high levels of income inequality and low levels of human rights protection.

The key challenge to any bivariate analysis is that it might leave out important considerations and yield what is called a 'spurious' relationship between two variables. This means that a relationship between two variables that appears to be statistically significant is actually due to a third factor that has not been included in the analysis. Some variable X is specified to have a direct relationship with Y. Data collected on X and Y could then be plotted or analysed using what is called correlation analysis and a strong and significant relationship could be found. But it might be that some factor Z that is actually responsible for both X and Y, and that any direct relationship between the X and Y is non-existent.

For example, a study may show that economic development and human rights are positively related, where wealthier countries have better human rights protection. But we also know that wealthier countries also tend to be democracies and we know that democracies are better at protecting certain sets of human rights. There may be other factors beyond the level of development and democracy that explain the variation in the protection of human rights, and thus any systematic statistical study uses what is called multivariate analysis which estimates the independent effect of variables such as economic development, democracy, and conflict on the protection of human rights, while holding other variables constant. The technique is made possible through the use of large data sets with many observations and the typical unit

42 See Neil Mitchell and James M. McCormick, 'Economic and Political Explanations of Human Rights Violations' (1988) 40 *World Politics*, 476.

43 Poe and Tate (n 8).

44 Landman, *Protecting Human Rights* (n 1); Simmons (n 11); Fariss, 'Are Things Really Getting Better?' (n 11); Fariss, 'The Changing Standard' (n 11).

45 Jackie Smith, Melissa Bolyard and Anna Ippolito, 'Human Rights and the Global Economy: A Response to Meyer' (1999) 21(1) *Human Rights Quarterly*, 207.

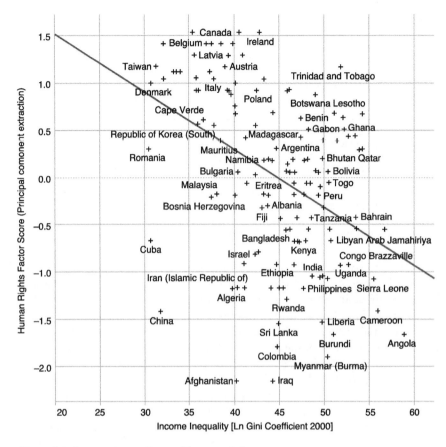

Figure 6.1 Income inequality and human rights.

Source: Landman and Larizza (2009).

of analysis is the country-year; a data point for each country for each year in a time-series collection of data.

Figure 2 summarises the main findings from many years of multivariate analysis on human rights that extends from the 1980s[46] to the latest work on treaty ratification and human rights.[47] Across all this work, multivariate analysis has been used on increasingly more complex data sets made up of more countries over longer periods of time. The figure shows that the 'basic' model that has been developed includes variables such as economic development, democracy, population size, civil war, and authoritarianism, each with

46 For example, Mitchell and McCormick (n 42).
47 Fariss, 'Are Things Really Getting Better?' (n 11).

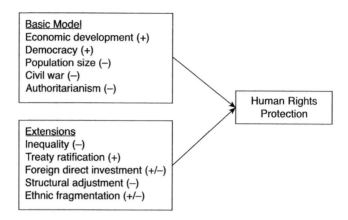

Figure 6.2 Summary of quantitative cross-national analysis of human rights.

its own positive or negative relationship with human rights.[48] Extensions of the basic model have included such variables as inequality, treaty ratification, foreign direct investment, structural adjustment policies, and ethnic fragmentation. Simple and more complex regression analysis has been used to estimate the different relationships and revealed the direction (+ or −), magnitude, and level of statistical significance of each of the different variables.

Descriptive, bivariate, and multivariate analysis also form part of the toolchest for what has become known as 'data analytics' popular in the analysis of big data on a wide range of topics including consumer behaviour analysis, mobile phone tracking, sentiment analysis, and image and video analysis. These techniques combine different sources of data, measure the density of reporting and the geographical location of reporting, triangulate these data with other data on the meanings of words used in 'tweets' (and other social media platforms) and images and videos of events with real consequence for human rights (e.g. police shootings in the United States, violence in Syria and the Middle East, and protest events in Istanbul, among many others). Data analytics are used to harvest meaning, understanding and explanation from vast quantities of data, but these data carry with them many problems of bias, incompleteness, and unrepresentativeness, all of which must be taken into account by the analyst in ways that reduce uncertainty and maximise the inferences they make possible.

---

48 See also, Landman, *Protecting Human Right* (n 1); Landman, *Studying Human Rights* (n 19); Landman, 'Rigorous Morality' (n 4).

5 Lacunae and future developments

There has been much progress in the quantitative analysis of human rights, where scholars and practitioners have developed ingenious ways to measure, map, count, plot, and interrogate a wide variety of data sources to make meaningful descriptive and analytical inferences about the patterns, perpetrators, victims, and conditions that characterise different categories and dimensions of human rights around the world. Attention remains focussed on the analysis of civil and political rights, but new measures and new methods have turned to a wider range of human rights using a wider and more lateral range of data relevant to human rights. Despite the extraordinary progress that has been made since the 1980s in this area of work, there remain many challenges and lucanae that need to be addressed.

First, any data project on human rights needs to accept and confront the fact that a large part of the work is dealing with what political scientist Will Moore calls 'the fundamental problem of unobservability', in other words, the methodological difficulty of counting and analysing a set of practices and social phenomena that remain obscured from direct observation by the analyst. Human rights violations are often committed behind closed doors, within secret detention facilities, or during complicated periods of violent conflict. Patterns of discrimination and unequal treatment can have subtle and unobserved elements with many different mediating factors that hide the intentionality of committing violations, or involve the disproportionate maltreatment of particular groups within society. The task of the data analyst through the collection and analysis of human rights and other measures is to engage in a systematic process of revelation. Indeed, the process of making an inference is 'the process of using facts we know to learn about facts we do not know'.[49] In this way, the human rights data analyst is using facts about human rights that he or she knows to learn something about the facts not yet known, where both the process of collecting facts and making inferences needs to be as systematic and rigorous as it can be. The less systematic and rigorous any analysis is, the weaker and more uncertain the inferences are. Strong inferences based on systematic and rigorous methods reveal things about patterns and contours of human rights that have not been known hitherto. In this way, quantitative human rights analysis is a process of revelation.

Second, any successful data project relies on maximising the quality of the data at every stage of the analytical project. Human rights data and measures vary with respect to how different categories and dimensions of human rights are operationalized (events, standards, surveys, socio-economic and administrative statistics, and big data), the validity and reliability of these data, the quality of the original source material and how that is used to produce quantitative indicators for first and second order analysis. There is the potential for

49 King, Keohane and Verba (n 17) 46.

error to be introduced at any stage of the process, which can have both independent and cumulative effects on the reliability of the findings and conclusions of any data project. Any analyst needs to be fully conscious of the potential for bias to be introduced across a project and the ways in which bias can be reduced. From the selection of data sources, to the coding of variables, to the building of multivariate models, choices that are made without care can lead to unsafe or insecure inferences, which is particularly problematic for work in a field seeking to advocate for change that leads to better protection of human rights.[50]

Third, quantitative analysis relies on what I call statistical conservatism and the use of precise language about what the analysis can actually tell us, rather than stretching the interpretation of findings in ways that are simply not possible given the data that analysts have and the results obtained. In my own work on treaty ratification and human rights, I conclude that there is a 'significant but limited effect between norms and rights',[51] which means that there was a positive and significant relationship between the treaty ratification behaviour of states and their protection of civil and political rights. The use of the word 'significant' means that the findings that were obtained occurred beyond mere chance, and that other studies using similar data and methods would have a strong probability of obtaining similar findings. In fact, Simmons and Fariss have done precisely this and their findings are consistent with mine.[52] The use of the word 'limited' means that the magnitude of the relationship was small, while the inclusion of additional variables means that there are other independent factors that account for the overall variation in the protection of human rights and that treaty ratification is but one of those many different factors.

This final point is absolutely crucial. Quantitative analysis of human rights provides a certain set of tools that can help us understand and explain the variation and patterns in the protection of different sets of human rights. They provide partial evidence for that variation and help us build larger sets of explanations for the human rights problems we observe and study. They do not provide the final proof of something, not the definitive answer. Rather, they provide a systematic and rigorous way to analyse different areas of concern in the larger field of human rights. For legal practitioners, statistics on human rights and the different quantitative techniques set out in this chapter can help build the evidence for a particular human rights campaign, case, or project. Used alongside narrative analysis, ethnographic research, forensic anthropology, testimonials, archival research and other approaches to analysing social and political phenomena, statistics and quantitative analysis have an important role to play, but not the only role.

50 Landman, *Human Rights and Democracy* (n 1).
51 Landman, *Protecting Human Rights* (n 1) 164.
52 Simmons (n 11); Fariss, 'Are Things Really Getting Better?' (n 11).

I remain confident and optimistic that quantitative techniques will continue to be improved upon and that data on human rights will continue to be generated in new and innovative ways. The advent of big data, data analytics, textual analysis, and geospatial techniques mean that now more than ever, scholars and practitioners have a wide range of tools at their disposal, not only to carry out increasingly sophisticated analyses of human rights problems, but they also have an important role to play in providing answers to some of these problems in ways that means making real people's lives better. This chapter has made clear that only through careful attention to all stages of the quantitative process can we reduce bias, minimise uncertainty, and maximise the utility of the inferences we make about human rights.

Further reading

Rodwan Abouharb and David Cingranelli, *Human Rights and Structural Adjustment* (Cambridge: Cambridge University Press, 2007).

Philip Alston and Sarah Knuckey (eds), *The Transformation of Human Rights Fact Finding* (Oxford: Oxford University Press, 2015).

Christopher J. Anderson, Aida Paskeviciute, Maria Elena Sandovici and Yuliya V. Tverdova, 'In the Eye of the Beholder? The Foundations of Subjective Human Rights Conditions in East-Central Europe' (2005) 38 *Comparative Political Studies*, 771.

Kevin Bales, Olivia Hesketh and Bernard Silverman, 'Modern Slavery in the UK: How Many Victims?' (2015) 12(3) *Significance*, 16.

Patrick Ball, Jana Asher, David Sulmont and Daniel Manrique, 'How Many Peruvians Have Died?' (Washington, DC: American Association for the Advancement of Science, 2003) <http://shr.aaas.org/hrdag/peru/aaas_peru_5.pdf> accessed 7 February 2017.

Patrick Ball, Herbert Spirer and Louise Spirer, 'Making the Case: Investigating Large Scale Human Rights Violations Using Information Systems and Data Analysis' (Washington, DC: American Association for the Advancement of Science, 2000).

Richard P. Claude and Thomas B. Jabine, 'Exploring Human Rights Issues with Statistics' in Thomas B. Jabine and Richard P. Claude (eds), *Human Rights and Statistics: Getting the Record Straight* (Philadelphia: University of Pennsylvania Press, 1992).

Christopher Fariss, 'Respect for Human Rights has Improved Over Time: Modelling the Changing Standard of Accountability' (2014) 108(2) *American Political Science Review*, 297.

Christopher Fariss, 'Are Things Really Getting Better?: How to Validate Latent Variable Models of Human Rights' (2018) 48(1) *British Journal of Political Science*, 275–282.

Christopher Fariss, 'The Changing Standard of Accountability and the Positive Relationship between Human Rights Treaty Ratification and Compliance' (2018) 48(1) *British Journal of Political Science*, 239–271.

Joe Foweraker and Todd Landman, *Citizenship Rights and Social Movements: A Comparative and Statistical Analysis* (Oxford: Oxford University Press, 1997)

Joe Foweraker and Todd Landman, 'Individual Rights and Social Movements: A Comparative and Statistical Inquiry' (1999) 29 *British Journal of Political Science*, 291.

Sakiko Fukuda-Parr, Terra Lawson-Remer and Susan Randolph, *Fulfilling Social and Economic Rights* (Oxford: Oxford University Press, 2015).

Raymond D. Gastil, *Freedom in the World: Political Rights and Civil Liberties 1978* (Boston: GK Hall, 1978).

Raymond D. Gastil, *Freedom in the World: Political Rights and Civil Liberties 1980* (Westport, CT: Greenwood Press, 1980).

Raymond D. Gastil, *Freedom in the World: Political Rights and Civil Liberties 1986–1987* (New York: Freedom House, 1988).

Raymond D. Gastil, 'The Comparative Survey of Freedom: Experiences and Suggestions' (1990) 25 *Studies in Comparative International Development*, 25.

Mark Gibney and Michael Stohl, 'Human Rights and US Refugee Policy' in Mark Gibney (ed.), *Open Borders? Closed Societies? The Ethical and Political Issues* (Westport, CT: Greenwood Press, 1988).

Oona Hathaway, 'Do Treaties Make a Difference? Human Rights Treaties and the Problem of Compliance' (2002) 111 *Yale Law Journal*, 1932.

Oona Hathaway, 'The Cost of Commitment' (2003) 55 *Stanford Law Review*, 1821.

Oona Hathaway, 'Why Do Countries Commit to Human Rights Treaties?' (2007) 51(4) *Journal of Conflict Resolution*, 588.

Ronald Inglehart, *Modernization and Postmodernization* (Princeton: Princeton University Press, 1997).

Ronald Inglehart, *Culture and Social Change: Findings from the Value Surveys* (Leiden: Brill, 2003).

Ronald Inglehart and Pippa Norris, *Rising Tide: Gender Equality and Cultural Change Around the World* (New York: Cambridge University Press, 2003).

Max Kaase and Kenneth Newton, *Beliefs in Government* (New York: Oxford University Press, 1995).

Gary King, Robert O Keohane and Sidney Verba, *Designing Social Inquiry: Scientific Inference in Qualitative Research* (Princeton: Princeton University Press, 1994).

Todd Landman, 'Comparative Politics and Human Rights' (2002) 43(4) *Human Rights Quarterly*, 890.

Todd Landman, 'Measuring Human Rights: Principle, Practice and Policy' (2004) 26 *Human Rights Quarterly*, 906.

Todd Landman, *Protecting Human Rights: A Global Comparative Study* (Washington DC: Georgetown University Press, 2005).

Todd Landman, 'Review Article: The Political Science of Human Rights' (2005) 35(3) *British Journal of Political Science*, 549.

Todd Landman, *Studying Human Rights* (Abingdon: Routledge, 2006).

Todd Landman, *Human Rights and Democracy: The Precarious Triumph of Ideals* (London: Bloomsbury, 2013).

Todd Landman, 'Rigorous Morality: Norms, Values and the Comparative Politics of Human Rights' (2016) 38(1) *Human Rights Quarterly*, 1.

Todd Landman and Edzia Carvalho, *Measuring Human Rights* (Abingdon: Routledge, 2009).

Todd Landman and Anita Gohdes 'A Matter of Convenience: Challenges of Non-Random Data in Analyzing Human Rights Violations during Conflicts in Peru and Sierra Leone' in Taylor Seybolt, Jay Aronson and Baruch Fishoff (eds), *Counting Civilian Casualties* (Oxford: Oxford University Press, 2013).

Todd Landman, David Kernohan and Anita Gohdes, 'Relativising Human Rights' (2012) 11(4) *Journal of Human Rights*, 460.

Todd Landman and Larissa Kersten 'Measuring Human Rights,' in Michael Goodhart (ed.), *Human Rights: Politics and Practice*, 3rd edn. (New York: Oxford University Press, 2015).

Todd Landman and Marco Larizza, 'Inequality and Human Rights: Who Controls What When and How' (2009) 53(3) *International Studies Quarterly*, 715.

Christopher Mitchell, Michael Stohl, David Carleton and George Lopez 'State Terrorism: Issues of Concept and Measurement' in Michael Stohl and George Lopez (eds) *Government Violence and Repression: An Agenda for Research* (New York: Greenwood Press, 1986).

Neil Mitchell and James M McCormick, 'Economic and Political Explanations of Human Rights Violations' (1988) 40 *World Politics*, 476.

Steven C. Poe and C. Neal Tate, 'Repression of Human Rights to Personal Integrity in the 1980s: A Global Analysis' (1994) 88(3) *American Political Science Review*, 853–872.

Megan Price, Jeff Klinger, Anas Qtiesh and Patrick Ball, 'Updated Statistical Analysis of Documentation of Killings in the Syrian Arab Republic' (San Francisco: Human Rights Data Analysis Group, 2013).

James Ron, Shannon Golden, David Crow and Archana Pandya, *Taking Root: Public Opinion and Human Rights in the Global South* (Oxford: Oxford University Press, 2017).

Barnett R. Rubin and Paula R. Newberg, 'Statistical Analysis for Implementing Human Rights Policy' in Paula R. Newberg (ed.) *The Politics of Human Rights* (New York: New York Press, 1980).

Taylor Seybolt, Jay Aronson and Baruch Fishoff (eds), *Counting Civilian Casualties* (Oxford: Oxford University Press, 2013).

Beth Simmons, *Mobilizing for Human Rights: International Law in Domestic Politics* (Cambridge, Cambridge University Press, 2009).

Jackie Smith, Melissa Bolyard and Anna Ippolito, 'Human Rights and the Global Economy: A Response to Meyer' (1999) 21(1) *Human Rights Quarterly*, 207.

Christian Welzel and Ronald F. Inglehart, 'Agency, Values, and Well-Being: A Human Development Model' (2010) 97(1) *Social Indicators Research*, 43.

Paul Whiteley, 'The Origins of Social Capital' in Jan Van Deth, Marco Maraffi, Kenneth Newton and Paul Whiteley (eds), *Social Capital and European Democracy* (London: Routledge, 1999).

Paul Whiteley, 'Economic Growth and Social Capital' (2000) 48 *Political Studies*, 443.

7 Critical ethnography and human rights research

William Paul Simmons and
Lindsey Raisa Feldman

1 Introduction

A range of qualitative research methods can be fruitfully employed in human rights research. Here we focus on critical ethnography which shares a similar ethos to many other cutting-edge qualitative methods with its emphasis on self-reflexivity, researcher positionality, and including the privileging of the voices of all participants in the research process. Until recently critical ethnography and similar qualitative methods have not often been explicitly used in human rights research. In fact, there is still a tendency not to equate qualitative projects, which delve into topics central to human rights, as human rights research *per se*.

To better understand this reticence, in the next section we trace the trajectory of anthropology's relationship to human rights. Anthropology, the discipline in which ethnography finds its methodological and conceptual home, has had an ambivalent relationship with human rights. Next, we provide three examples of critical ethnography that, although they do not claim to be human rights research, shed light on important questions related to human rights. We then briefly discuss two recent approaches to human rights—rights based development and transformative human rights education—that share a similar ethos with critical ethnography to show that such an approach is not entirely foreign to human rights work. Finally, we step back and further discuss the general ethos of critical ethnography, its challenges, and its potential to enhance any human rights related research.

2 The disconnect between human rights and qualitative research: a case study of the American Anthropological Association

If, as we argue, qualitative research methods are so well suited for the study of human rights, why has it been mostly neglected up to now? Two main factors account for this relative neglect. First, social science fields like anthropology, which rely heavily on qualitative methods, have had a rocky relationship with the study and practice of human rights. Second, the fields that have dominated the study of human rights, mostly law, political science, and philosophy, have until recently been dominated by empirical, positivist, and analytical approaches and methodologies that are called into question by critical ethnography and related approaches. The schism between anthropology and human rights, only recently having been stitched back together, serves as the jumping off point for the rest of the chapter, where we will describe a new era in which qualitative methods are poised to occupy a central place in human rights research.

2a AAA, relativism, and human rights

A major epistemological specter haunts the field of anthropology (and that of human rights), one that has been laid to rest and then unearthed time and time again. Anthropologists debate whether they can, and should, draw threads of connection within and across societies to describe broader meanings of human experience. For both individual anthropologists and the American Anthropological Association, this debate regarding universalism and relativism has shaped its relationship with human rights.

The American Anthropological Association (AAA), founded in 1902, serves as a democratic umbrella organization for practicing anthropologists and those interested in the field. According to Mark Goodale, there are three distinct periods of AAA's engagement with human rights:

1. 1945–1950: formal and public consideration of the Universal Declaration on Human Rights, rejection of it, denial of possibilities for engagement;
2. 1950–1987: anthropological absence from important developments as an international and transnational human rights discourse emerged and became preeminent; and
3. 1987–present.[1]

Goodale argues that, in the first period, the AAA rejected the United Nation's Universal Declaration of Human Rights on both 'empirical and ethical grounds'.[2] This stemmed from the discipline's adoption of cultural relativism as an epistemological framework. Cultural relativism, or the challenging of a 'presumed universality of standards that actually only belong to one culture',[3] is a central proposition of the AAA's official 1947 statement on human rights. It states,

---

1 Mark Goodale, 'Towards a Critical Anthropology of Human Rights' (2006) 47(3) *Current Anthropology*, 485, 488.
2 Ibid. 486.
3 Alison Dundes Renteln, 'Relativism and the Search for Human Rights' (1988) 90 *American Anthropologist*, 56, 58.

Standards and values are relative to the culture from which they derive so that any attempt to formulate postulates that grow out of the beliefs or moral codes of one culture must to that extent detract from the applicability of any Declaration of Human Rights to mankind as a whole.[4]

The position of ethical relativism led to the conclusion that any sort of statement of universal standards veers into moral imperialism, and thus could not be supported by a discipline intent on moving away from this damaging framework. The AAA's 1947 Statement led to a three-decade period marked by the 'absence of anthropologists from discussions' of human rights issues.[5] Meanwhile, in the same timeframe, the United Nations' universal declaration served as the foundation for an explosion of discourses surrounding human rights across the academy and beyond, in the form of publications, human rights instruments and NGOs.

In the early 1990s, aligning with the reflexive turn of the anthropological discipline as a whole, scholars began historicizing the role of anthropology in the field of human rights. Even if the exact term *human rights* was rarely employed since the 1947 Declaration, anthropologists were actively engaged in parallel projects, like those that developed categories of collective rights and fused anthropological knowledge with human rights activism.[6]

Since the 1990s, anthropology's increased engagement with human rights has taken on two central foci. The first is what Goodale calls an 'emancipatory cultural politics,' in which 'anthropologists use their knowledge of specific cultural processes and meanings—and the broader relationships of power through which these processes and meanings are necessarily embedded—to reinforce specific projects for social change'.[7] The second focus is less political; it is to study human rights both critically and empirically through the use of ethnography.

According to Goodale, ethnography is necessary in order to critically engage with the discourses and effects of human rights in practice. The ethnographic approach allows the researcher to understand human rights as 'a type of politically consequential normative framework that is constituted through social practice,' and thus for ethnographers, 'to study what human rights do is also to study what human rights are'.[8] Therefore, ethnographies about human rights are useful for understanding ways that human rights have proven useful

4 American Anthropological Association (AAA), 'Statement of Human Rights' (1947) 49 *American Anthropologist*, 539.
5 Ronald Cohen, 'Human Rights and Cultural Relativism: The Need for a New Approach' (1989) 91 *American Anthropologist*, 1014–1015.
6 Ellen Messer, 'Anthropology and Human Rights' (1993) 22 *Annual Review of Anthropology*, 221.
7 Mark Goodale, 'Introduction to Anthropology and Human Rights in a New Key' (2006) 108 *American Anthropologist*, 1, 3.
8 Ibid. 4.

in disparate contexts, but 'without having to resort to the kinds of abstracted theories of universality that underpin major human rights instruments and institutions'.[9]

The historical estrangement from human rights that the discipline of anthropology engendered through its own epistemological stance serves as a historical backdrop for why qualitative methods are, in part, missing from human rights projects. At the same time, as Goodale contends, conducting ethnographies of human rights allows for rich descriptive empiricism that leads to fecund critical inquiry. A researcher can describe the ways specific groups and societies impact and are impacted *by* normative frameworks of human rights discourse. Goodale therefore situates ethnography, after nearly 100 years of theoretical and methodological ambivalence, as the central tenet of anthropology's potential engagement with human rights in the twenty-first century. In the next section, we will push this further and argue that recent advances in critical ethnography are especially appropriate for human rights, especially the critical approaches to human rights now being adopted.

3 From ethnography to critical ethnography and critical human rights research

The reflexive turn in anthropology, often associated with the release of Clifford and Marcus's seminal 1986 collection *Writing Culture*,[10] brought with it new acknowledgements regarding the researcher's primacy in ethnographic accounts, that have led to a critical ethnographic approach. The reflexive turn was inspired by the acknowledgement of a post-colonial era and the eminence of post-modern and post-structuralist scholarship. It caused anthropologists to interrogate their own role in subject-making, the questionable goal of objectivity, and the ethical responsibilities of ethnographers. Prior to this turn, anthropology and ethnography were largely deemed scientific, non-political pursuits. Yet the reflexive era is defined by complicated methodological and philosophical considerations about the very nature of ethnography.

For example, anthropologists began exploring whether its central concept 'culture', as an ultimately structured, definable entity was insufficient to describe the experiences of individuals and groups in a globalizing world.[11] This questioning was met with fierce resistance, with its sharpest critics labeling the reflexive era the 'death knell' of anthropology as a relevant discipline.[12] This era also made space for new ethnographic styles, and particular underrepresented

---

9 Goodale, 'Towards a Critical Anthropology' (n 1) 507.
10 James Clifford and George E. Marcus (eds), *Writing Culture: The Poetics and Politics of Ethnography* (Berkeley: University of California Press, 1986).
11 Arjun Appadurai, *Modernity at Large: Cultural Dimensions of Globalization* (Minneapolis: University of Minnesota Press, 1996).
12 Steven Sangren, 'Rhetoric and the Authority of Ethnography: "Postmodernism" and the Social Reproduction of Texts' (1988) 29(3) *Current Anthropology*, 405.

groups of researchers to emerge. Literary ethnography, dialogic ethnography, auto-ethnography, and ethnographic fiction are a few of the genres that emerged from this period, throwing the role of the ethnographer and the material and symbolic impact of *doing* ethnography into high relief.

For instance, Taussig's theory of ethnography-as-mimesis argues that in writing ethnographies, we produce reproductions of what we have experienced. Through this process of mimesis, wherein researchers join with what they copy, ethnographies shift the focus from interpreting the formal unity of a culture to elaborating the lines of sensual and imaginative relationships we co-create with our subjects. He writes, 'What happens is that the very concept of "knowing" something becomes displaced by a "relating to"'.[13] This summarizes an ultimate aim of the reflexive era, which anthropologists and ethnographers across the social sciences have begun to internalize in the act of writing ethnographies. By relating to someone, as opposed to knowing something, this new era of ethnography attempts humility, dismantling the penetrative gaze of the ethnographer into the lives of others.

Critical ethnography as an ethos, more than a specific method or even a set of methods, requires a fundamental shift in worldview about the role of the researcher in relationship to the subject matter of research. Chapters in a popular ethnography guidebook include such phrases as 'walking in rhythm', 'recording the miracle' and 'walking softly through the wilderness',[14] while the standard work of critical ethnography includes such phrases as 'world traveling', 'loving perception', 'positive naiveness', and 'wild mind and monkey mind'.[15] This is a far cry from the view that 'scholarship must be "scientific", impartial, and therefore safely removed from everyday life'.[16] Instead, critical ethnography requires the researcher to immerse themselves in 'the actual experience of something, we [the researchers] intuitively apprehend its essence; we feel, enjoy and understand it as reality, as we thereby place our own being in a wider, more fulfilling context'.[17]

This ethos of critical ethnography is inspired by ongoing developments in disparate theoretical approaches such as feminist and indigenous epistemology, postcolonialism, and critical race theory. These movements all share a deep skepticism of universal objective truths in lieu of a deep, subjective immersion in concrete situations. They call for a weakening of traditional authority including the objective and Archimedean position of academic researchers including ethnographers, to the point of arguing for a privileging

---

13 Michael Taussig, *Mimesis and Alterity: A Particular History of the Senses* (New York: Routledge, 1993) p. 21.

14 David M. Fetterman, *Ethnography: Step by Step*, 2nd edn. (Thousand Oaks, CA: Sage, 1998).

15 D. Soyini Madison, *Critical Ethnography: Method, Ethics, and Performance* (Thousand Oaks, CA: Sage, 2005).

16 Margaret Randall, 'Foreword' in Julie Shayne (ed.), *Taking Risks: Feminist Activism and Research in the Americas* (Albany: State University of New York Press, 2014) p. xii.

17 Ibid. xxiv (quoting Orlando Fals-Boda).

of non-researcher knowledge. Critical ethnography, in this vein, does not proceed according to specific rules laid out beforehand, but involves learning from marginalized voices. It is entering research with humility and generosity, what Gayatri Spivak has called a 'learning to learn from the voice' of the Other.[18] It is a patient listening that is ever-conscious of intractable power relations that will always bias researchers' observations and can only be addressed by recognizing our own positionality.

4 Examples of critical ethnography to advance human rights work

Here we present three compelling examples of critical ethnography, none of which has been labeled a human rights project by its author. However, these three give important insights into the mindsets of human rights perpetrators, document how human rights activists actually perpetuate stigmatization and marginalization, and how a neo-liberal policy that further exploits prison inmates can actually open up a space for inmates to find dignity and reverse stigmatization. Taken together they show that critical ethnographies can move the researcher to reflect on their own positionality and immerse themselves in a research project to move past prevailing conceptions of little understood populations. Note that each of these projects are multi-method; relying on a number of data collection techniques including qualitative interviews, participant observation, content analysis, focus groups, and even quantitative surveys.

4a John Steiner and the SS

We begin with a highly unusual and little known early research project by John M. Steiner that would probably be classified as traditional ethnography, though it contains some elements of critical ethnography.[19] Steiner, who had survived five concentration camps and two death marches during the Holocaust, later earned his PhD in Sociology from Freiburg University. He undertook a 20-year ethnography from 1958 to 1978 to determine the background motivations of Nazi officials, especially SS officers. He hung out with them at their reunions and other festivities as well as engaging in 300 interviews, soliciting 50 life histories, and conducting hundreds of surveys of them. Steiner was able to build excellent rapport and trust with the participants as evidenced by even being invited to give a short address at an annual SS

18 William Paul Simmons, *Human Rights Law and the Marginalized Other* (New York: Cambridge University Press, 2011) pp. 160–188.
19 John M. Steiner, 'The SS Yesterday and Today: A Sociopsychological View' in Joel E. Dimsdale (ed.), *Survivors, Victims, and Perpetrators: Essays on the Nazi Holocaust* (Washington: Hemisphere Publishing Corporation, 1980).

meeting. Steiner must have been very conscious of his positionality as a Holocaust survivor throughout his study though he does not discuss it in much detail and we must imagine his research required an extremely patient listening to the Other, what Spivak called a 'self-suspending leap into the other's sea'.[20]

Not surprisingly Steiner found a complex interaction between individual and social factors that were common to members of the SS. The officers gravitated toward the Prussian militaristic ideology preached by Hitler with its 'rigidly structured thought processes and behavioral expectations'[21] based upon 'loyalty and obedience'.[22] They joined the SS because it 'would facilitate a legitimate and socially acceptable shedding of their unwanted identity as well as the acquisition of a more satisfying self'.[23]

Steiner's research corroborates the well-known findings of Milgram, Zimbardo, and others that there is a 'latent Eichmann residing in most of us' waiting for the appropriate circumstance.[24] 'All of us under certain situations may find ourselves in a position where we will behave inhumanely'. Steiner moves past Milgram though, in that his work provides an explanation for the emergence of joyful sadism beyond someone following orders in otherwise ordinary individuals. The new identity of the SS officers brought a release, a 'feeling of belonging and euphoria, resulting in strong emotional ties'.[25] This feeling of euphoria was found to especially effect 'vocal young dissidents with a tendency to go to the extreme'.[26] Combined with their adherence to the 'Prussian' ideology it created a movement that lacked 'sensitivity or self-effacing charm'.[27] These officers when placed in a 'total institution' like the SS that legitimized violence, and as they gained 'considerable power', became especially cruel. This cruelty was accompanied by feelings of 'elation or ecstatic joy'.[28]

Steiner labels these former sadistic perpetrators as sleepers, because before joining the SS they were mostly normal, and after the war, they were 'law-abiding citizens, socioeconomically more successful' and with shockingly low crime rates.[29] But placed in the appropriate circumstance when given the opportunity, there was 'a self-selection process for brutality'. When the

20 Laura Lyons and Cynthia Franklin, 'On the Cusp of the Personal and the Impersonal: An interview with Gayatri Chakravorty Spivak' (2004) 27 *Biography*, 203, 207–208.
21 Steiner (n 19) 411.
22 Ibid. 414.
23 Ibid. 416.
24 Ibid. 431.
25 Ibid. 419.
26 Ibid. 422.
27 Ibid. 423.
28 Ibid. 431.
29 Ibid. 441.

opportunity arose, they became 'quasi-executioners in feeling as well as action'.[30]

Steiner's early ethnography complements recent psychological and philosophical works on human rights perpetrators. He shows that when given loose rein many of the SS officers, 'tend to feel free from cumbersome moral restrictions, technical legalities, or a preoccupation with questions as to what is right or wrong'.[31] Political Scientist Fred Alford, in his recent reconsideration of the famous Milgram experiments, focuses on the subject's laughter as they believe they are giving life-threatening shocks to another individual.[32] Milgram had quickly dismissed this as nervous laughter, but Alford asks 'what if these men are giggling in embarrassed pleasure at being given permission to inflict great pain and suffering on an innocent and vulnerable man?' Alford echoes Steiner's conclusions by wondering 'What if this is what the teachers (subjects) really want, what they long for, what satisfies . . . permission to hurt someone?' This is not being forced to do something but being provided with carte blanche to do something that is forbidden but enjoyable without suffering the opprobrium of society. They are reluctantly being forced to do something that they've always wanted to do. They are free to express 'embarrassed pleasure, guilty pleasure, but it is still pleasure'.[33] Steiner's highly unusual ethnography leads to the finding that authoritarian personalities and even sadists are looking for justification, but also freedom, and when they get freedom, they are able to shed their previously restricted personalities and change from 'ordinary men' to 'willing executioners', and when some individuals are given permission to be willing executioners they go beyond what is sanctioned to become joyful sadists.

4b Laura Maria Agustín and the 'rescue' of sex workers

Laura Maria Agustín, long an activist working at the US-Mexico border, the Caribbean, and other places throughout the western hemisphere, often encountered migrants who also sold sex. She was often surprised to find sex workers portrayed as victims and stigmatized by the very people purporting to provide them social services. She decided to conduct extensive field work in Europe by working with the social sector that sought to help migrants and sex workers. By doing so, she was able to examine 'the texture and atmosphere as well as the words and gestures, making up their practice'.[34] To ground her research, she was drawn to anthropological theories and methods especially

---

30 Ibid. 433.
31 Ibid. 438.
32 C. Fred Alford, *What Evil Means to Us* (Ithaca: Cornell University Press, 1997).
33 Ibid. 26.
34 Laura María Agustín, *Sex at the Margins: Migration, Labour Markets, and the Rescue Industry* (London: Zed Books, 2007) p. 136.

because of their embrace of cultural relativism. They 'would allow me to resist moralizing as well as western cultures' claim that its values are best'.[35] With such an approach she would be able 'to study migrants and helpers, their words and actions, in the same kinds of ways, evaluating these within their own groups' logic'.[36]

Agustín, like many ethnographers, took on the role of a trickster, adopting different positionalities at different times: 'a mix of insider, outsider, stakeholder, political actor and researcher-with-a-self-interest, and shifted according to the conditions of the moment'.[37] She is quite conscious of her positionality as a researcher with certain privileges and certain obligations including publishing in outlets that most likely will not be read by her subjects. She was also humble from the start about her inability to grasp the entire picture of the pheno-menon under study, even though she was immersed in it. She consciously follows the insights of the seminal book *Writing Culture* and presents her find-ings mostly through verbatim narratives bookended by contextual descriptions and analysis.

Consider her first vignette which is entitled 'Imposing Solidarity'. Agustín describes the scene of working with an aid organization patrolling an urban park in a Spanish city, driving up to groups of West African migrant sex workers. While distributing bags of condoms the aid workers give out lectures on the 'principles of solidarity and cooperation', even while berating one woman for allegedly asking for an extra bag of condoms.[38] Agustín and other aid workers are embarrassed by the spectacle and vow not to further help the organization. She stays and chats with the sex workers who question why that aid organization is even there. They do not offer anything of value to the sex workers as they already have good access to condoms. It is clear that the aid organization does not fully appreciate the identities, circumstances, or needs of the migrant sex workers. Leaders of the aid organization later admit that the sex workers do not really need more condoms but that providing condoms opens 'a way in' to the women. The leaders further express confidence that the migrant sex workers share their worldview, that they are all sisters. This claim for solidarity remains 'unreflexive'[39] as it is between those seeking to rescue prostitutes, when most of the migrant women did not refer to themselves as prostitutes or even commercial sex workers, but as migrants who need to sell sex in order to become established economically in a new country. The migrant women understood a key insight of recent feminist theory better than the aid workers, that their essence was not fixed. Further, few of the migrant sex

35 Ibid. 137.
36 Ibid.
37 Cf Toon Van Meijl, 'The Critical Ethnographer as Trickster' (2005) 15(3) *Anthropological Forum*, 232.
38 Agustín (n 34).
39 Ibid. 157.

workers understood Spanish well enough to communicate in a meaningful way with the aid workers, and very few saw the mostly white, middle class aid workers as their allies.

Agustín's ethnography also explores the professional conferences and publications that similarly draw conclusions about sex workers without really listening to their voices. She meets feminists who forcefully claim 'that prostitution is always, in all situations, abuse and violence . . . and the men are cruel egotistical perverts who should be in prison'.[40] She reviews safe sex flyers that paint migrant sex workers as having no agency: 'as tremendously disadvantaged: poor, oppressed, coming from violent societies, having no choices. They are never described as feminists and rarely as politically active or possessing consciousness of their own situation'.[41]

Agustín's ethnography offers a much more nuanced account of migrants' lives and their vulnerabilities, but also provides a critique of a colonial way of doing human rights.[42] Agustín situates the anti-human trafficking discourse of the past two decades historically alongside the white slave crusades of the early twentieth century that swept the US and other countries. While not minimizing the fact that some migrants and some sex workers are exploited, her careful ethnography shows that even exploitation has many different shades, with some migrants aware that they would need to be exploited in order to get a foothold in the new country. Even the debt that migrants are 'forced' to pay, which many rescuers claim proves the existence of human trafficking, has to be problematized. One woman says 'I never considered it to be a debt. For me it was like a favour that they did for me'.[43] Such nuanced understandings of the migrant and sex worker experience stand in stark contrast to the perceptions of the rescue industry. It also expands the field of migration studies which 'is guilty of ignoring women who sell sex and consigning them to the miserable field of "victims of trafficking"'.[44]

Of course, this human rights crusade is not without consequence, as seen in its continuing impacts. For instance, in our home state of Arizona, under the guise of finding sex trafficking victims a university social work professor teamed with local police to round up large numbers of sex workers. Instead of finding such victims, they ended up harming a number of sex workers, mostly women of color and transgendered women, who are already stigmatized and persecuted in a number of ways by law enforcement and by the larger society.[45]

40 Ibid. 173.
41 Ibid. 179.
42 Cf Erica Lorraine Williams, 'Feminist Tensions: Race, Sex Work, and Women's Activism in Bahia' in Shayne (n 16).
43 Agustín (n 34) 34; Cf ibid. 217.
44 Agustín (n 34) 47.
45 Stéphanie Wahab and Meg Panichelli, 'Ethical and Human Rights Issues in Coercive Interventions With Sex Workers' (2013) 28 *Affilia*, 344; ACLU Blog of Rights, 'Arrested for Walking While Trans: An Interview with Monica Jones' (2 April 2014) <https://www.

Those arrested would only be given social services, notably only provided by Christian churches and charities, if they accept the victimization framework by claiming to be victims.

Interestingly Agustín, in a personal conversation, says she does not see herself as doing human rights work. Yet, by deconstructing prominent narratives in human rights work, she is pointing out human rights abuses that are rarely considered and finding one of their chief causes in a purported human rights movement.

4c Lindsey Feldman and prison labor: a personal reflection[46]

Just as Agustin does not see herself as doing human rights work, I am hesitant to label my research, a multi-year anthropological inquiry into the lived experiences of incarceration, a human rights project. Yet, as I have come to realize, projects can contribute to human rights discourses even without the researcher labeling them as human rights projects. I will reflect on the necessary connections between prison research and human rights, as well as the ways that doing a critical ethnography led my work to unexpected connections with certain, more radical human rights discourses. I hope my research provides all readers who are interested in qualitative research an example of how critical ethnography can support key tenets of human rights work.

My project began as a straightforward approach to studying prison labor in Arizona—namely, how individuals who experience working in prison daily make sense of their role in the Prison Industrial Complex. Much prison labor is non-skilled, factory style work. However, a small set of skilled labor programs, ranging from auto mechanic certification to wildland firefighting programs, has integrated rehabilitative qualities into a markedly punitive system. I decided to focus on one particular skilled labor program, the Inmate Wildfire Program (IWP), consisting of 11 prison crews who fight over 100 wildfires per year, in order to understand how individuals make sense of the severe economic and social realities of the era of mass incarceration, as seen in their low pay for the dangerous work of fighting wildfires.

Yet, it was only through the actual *doing* of critical ethnography that my project became more complex and ultimately, one that spoke to the concepts of dignity and humanity that are at the core of prison-related human rights discourses. What I found, through ethnographic fieldwork embedded with several prison fire crews, is that in the face of the inherently exploitative nature of prison labor, the IWP offers individuals deeply meaningful experiences that provide its participants a subtle but meaningful resistance to the overwhelmingly punitive reality of Arizona prisons.

aclu.org/blog/lgbt-rights-criminal-law-reform-hiv-aids-reproductive-freedom-womens-rights/arrested-walking> accessed 7 February 2017.

46 Note that this section is written in the first person, as it is an ongoing reflection of the second author on her current research project.

The turning point in my methodology was when I decided to become a wildland firefighter, and in so doing, decided to engage in a more critical ethnographic technique. I was urged to become a firefighter by the prison crews themselves, when I first went to visit them on the yard. Both the prisoners and the Correctional Officers told me that what the crews experience on the fireline was somewhat indescribable, and if I was to examine the meanings of skilled work for incarcerated people, I needed to be next to them for days on end. This decision resulted in inserting myself into the ethnographic field, and as such, radically altered my project in many ways.

First, I had to accept that my fieldwork would be much longer and more intensive than I originally expected. My fieldwork expanded to 15 months, through two active fire seasons and over 20 fires and counting that I fought alongside the prison crews as a certified wildland firefighter. Initially overwhelmed by this prospect, I came to embrace this long-form qualitative method, a practicing of a 'slow science' that is increasingly rare in the deadline-heavy, product-oriented world of graduate school.[47] It also required a more insistent self-reflexivity than if I had not dived in headfirst. Choosing to participate in such an extreme way required me to acknowledge my own biases, limitations, and privilege throughout the project. It also meant that I had to abandon any claim to detachment or objectivity, and embrace the ethnographic power that being physically and emotionally linked to my project provided for my argument.

Second, this decision fundamentally changed the questions I asked, and ultimately, the argument I am making in my research project. The physical intimacy of engaging in life-threatening and physically punishing work led to an emotional intimacy with the prison crews, and resulted in much deeper and more profound discussions with the men I worked with. The topics we discussed, and that I wrote down in fieldnotes as well as during formal interviews, were more personal and emotionally driven than I would have expected if I had just stayed in the restrictive spaces often given to prison researchers. Through these discussions, I realized the profound meanings that the Inmate Wildfire Program provides for many of the individuals who participate in it, from the radically (at least in the prison context) vulnerable and inclusive friendships formed on the crews, to the symbolic re-inscription of the category 'criminal' as they interacted with the public. These meanings, and how they resist the punitive nature of Arizona's prison system, now form the center of my project, and would not have appeared to me if I had not spent days and weeks with these crews on the fireline.

Finally, shifting to a more critical, rather than straightforward ethnographic method—with an emphasis on inductive data collection, self-reflexivity, and

---

47 Kristel Beyens, Philippe Kennes, Sonja Snacken and Hanne Tournel, 'The Craft of Doing Qualitative Research in Prisons' (2015) 4(1) *International Journal for Crime, Justice, and Social Democracy*, 66.

emotional involvement—led to a correlation with human rights discourses. I decided not only to write a manuscript from this research, but also a set of policy recommendations, because of the blatant human rights degradations I witnessed in Arizona's prison system. But more broadly, I am aiming to acknowledge these prisoners' rights to dignity and humanity, even in the face of their loss of liberty for having committed a crime. One of the most meaningful aspects of the IWP, according to the men with whom I worked, is that they are treated as human beings. Through my ethnographic project, I aim to express this humanity by using their words and actions that I was lucky enough to witness. In this way, I am contributing to a new era of human rights discourses that stem from the voices of those who are notoriously kept silent, especially when behind bars.

5 Analogous radical approaches to human rights

Increasingly the ethos of critical ethnography described above is mirrored in human rights research and activism such as various strands of human rights from below,[48] more radical rights-based approaches to development, and transformational human rights education. Such a perspective challenges traditional notions of human rights. For instance, activities at transnational levels among elites, though amenable to ethnographic analysis as shown by Merry, are not privileged over grassroots activism.[49] Everyday actions become the focus, and human rights are not defined by the privileged, especially with static definitions, but are contested concepts that are discovered in on-the-ground struggle. Like critical ethnographers, radical human rights focuses on positionality and self-reflexivity, understanding intractable power relations, patient listening to the voices of the marginalized, and immersion in a particular situation. Here we briefly describe radical forms of rights-based development and transformative human rights education.

5a Participatory development and working with the Other

Participatory development, where the poor have a voice in development projects affecting them, has been embraced by almost the entire development community including the World Bank and national development agencies like USAID and DFID. The *Voices of the Poor*, published by the World Bank,

---

48 Simmons (n 18); Upendra Baxi, *Human Rights in a Post Human World: Critical Essays* (Oxford: Oxford University Press, 2009); David Scott, 'Regarding Rights for the Other: Abolitionism and Human Rights from Below' in Leanne Weber, Elaine Fishwick and Marinella Marmo (eds), *The Routledge Handbook of Criminology and Human Rights* (Abingdon: Routledge, 2016).

49 Sally Engle Merry, *Human Rights and Gender Violence: Translating International Law into Local Justice* (Chicago: University of Chicago Press, 2006).

boldly claims 'there are 2.8 billion poverty experts, the poor themselves'.[50] It is almost impossible to imagine any mainstream development agency now signing off on a project that is top-down and imposed upon the marginalized, as was the norm with the mega-development projects in the post-World War II era. Participatory development's discourse is directly tied to human rights-based principles as it consciously seeks to empower and increase the dignity of the most marginalized. At its best, participatory development is self-reflective and self-critical: 'this generates an ongoing dialogue between practitioners on the quality, validity and ethics of what they are doing, which is intended to guard against slipping standards, poor practice, abuse or exploitation of the people involved'.[51]

This 'participatory development orthodoxy' has recently been subjected to strong critiques by academics and practitioners that mirror the critiques of traditional ethnographies by critical ethnographers. These critiques center on the failure of participatory techniques to adequately understand hegemonic power relationships. Participatory processes which are designed to re-structure power relationships, end up perpetuating and entrenching pre-existing power relationships. Instead of using the 'voices of the poor' to modify the development enterprise, these voices are used to implement pre-existing development agendas. 'What people are empowered to do is to take part in the modern sector of developing societies'.[52] Power and the system are never interrogated. The practitioners empower the marginalized to critique themselves, but not to turn the critical gaze back on the development enterprise and its institutions.

Scholars and practitioners are attempting to move past these critiques of participatory development by immersing themselves with humility and generosity into the development enterprise. This is a more radical rights-based approach to development that is hyper-critical of its practices and involves a patient listening to the voice of the Other. It is working with the impacted communities to interrogate existing power relations and structural violences. This is a fraught enterprise which

> must be interrogated for the extent to which it enables those whose lives are affected the most to articulate their priorities and claim genuine accountability from development agencies, and also the extent to which the agencies become critically self-aware and address inherent power inequalities in their interaction with those people.[53]

50 Deepa Narayan, Raj Patel, Kai Schafft, Anne Rademacher and Sara Koch-Schulte, *Can Anyone Hear Us? Voices of the Poor* (New York: World Bank, 2000) p. 2.

51 Bill Cooke and Uma Kothari, *Participation: The New Tyranny?* (London: Zed Books, 2001) p. 5.

52 Glyn Williams, 'Evaluating Participatory Development: Tyranny, Power and (Re) Politicisation' (2004) 25(3) *Third World Quarterly*, 557, 563.

53 Celestine Nyamu-Musembi and Andrea Cornwall, 'What is the "Rights-Based Approach" All About? Perspectives from International Development Agencies' IDS Working Paper 234 (Brighton: Institute of Development Studies, 2004) p. 47.

Development is no longer just about economic development but about political action and structural change. Similar to critical ethnography, the process is just as important if not more important than the final product. Now development projects are evaluated by 'the degree to which they contribute to the mobilization and sustained political action of the poor'.[54]

5b Transformative human rights education

International human rights institutions and documents have had mixed results at best in improving human rights situations on the ground, especially for marginalized communities. 'In many situations this evidence suggests that the human rights practices of States that ratify such treaties may actually worsen after ratification'.[55] However, more nuanced studies by Katherine Sikkink and her colleagues have shown that international norms can lead to domestic change, but this requires a complex dance between transnational NGOs, local policy entrepreneurs, the diffusion of international norms, and favorable country conditions.[56]

Though human rights documents have had limited effects on macro-level national policies and practices, a growing body of studies has shown that when translated into local social and cultural conditions, a process known as vernacularization,[57] human rights documents can have profound impacts on the rights consciousness and empowerment of marginalized groups. For instance, many studies have shown that the UN Convention for the Elimination of Discrimination against Women (CEDAW) 'has inspired feminist activism around the world and helped raise women's legal consciousness'.[58]

To better understand how vernacularization of human rights documents can be most successful, we turn to the burgeoning field of human rights education (HRE). Amnesty International's definition of HRE emphasizes participation and empowerment. 'Human rights education is a deliberate, participatory practice aimed at empowering individuals, groups, and communities through fostering knowledge, skills, and attitudes consistent with internationally

---

54 Williams (n 52) 567.
55 Alex Geisinger and Michael A. Stein, 'A Theory of Expressive International Law' (2007) 60 *Vanderbilt Law Review*, 77.
56 Thomas Risse, Kathryn Sikkink and Stephen C Ropp (eds), *The Power of Human Rights: International Norms and Domestic Change* (Cambridge: Cambridge University Press, 1999).
57 Lynette J. Chua, 'The Vernacular Mobilization of Human Rights in Myanmar's Sexual Orientation and Gender Identity Movement' (2015) 49(2) *Law & Society Review*, 299; Cf Merry (n 49).
58 Lisa R. Pruitt and Marta R. Vanegas, 'CEDAW and Rural Development: Empowering Women with Law from the Top Down, Activism from the Bottom Up' (2012) 41 *Baltimore Law Review*, 263, 267; Cf Peggy Levitt and Sally Engle Merry, 'Vernacularization on the Ground: Local Uses of Global Women's Rights in Peru, China, India and the United States' (2009) 9(4) *Global Networks*, 441.

recognized principles'.[59] This definition highlights what has been labeled 'HRE for Transformative Action' and it has been found that for victims of human rights abuses such education 'can foster a sense of transformative or strategic agency'.[60] Transformational HRE can have a wide impact. One study in Turkey found that such human rights education has profound impacts at the local level and even enacted change at the national level. After training on CEDW 'women are able to stand up for their rights together, challenge and eliminate discrimination against themselves in a wide-range of fields and promote women's human rights and equality in their communities and on the national level'.[61]

Proponents of human rights education for transformation have adopted a number of participatory, learner-centered, active learning strategies, including socio-drama, participatory workshops, creating learning materials collectively, theatre, testimonies, deep listening activities such as talking circles, personal and group reflections on specific events, and collective protests.[62] Note that similar strategies have been successfully used in the related fields of legal empowerment,[63] health communication,[64] and participatory rights-based development.[65] What we learn from each of these literatures is to emphasize dignity, empowerment, and inclusion.

6 A method and ethos of qualitative human rights research

As we stated at the outset of this chapter, and as described in Lindsey Feldman's reflection of doing ethnography, there is no prescribed step-by-step process for the qualitative methods of critical ethnography. However, here we will

59 Amnesty International, 'Promoting Human Rights Education & Capacity Building' <http://amnestymena.org/en/WhoWeAre/HumanRightsEducation.aspx?media=print> accessed 7 February 2017.

60 Monisha Bajaj, *Schooling for Change: The Rise and Impact of Human Rights Education in India* (New York: Bloomsbury, 2012) p. 26.

61 Liz Ercevik Amado, *The Human Rights Education Program for Women (HREP) Utilizing State Resources to Promote Women's Human Rights in Turkey* (Nancy L. Pearson, ed., 2005) p. 15 <http://www.newtactics.org/sites/default/files/resources/Human-Rights-Education-EN. pdf> accessed 7 February 2017.

62 Equitas, 'Evaluating Human Rights Training Activities A Handbook for Human Rights Educators'(2011)<https://equitas.org/en/popular/may-10-2011-publication-of-evaluating-human-rights-training-activities-a-handbook-for-human-rights-educators/> accessed 7 February 2017

63 Stephen Golub, 'What is Legal Empowerment? An Introduction' in Stephen Golub (ed.), *Legal Empowerment: Practitioners' Perspectives* (Rome: International Development Law Organization, 2010).

64 See Luuk Lagerwerf and Henk Boer, *Health Communication in Southern Africa: Engaging with Social and Cultural Diversity* (Amsterdam: Rozenberg, 2009).

65 Sam Hickey and Diana Mitlin, *Rights-Based Approaches to Development: Exploring the Potential and Pitfalls* (Sterling, VA: Kumarian Press, 2009).

emphasize two methodological considerations that researchers should acknowledge when deciding to use qualitative methods in human rights work.

The first consideration for qualitative researchers is their own positionality. When conducting fieldwork—whether it is participant observation, formal interviewing, or surveying—researchers must actively and continually place themselves within the research project. Researchers should recognize how their role, most typically in this case as an extension of an academic institution, *a priori* shapes their interactions with those with whom they work. Further, the researcher's gender, race, and class shape these interactions in critical ways. Continually recognizing how one's own position affects the research process allows for a self-reflexive qualitative methodology that challenges the classical hegemonic 'researcher-as-authority' positionality.

Second, critical ethnography resists the imposition of models or theories into the field to be tested. Instead, a loosely formulated set of research questions help to frame the project, and are then fleshed out, contradicted, or expanded on by the empirical data collected through qualitative methods like radical participatory research, or critical ethnographic interviewing. This approach is undoubtedly messier and more challenging than quantitative approaches, and requires the researcher to change project outcomes or theoretical arguments based on what they have learned from those they work with. Yet, an inductive approach also more accurately reflects the nature of a radical approach to human rights, which opens spaces for the voices of Others to be central to the final product.

In many ways, the actual methodological action plan is of secondary importance to an appreciation of the ethos of radical approaches to qualitative research. Here, we turn to Nagar's recent writings to reflect on a Western academic working closely with a rural feminist group in India, detailing the various pitfalls of decades-long work, together navigating their various forms of privileges. In order to co-author feminisms involves thousands of decisions, building relationships, learning from, listening to, admitting mistakes. As she writes,

> These are journeys enabled by trust with the ever-present possibility of distrust and epistemic violence; journeys of hope that must continuously recognize hopelessness and fears; and journeys that insist on crossing borders even as each person on the journey learns of borders that they cannot cross—either because it is impossible to cross them, or because it does not make sense to invest dreams and sweat in those border crossings.[66]

This is a journey of vulnerability and love, of telling stories, of poetry, of tears and smiles, of trust and hope, distrust and hopelessness. This is work, co-authored, reflective, and reflexive. 'If alliance work can be imagined as dance

66 Richa Nagar, *Muddying the Waters: Coauthoring Feminisms across Scholarship and Activism* (Urbana: University of Illinois Press, 2014) 6.

choreography, then co-authorship in alliance work is precisely about building singularities that roil and clash and teem with life'.[67] This is employing research methodologies, theoretical advances, and academic knowledge in solidarity with marginalized communities. But, it is not applying these tools uncritically. It is not employing them on a group as analysis from the outside, but employing them in solidarity with them. Likewise, it is employing human rights and jurisprudence with the same self-criticism and with solidarity. This is not done in an instant, it is done over years. It is not done with no second chance as the heroic act. It is done knowing it will probably need to be re-done, that no step is final. It is creation.

It is not surprising that a recent edited collection on such scholar activism is entitled *Taking Risks*.[68] Doing critical ethnography in human rights research as we outline above involves a great deal of risk taking. In Lindsey's extreme case it involves very real physical risks of fighting fires in the desert and mountains of Arizona. Such work also involves substantial emotional labor as it requires building relationships grounded on trust, openness to new ideas, and generosity. It requires shedding or at least interrogating, as much as possible, the many privileges that academics and activists have accrued over years. It is often a lengthy process with uncertain outcomes, which might not fit the career trajectories and timetables of scholars in our neo-liberal universities. It also risks a feeling of betrayal as one must navigate multiple roles in a research project, and might ultimately have to use narratives from co-participants for publications to advance one's own career.[69] This is research that is truly falsifiable as the researcher sets aside much of their knowledge to take a 'self-suspending leap into the other's sea'.[70] Thus, one of the chapters in a recent volume on scholar-activism is entitled 'When Research Challenges Everything You Thought You Knew'.[71] Understanding that such critical and radical approaches are not for everyone, we urge human rights research to adopt such an ethos into their projects as much as possible: to question their positionality, patiently listen to others, be radically vulnerable, and have good humor.

Further reading

Laura María Agustín, *Sex at the Margins: Migration, Labour Markets, and the Rescue Industry* (London: Zed Books, 2007).
C. Fred Alford, *What Evil Means to Us* (Ithaca: Cornell University Press, 1997).
Liz Ercevik Amado, *The Human Rights Education Program for Women (HREP) Utilizing State Resources to Promote Women's Human Rights in Turkey* (Nancy L. Pearson, ed., 2005) <http://www.newtactics.org/sites/default/files/resources/Human-Rights-Education-EN.pdf> accessed 7 February 2017.

---

67 Ibid. 168.
68 Shayne (n 16).
69 Nagar (n 66) 61.
70 Lyons and Franklin (n 20).
71 Williams (n 42) 230.

American Anthropological Association (AAA), 'Statement of Human Rights' (1947) 49 *American Anthropologist*, 539.

American Civil Liberties Union (ACLU) Blog of Rights, 'Arrested for Walking While Trans: An Interview with Monica Jones' (2 April 2014) <https://www.aclu.org/blog/lgbt-rights-criminal-law-reform-hiv-aids-reproductive-freedom-womens-rights/arrested-walking> accessed 7 February 2017.

Amnesty International, 'Promoting Human Rights Education & Capacity Building' <http://amnestymena.org/en/WhoWeAre/HumanRightsEducation.aspx?media=print> accessed 7 February 2017.

Arjun Appadurai, *Modernity at Large: Cultural Dimensions of Globalization* (Minneapolis: University of Minnesota Press, 1996)

Monisha Bajaj, *Schooling for Change: The Rise and Impact of Human Rights Education in India* (New York: Bloomsbury, 2012).

Upendra Baxi, *Human Rights in a Post Human World: Critical Essays* (Oxford: Oxford University Press, 2009).

Kristel Beyens, Philippe Kennes, Sonja Snacken and Hanne Tournel, 'The Craft of Doing Qualitative Research in Prisons' (2015) 4(1) *International Journal for Crime, Justice, and Social Democracy*, 66.

Lynette J Chua, 'The Vernacular Mobilization of Human Rights in Myanmar's Sexual Orientation and Gender Identity Movement' (2015) 49(2) *Law & Society Review*, 299.

Robin Patric Clair, *Expressions of Ethnography: Novel Approaches to Qualitative Methods* (Albany: SUNY Press, 2012).

James Clifford and George E. Marcus (eds), *Writing Culture: The Poetics and Politics of Ethnography* (Berkeley: University of California Press, 1986).

Ronald Cohen, 'Human Rights and Cultural Relativism: The Need for a New Approach' (1989) 91 *American Anthropologist*, 1014.

Bill Cooke and Uma Kothari, *Participation: The New Tyranny?* (London: Zed Books, 2001).

Equitas, 'Evaluating Human Rights Training Activities A Handbook for Human Rights Educators' (2011) <https://equitas.org/en/popular/may-10-2011-publication-of-evaluating-human-rights-training-activities-a-handbook-for-human-rights-educators/> accessed 7 February 2017.

David M Fetterman, *Ethnography: Step by Step*, 2nd edn. (Thousand Oaks, CA: Sage, 1998).

Stephen Golub, 'What is Legal Empowerment? An Introduction' in Stephen Golub (ed.), *Legal Empowerment: Practitioners' Perspectives* (Rome: International Development Law Organization, 2010).

Mark Goodale, 'Introduction to Anthropology and Human Rights in a New Key' (2006) 108 *American Anthropologist*, 1.

Mark Goodale, 'Towards a Critical Anthropology of Human Rights' (2006) 47(3) *Current Anthropology*, 485.

Sam Hickey and Diana Mitlin, *Rights-Based Approaches to Development: Exploring the Potential and Pitfalls* (Sterling, VA: Kumarian Press, 2009).

Luuk Lagerwerf and Henk Boer, *Health Communication in Southern Africa: Engaging with Social and Cultural Diversity* (Amsterdam: Rozenberg, 2009).

Peggy Levitt and Sally Engle Merry, 'Vernacularization on the Ground: Local Uses of Global Women's Rights in Peru, China, India and the United States' (2009) 9(4) *Global Networks*, 441.

Laura Lyons and Cynthia Franklin, 'On the Cusp of the Personal and the Impersonal: An Interview with Gayatri Chakravorty Spivak' (2004) 27 *Biography*, 203.

D. Soyini Madison, *Critical Ethnography: Method, Ethics, and Performance* (Thousand Oaks, CA: Sage, 2005).

Sally Engle Merry, *Human Rights and Gender Violence: Translating International Law into Local Justice* (Chicago: University of Chicago Press, 2006).

Ellen Messer, 'Anthropology and Human Rights' (1993) 22 *Annual Review of Anthropology*, 221.

Richa Nagar, *Muddying the Waters: Coauthoring Feminisms across Scholarship and Activism* (Urbana: University of Illinois Press, 2014).

Deepa Narayan, Raj Patel, Kai Schafft, Anne Rademacher and Sara Koch-Schulte, *Can Anyone Hear Us?: Voices of the Poor* (New York: World Bank 2000).

Celestine Nyamu-Musembi and Andrea Cornwall, 'What is the "Rights-Based Approach" All About? Perspectives from International Development Agencies' IDS Working Paper 234 (Brighton: Institute of Development Studies, 2004).

Lisa R. Pruitt and Marta R. Vanegas, 'CEDAW and Rural Development: Empowering Women with Law from the Top Down, Activism from the Bottom Up' (2012) 41 *Baltimore Law Review*, 263.

Margaret Randall, 'Foreword' in Julie Shayne (ed.), *Taking Risks: Feminist Activism and Research in the Americas* (Albany: State University of New York Press, 2014).

Alison Dundes Renteln, 'Relativism and the Search for Human Rights' (1988) 90 *American Anthropologist*, 56.

Thomas Risse, Kathryn Sikkink and Stephen C Ropp (eds), *The Power of Human Rights: International Norms and Domestic Change* (Cambridge: Cambridge University Press, 1999).

Steven Sangren, 'Rhetoric and the Authority of Ethnography: "Postmodernism" and the Social Reproduction of Texts' (1988) 29(3) *Current Anthropology*, 405.

David Scott, 'Regarding Rights for the Other: Abolitionism and Human Rights from Below' in Leanne Weber, Elaine Fishwick and Marinella Marmo (eds), *The Routledge Handbook of Criminology and Human Rights* (Abingdon: Routledge, 2016).

Julie Shayne (ed.), *Taking Risks: Feminist Activism and Research in the Americas* (Albany: State University of New York Press, 2014).

William Paul Simmons, *Human Rights Law and the Marginalized Other* (New York: Cambridge University Press, 2011).

John M. Steiner, 'The SS Yesterday and Today: A Sociopsychological View' in Joel E. Dimsdale (ed.), *Survivors, Victims, and Perpetrators: Essays on the Nazi Holocaust* (Washington: Hemisphere Publishing Corporation, 1980).

Michael Taussig, *Mimesis and Alterity: A Particular History of the Senses* (New York: Routledge, 1993).

Toon Van Meijl, 'The Critical Ethnographer as Trickster' (2005) 15(3) *Anthropological Forum*, 232.

Stéphanie Wahab and Meg Panichelli, 'Ethical and Human Rights Issues in Coercive Interventions With Sex Workers' (2013) 28 *Affilia*, 344.

Erica Lorraine Williams, 'Feminist Tensions: Race, Sex Work, and Women's Activism in Bahia' in Julie Shayne (ed.) *Taking Risks: Feminist Activism and Research in the Americas* (Albany: State University of New York Press, 2014).

Glyn Williams, 'Evaluating Participatory Development: Tyranny, Power and (Re) Politicisation' (2004) 25(3) *Third World Quarterly*, 557.

8 Comparative approaches to human rights

Sue Farran

1 Introduction

The comparative approach involves considering the ways in which different legal systems or different sources of law deal with a particular subject. The process of comparison can take many forms and involve diverse comparators, for example language, ideologies, concepts, jurisdictional styles, legal traditions, rules, forums for adjudication, procedural and/or substantive law. Some of these will be considered in the examples section of this chapter.

Comparative law as a distinct discipline emerged in the late nineteenth century and was dominated by two approaches. The first was to describe and categorise the legal systems of the world, and so we find discussion of legal families in classic comparative writers such as Rene David and John Brierley,[1] Konrad Zweigert and Hein Kötz[2] and Patrick Glenn.[3] This classification imposed a sense of order on diversity – although it was far from comprehensive in its scope,[4] and allowed comparativists to draw comparisons between different legal families, such as the legal systems of the common law family (England and Wales, the United States, Australia, etc.) and the civil law family (France, Spain, Italy, etc.).[5] At the time of the earliest classifications it

1 René David and John Brierley, *Major Legal Systems in the World Today*, 2nd edn. (London: Stevens and Sons, 1978).
2 Konrad Zweigert and Heinz Kötz, *An Introduction to Comparative Law*, 3rd edn. (Tony Weir tr.) (Oxford: Clarendon Press, 1998).
3 H. Patrick Glenn, *Legal Traditions of the World*, 5th edn. (Oxford: Oxford University Press, 2014).
4 See for example Mauro Bussani and Ugo Mattei (eds), *The Cambridge Companion to Comparative Law* (Cambridge: Cambridge University Press, 2012).
5 These families were gradually expanded to recognize mixed legal systems and these in turn were expanded to include different types of mixed systems which departed from the classic common law/civil law mix as found in Quebec, Louisiana, Scotland, etc. See for example Esin Örücü, 'What is a Mixed Legal Systems: Exclusion or Expansion'(2008) 12(1) *Electronic Journal of Comparative Law* <http://www.ejcl.org> accessed 7 February 2017; See also JuriGlobe, *Mixed Legal Systems*, University of Ottawa <www.juriglobe.ca> accessed 7 February 2017; and Vernon Valentine Palmer, Mohamed Y Mattar and Anna Koppel (eds), *Mixed Legal Systems, East and West* (Abingdon: Routledge, 2014).

was also possible to talk of the socialist family of law,[6] and in a rather more limited way 'mixed legal families'.[7] The second approach was to use comparative law less scientifically and more pragmatically to construct or improve national laws, drawing on the wealth of foreign models and foreign experience (something we still find occurring in the work of law reform commissions).

Glenn makes two observations that are relevant to the use of comparative methodology in the context of human rights.[8] The first is that the focus of comparative law was initially on private law[9]; the second is that there was no place for international human rights in comparative law because rights were determined by national law and international law governed the relationship between states. He goes on to add 'comparative law in the field of human rights is very recent'.[10] While both of his observations remain true, they are no longer absolute. Law is less territorially bounded, due in part to the mobility of people, modern technology and the movement of ideas, the development of mutual legal arrangements, and the recognition that international law pertaining to human rights is no longer just about the relationship between states. There is a need, as Glenn points out, for 'government lawyers to respond to current and highly fluid empirical situations'[11] and this has led to the emergence of what he refers to as 'applied comparative human rights law', which extends 'beyond the legislative, consultative and advisory process . . . to the adjudicative process'.[12] We might therefore expect to find comparative law being used in law-making, in law reform or review, in policy framing and in adjudication, for example by courts – and examples of these will be considered below.

So it would seem that comparative law or a comparative legal approach may be used in a theoretical and/or practical way and that its scope has evolved so that it is a liberal process which may be useful in a range of circumstances. But what does it entail? Essentially a comparative approach involves looking at 'the other' and often stepping outside what is familiar to engage with what is unfamiliar. The rationale for such an approach may be that by better understanding the 'other' we can understand and appreciate how things work

---

6 See for example John Quigley, 'Socialist Law and the Civil Law Tradition' (1989) 37(4) *The American Journal of Comparative Law*, 781–808.

7 See for example Kenneth Reid, 'The Idea of Mixed Legal Systems' (2003–2004) 78 *Tulane Law Review*, 5–40; Jacques du Plessis, 'Comparative Law and the Study of Mixed Legal Systems' in Mathias Reiman and Reinhard Zimmermann (eds), *The Oxford Handbook of Comparative Law* (Oxford: Oxford University Press, 2012).

8 H. Patrick Glenn, 'Comparative Law, Immigration and Human Rights' (1991) 2 *African Journal of International and Comparative Law*, 668–679.

9 See for example chapters in Peter de Cruz, *Comparative Law in a Changing World* (Abingdon: Routledge, 2007); and in Matthias Siems, *Comparative Law* (Cambridge: Cambridge University Press, 2014).

10 Glenn, 'Comparative Law' (n 8) 678.

11 Ibid. 675.

12 Ibid. 677.

or do not work elsewhere and by reflection be more critically aware of the legal approach in our own system. We might also realise that there is more than one way to regulate conduct and that sometimes the way in which this is done elsewhere is instructive or inspirational. There has been some criticism that this perspective has been one way, with the developed or western world adopting the view that nothing can be learned from the legal systems of less developed societies or those countries which are sometimes colloquially referred to as the 'global south'. However, that attitude is changing, as evidenced, for example, by considerations of alternative dispute resolution mechanisms, or non-custodial forms of punishment.

A comparative approach might also be adopted to determine differences and/or similarities so that if some kind on consensus is being sought, for example to develop a uniform legal approach to an issue, or to arrive at a trans-national agreement on certain legal questions, the challenges and obstacles can be identified from the outset. This is not to suggest that the comparative approach always involves two or more legal systems. It need not. Comparisons can take place within systems, for example one might compare the assessment of damages in tort or delict with those in contract for the purposes of insuring against risk, or, especially where the legal system is plural and has a number of different laws governing the same area of activity, by comparing the operation of those internal laws. For example, is the right to family life the same for those who are married, those in a civil partnership and those who cohabit without marriage or a civil partnership? We may also make temporal comparisons within a single legal system, for example the legal regime before and after a particular piece of legislation or seminal court decision.

In all of the above we should be clear why the approach is being adopted and what we want to learn from it. The motivation may be simply curiosity, for example how does a criminal justice system work without jury trial? This spirit of enquiry is perfectly acceptable and falls under what Siems categorises as 'knowledge and understanding',[13] but does not really advance an answer to 'what do you want to gain from this comparative approach?' While not suggesting that all research methodologies must be driven by utilitarianism we might want to ask why achieving a better understanding of the other is valuable? This takes us back to Glenn's observation regarding the application of comparative law, so for example, one answer might be the practical use of the comparative method to national legislation, or by the courts to address a novel but not unique problem. In the context of human rights, a comparative approach may inform international agencies of the extent (or absence) of a perceived problem or issue. A further practical use might be at the regional level to support the development of a regional 'common law' to address a

13 Siems (n 9) 3.

shared concern, to unify disparate laws, or to inform strategies to resolve conflicts of laws. Peter Quint for example, has pointed out that:

> In the development of international law on the European level, comparative law has become a factor of increasing importance. . . . In Europe therefore, principles and doctrines that are gathered from various domestic legal systems by way of a method of comparative law often form the crucible and basis of international human rights – first, to some extent in the delineation of the general written principles of the human rights guarantees, and then, with increasing importance, in the later judicial interpretation of those principles.[14]

Comparative insights might also provide a deeper and broader appreciation of how the law works in different contexts. This is particularly relevant to human rights, because the context requires us to take into account political, cultural and socio-economic factors. As Schwelb points out:

> The promotion of respect for human rights through the instrumentality of international conventions is a very slow process. The difficulties are compounded when an attempt is made to attack a problem which is intimately connected with mores of the various communities and with religious traditions.[15]

In the context of human rights, especially if we accept, at least at an ideological level, that these should be universal, the comparative approach enables us to appreciate why the experience of human rights is uneven, why there are challenges to the content and realisation of rights in different countries, and for different communities and sub-groups and individuals within these communities. This understanding can then be used to inform opinion and policy options including interventions and support initiatives. At the same time, a comparative approach may reveal that despite apparent diversity there are common core values that can be utilised to form the basis of human rights advocacy. For example, there may be a resistance to individual human rights where societies focus on the group as a unit of social cohesion and stability, but at the same time the importance of intra-personal obligations may be recognised.

By stepping beyond our own (legal) conceptual and ideological shores we soon realise that the comparative approach to studying and understanding human rights may need to go beyond the black letter of the law however. While we could, for example, compare different international instruments

14 Peter E. Quint, 'International Human Rights: The Convergence of Comparative and International Law' (2001) 36 *Texas International Law Journal*, 605, 607.
15 Egon Schwelb, 'Marriage and Human Rights' (1963) 12 *American Journal of Comparative Law*, 337, 381.

to determine which offers, for example, the best protection to the rights of indigenous people to safeguard their natural resources, law does not exist in a vacuum. Especially in the context of human rights, many other factors are relevant: religion, political structures, the economic environment and development status of the country, its history and the organisation of society all play a role.

The comparative approach therefore provides a key which opens a door, but it may be a 'Pandora's box'. How then should we use this approach and what challenges and potential pitfalls should we be mindful of? Although one finds references to 'comparative law' it is really a method of looking at law in so far as there is no clear identifiable content which marks it out as a substantive subject, compared to for example, the law of contract. At the same time however, rather like human rights, one might argue that as a subject it can be pervasive and need not be self-contained. It is suggested therefore that the comparative approach is fluid and versatile. Although historically, comparatists from the late nineteenth and twentieth centuries focussed largely on the comparison of legal systems, noting in particular differences and similarities between different legal 'families' and making macro-comparisons, we also find micro-comparative studies focussing on single areas of law (see Schwelb below), or single legal institutions.

2 Drawbacks and common pitfalls

One of the first challenges in using a comparative approach is 'what to compare'? Traditionally comparisons have been made between different legal systems, notably those of the common law and those of the civil law; or between codified and non-codified systems. This may mean from the outset that very different systems are being compared, using different language, different concepts and different structures. This comparative approach has a number of potential pitfalls.

2a Language

Nowadays there is considerably more material available in translation than there used to be. For example, it is possible to find information in English on the legal systems of continental Europe or of more exotic countries such as China and Russia, if one lacks the linguistic skills to read original material. Much of this material, especially in the field of human rights, may be published in several languages, for example UN documents, decisions of the European Court of Human Rights, and so on. Some legal concepts do not, however, translate easily or indeed at all if there is no word in the vocabulary for that idea, so it is important to beware of assuming equivalence.[16] This is particularly

---

16 See Simone Glanert (ed.) *Comparative Law – Engaging Translation* (Abingdon: Routledge, 2014).

important when making micro-comparisons of specific legal institutions, but even in macro-comparisons of systems. For example, the word 'loi' in French refers to certain forms of legislation, not, as might be thought from a literal translation 'law' in a more general sense. In the Pacific region research into gender discrimination revealed that many local languages did not have words for 'gender', 'domestic violence' or 'equality' and that often the words that had been chosen to translate these concepts conveyed very different messages from what was intended, sometimes leading to counterproductive consequences.

2b Transplants

Just as translation can change a concept, so too can the 'transplant' of a legal institution from its 'home' environment to a new one. This process is particularly found in countries historically brought under the control of others during the period of colonisation. An example would be the rules of evidence used in courts established in former British colonies. These transplants frequently give rise to legal pluralism in post-colonial states, or add an additional layer to those legal systems which were already plural. There are a number of problems associated with transplants, not least of which is the interrelatedness of one aspect of a legal system with other parts. For example, introducing legislation on a subject like adoption may make cross-reference to the opinion of experts such as social welfare services, child psychologists or others who simply do not exist in the receiving country. Similarly introduced legal procedures or forums may be premised on particular forms of legal training or legal thinking. A typical example is the reference in many post-colonial legal systems of the British Commonwealth to 'the principles of the common law and equity', despite the fact that these courts have not had the same historical development of the law as occurred in Britain. There is considerable literature on the role of transplants, much of it critical.[17]

Transplants do not have to be imposed, however. They might be adopted following comparative research because they are seen as a good or useful thing. Indeed, it is not unusual to find law reform commissions engaging in comparative exercises or courts adopting a comparative approach where novel cases present themselves and there are no or few domestic precedents to follow. Transplants may also be adopted as a consequence of a shared vision, for example in adopting human rights instruments.[18]

---

17 See for example, Alan Watson, *Legal Transplants: An Approach to Comparative Law* (Edinburgh: Scottish Academic Press, 1974); Otto Khan-Freund, 'On Uses and Misuses of Comparative Law' (1974) 37 *Modern Law Review*, 1; Jonathan Miller 'A Typology of Legal Transplants: Using Sociology, Legal History and Argentine Examples to Explain the Transplant Process' (2003) 51 *American Journal of Comparative Law*, 839.
18 See Merris Amos, 'Transplanting Human Rights Norms: The Case of the United Kingdom's Human Rights Act' (2013) 36 *Human Rights Quarterly*, 386.

Whether imposed or adopted, the comparatists should be wary of assuming that the law, legal institution or legal process is exactly the same in the country to which it was transplanted as in the country of origin. If transplants are to succeed they often have to be adapted or modified. This might be done consciously or might be brought about by the interaction of other parts of the legal system, or through the influence of non-legal forces. One consequence of this process might be the emergence of a hybrid process, institution or forum which, although superficially similar, may be rather different on closer examination. For example, in the Pacific region the court process is modelled on the common law adversarial system, but because litigants may be represented by relatively novice lawyers, judges will sometimes offer more guidance than might be expected in England and Wales, or indeed in other common law systems such as Australia and New Zealand. Similarly, those who represent litigants will be general law practitioners drawn from the single profession of solicitors. The comparatist should therefore be aware of these localised variations, and while it may not be necessary to have a full grasp of the whole of the substantive law of the legal system being compared, or from which comparisons are drawn, it is helpful to understand the basic structure of that legal system.

2c *Context*

A further caveat when comparing legal systems or parts of legal systems is the need to be aware of the influence of the historical past. For example, land law in England, Wales and Scotland would be difficult to comprehend without some understanding of feudalism, while understanding that Scotland has a different legal system from England and Wales is helped by appreciating the historical reasons for this. These past events have contemporary relevance.

Of course, the importance of historical perspective is not only relevant to, for example, comparing the law of France with that of England and Wales. Even in those countries of the common law 'family' the relevance of a colonial past remains significant. Indeed, within the same country historical background might be important for understanding present issues. For example, in the United States of America, slavery, its abolition and the subsequent struggle for equal rights is informed by the past. It is also important to realise that in federal systems, such as Switzerland, Australia, the United States, India, Canada and elsewhere there will be differences in the domestic laws of different states/provinces which may lend themselves to comparison, but which also may be informed by the particularities of the history of each state. Similarly, it is a mistake to assume that because countries occupy the same land mass or region their laws are the same. We cannot therefore refer to 'Africa' as if it is a homogenous legal system, any more than we can refer to 'the Pacific' as a homogenous legal system. Indeed, we cannot even refer to 'UK law', because there is no such thing. There is the law of England and Wales, the law of Scotland and the law of Northern Ireland, and with increasing devolution, today one has to be cautious about treating the law of England and Wales as identical, so that there is scope for comparison within the laws of the UK.[19]

Similarly, the economic and political environment in which the law operates is important and may be particularly relevant in the case of human rights, especially second generation rights.[20] It is all very well to advocate the universality of rights but different political ideologies will view rights in different ways, while the economic status of a country will determine what resources are available to support human rights, ranging from access to justice to the provision of healthcare. It is also important to realise the importance of religion in various parts of the world, not only as an integral part of the legal system but as a normative framework. In more secular western societies the influence of religion may be difficult to grasp. For example, in the UK human rights jurisprudence drawing on the right to freedom from torture and inhuman treatment has led to the abolition of corporal punishment. In the Pacific region however, even where there are laws prohibiting corporal punishment in school, strong adherence to biblical references such as 'spare the rod and spoil the child' are frequently used to justify the physical punishment of children in schools and at home.

The social structure is also relevant. One of the oft-cited criticisms of western rights statements is that these give too much prominence to the rights of individuals. In societies where individualism is overshadowed by collectivism or the importance of the community or group, the recognition and observance of obligations owed to the group may be more important. Social organisation may also explain status hierarchies and inequalities in society, and lead to accusations that individual rights discourse is destabilising because it undermines the very foundations of society.

For human rights educators and advocates it may also be important to understand the social structure for effective human rights training, because a programme that works in one country may not be received so positively in another if appropriate social and cultural protocols are not observed or the right persons of importance not involved. A comparatist in the field will be astute to identify differences as well as note similarities. This does not mean that the comparatists has to be an economist, a political and social scientist, and an historian as well as a legal scholar, but it does mean that the comparatist had to consider the things that influence similarities and/or differences. This

19 See for example, David Cabrelli and Sue Farran, 'Exploring the Interfaces between Contract Law and Property Law: A UK Comparative Approach' (2006) 13(4) *Maastricht Journal of European and Comparative Law*, 403–443.

20 See for example, Dominic O'Brien and Sue Farran, 'A New Dawn for Human Rights in Fiji: Learning from Comparative Lessons' (2015) 2(2) *Journal of International and Comparative Law*, 227–257; For a different comparative perspective see Andra Le Roux-Kemp 'The Recognition of Health Rights in Constitutions on the African Continent: A Systematic Review' (2016) 24 *African Journal of International and Comparative Law*, 142–157.

is particularly important if trying to understand why human rights are not experienced similarly across the globe.

3 Examples of good practice

There is a huge range of comparative human rights material available, ranging from national reports of law reform commissions which take a comparative approach, to the publications of international NGOs, as well as academic articles. Below are just a few to give an indication of the very varied approaches that can be adopted.

Dhand and Diab use the comparative method to examine whether Canada's revised provision of healthcare for immigrants (including refugees) meets its international and/or domestic human rights obligations under the 1981 Canadian Charter of Rights and Freedoms.[21] They limit their comparison to other common law countries with developed economies: the United States, the United Kingdom and Australia. In other words, they are comparing like with like, especially in respect of the application of international treaties in domestic law. The comparative discussion is embedded in an introductory description of the Canadian context and the revised healthcare policy. The comparative approach is used in order to establish a 'basic level of (healthcare) coverage common to each (comparator)'.[22] This is then used to determine if Canada meets this common basic level. While the comparative discussion is quite brief and limited in its consideration of material, it is clear that its purpose is to develop a tool which can be used to objectively test the revised healthcare provision. The application of this tool finds that the 2012 changes in Canada's healthcare coverage for refugees and other migrants: 'set Canada apart from the approach taken in the United States, the United Kingdom and Australia and raised questions in relation to Canada's obligation under international human rights law'.[23] Here, then, the comparative approach is used to support a critical analysis of domestic law, drawing on the fact that international human rights law has interpretive application for Canadian domestic law, and that even where international treaties are not explicitly recognised in domestic law – as with the comparators used here – they are used as a 'guide for interpreting *Charter* rights as well as domestic law and policy, giving rise to a preference for applications of the law that are consistent with the values and principles in treaties and covenants at issue'.[24] The comparative approach also draws on concrete examples of these international principles in a peer group of comparators.

21 Ruby Dhand and Robert Diab, 'Canada's Refugee Health Law and Policy from a Comparative, Constitutional, and Human Rights Perspective' (2015) 1 *Canadian Journal of Comparative and Contemporary Law*, 351–406.
22 Ibid. 364.
23 Ibid. 405.
24 Ibid. 402.

Comparing legal systems with shared experience, either historically or contemporaneously, can be a good use of the comparative approach. Maarten Kurrenbrouwer does this and also highlights the significance of political structures on human rights, reminding us that we cannot compare laws in a vacuum.[25] In this article the author sets out to compare the balance between human rights promotion and human rights violations in the Netherlands Indies, British India, French Indo-China and independent Thailand during the course of the nineteenth and twentieth centuries in the periods of early colonialism, later colonialism and post-colonialism, using a ranking system to map the progress of different rights over the course of history. His rationale is that: 'For better or worse, colonialism had a lasting consequence for human rights during the post-colonial period'.[26] This is what might be called a macro-comparison with a largely historical perspective, focussing predominantly on political structures in the metropolitan and colonial countries. There is a certain sparsity of detailed information, partly because the time period being covered is extensive and also the range of countries being considered. As with any historical research there are also challenges in respect of accessible and reliable material. What the article usefully does however, is to provide a comparative historical backdrop to the countries considered against which contemporary human rights issues could be considered.

A more micro-comparison is undertaken by Egon Schwelb, who focuses on the UN Convention on Consent to Marriage: Minimum Age for Marriage and Registration of Marriage.[27] Here the comparative approach is taken to examine the claim that this is a Convention which imposes a western view of marriage on non-western countries, and to answer the question: what is it that the Convention seeks to address, and what challenges might its implementation have in different legal systems? Schwelb covers a wide range of countries: Turkey, Tunisia, Iraq, Morocco, Pakistan, India Japan, China and Malaysia and includes consideration of Muslim, Hindu and customary laws. He considers consent comparatively as well as looking at arranged marriages, breach of promise to marry, marriage by proxy or agent, 'common law marriage' and forced marriage (e.g. 'shotgun marriages'). There is a wealth of detail in footnotes and some fascinating historical detail. While some of the material may today be a bit dated (he was writing in the early 1960s), his approach of taking one aspect of an international convention and looking across the legislation of all the comparators informs his analysis of the types of changes that will have to be considered to achieve compliance with the Convention in very different countries.

25 Maarten Kurrenbrouwer, 'Colonialism and Human Rights. Indonesia and The Netherlands in Comparative Perspective' (2003) 21 *Netherlands Quarterly Human Rights*, 203–224.
26 Ibid. 204.
27 Schwelb (n 15); The Convention had not come into force at the time Schwelb's article was punished, although it had opened for signature. It came into force on 9 December 1964.

Israel de Jesús Butler also focusses on international human rights instruments but he looks at the right of individual petition as a procedural mechanism in regional and international human rights provisions.[28] He takes a comparative view across Europe, South America and Africa and looks at UN Convention rights and Charter rights systems. His geographical comparison is accompanied by a temporal comparison whereby he takes a historical view through to the present day in order to examine if 'the position of the individual has changed conceptually and practically in international law'.[29] He not only considers the various mechanisms in the European, Inter-American and African systems but also looks at practical issues such as the forums (courts and/or commissions), access (including that of NGOs), procedure (including availability of legal aid and representation), and the remedies and compliance mechanisms. It is against this background that he evaluates the most effective system for individual petition. This process is then followed for both UN charter based mechanisms and UN treaty based mechanisms. Finally, he uses the comparative approach to draw out similarities and differences. For example, he concludes:

> The UN treaty bodies resemble the African and American Commissions in their proceedings (they are written), their remedies (because they direct a specific course of legislative or administrative action but are less likely to direct or less specific about the payment of costs or reparation), their enforcement mechanisms (because they have political bodies which fail to address specific states for their compliance with specific decisions), and their part-time nature. Both those UN Charter and UN treaty mechanisms which provide information on compliance seem to have a marginally higher success rate than the American system and a far greater success rate than the African system.[30]

This selection of one focus point can work well. Henk Botha takes the concept of dignity as a key human right and considers it comparatively looking at the South African Constitution and that of Germany, as well as its inclusion in a number of international human rights instruments.[31] He justifies his comparative approach as follows:

> South African constitutional scholars have largely failed to situate their analyses and critiques of the Court's dignity-based jurisprudence within

28 Israel de Jesús Butler, 'A Comparative Analysis of Individual Petition in Regional and Global Human Rights Protection Mechanisms' (2004) 23 *University of Queensland Law Journal*, 22–53.
29 Ibid. 22.
30 Ibid. 49.
31 Henk Botha, 'Human Dignity in Comparative Perspective' (2009) 20 *Stellenbosch Law Review*, 171–220.

the broader context of a transnational constitutional discourse on human dignity. This is surprising for a number of reasons. First, human dignity is central to the constitutions of many countries which have, over the past 60 years, emerged from dictatorship, oppression, totalitarianism, fascism, colonialism and discrimination. Secondly, section 10 of the Constitution of the Republic of South Africa, 1996 ('the Constitution'), which enshrines the right to human dignity, closely resembles the provisions of some of these constitutions. Thirdly, it is highly likely that the Constitutional Court's understanding of dignity as the most fundamental norm contained in the Constitution has been shaped, at least to some extent, by comparative case law and literature. And fourthly, foreign case law and academic literature offer rich resources for the conceptualization, analysis and critique of a dignity-based approach.[32]

Botha rationalises his choice of Germany as a comparator with South Africa on the grounds of the extensive jurisprudence on dignity developed by the German courts, the acknowledgment of this jurisprudence and reference to it by South African courts, and parallels that can be drawn between the historical circumstances surrounding the emergence of the German Basic Law and the South African Constitution. He starts with the recognition that,

> [d]ignity is a contested concept . . . . Behind the agreement on abstract notions of the inviolability of the dignity and worth of the human person lurks disagreement over the scope and meaning of dignity, its philosophical foundations, and its capacity to guide the interpretation of human rights and to constrain judicial law-making.[33]

He locates his two-country comparative study in the broader context of international human rights instruments which refer to dignity, especially in preambles, where he provides a descriptive comparative overview of the place of dignity in the international arena. He also provides an extensive overview of the place of dignity in national constitutions, from which he is able to conclude that 'human dignity is part and parcel of a shared constitutional vocabulary which cuts across national boundaries'.[34] At the same time, however, this comparative exercise alerts him to the high level of generality attaching to the concept of dignity and he argues that in order to understand its real significance concrete examples are needed, hence the detailed examination of the role of dignity in German and South African law: 'we need a better understanding of the ways in which dignity is concretized in particular

32 Ibid. 172.
33 Ibid. 171.
34 Ibid. 177.

constitutional systems'.[35] This leads to a 'drilling down' into these legal systems to critically analyse the concept and function of dignity, first in German law and then in South African law, drawing out similarities and differences between the two. The paper concludes with a micro-comparison of South African court decisions looking at how the courts have treated dignity differently in different contexts ranging from the death penalty to the transfer of football players. In some respects this last section could have been a comparative study in its own right, but its inclusion justifies the argument made that we need to concretize the use of rights terms and concepts if we are to understand them.

Clarke and Richards adopt a fairly traditional comparative approach but apply it to a very contemporary issue, that of forced marriage.[36] Looking at the civil law system of France and the common law system of England and Wales (therefore legal systems traditionally viewed as belonging to different families of law), the co-authors indicate the value of the comparative approach while also being mindful of the challenges when they write:

> Forced marriage raises immensely complex and sensitive problems, encompassing social, gender, ethnic, religious and economic issues which arise from intersecting questions of gender, culture and sexuality. It is an increasing problem in both France and England as both countries attempt to deal with the difficulties in a sensitive and multifaceted way. A comparative study in this regard can be of value to both jurisdictions, where the issues are similar but the solutions vary, especially due to the differences between the English common law and the French civil law systems.[37]

The authors adopt a closely woven approach comparing French and English systems at each point, both in stating the problem and in discussing responses to it. Similarities and differences are brought out as the article progresses. The authors conclude that:

> The blunt instrument of criminalization alone is not, in our view, the way to encourage such change in perceptions of what characterizes the consent required for arranged marriage and what constitutes an unconscionable invasion of rights. It would appear that, in this respect, despite the marked differences in the way in which the two legal systems function, both have recognized that it is possible by civil remedies to protect victims. . . . The comparison between the approach of France, a codified

35 Ibid. 178.
36 Brigitte Clark and Claudina Richards, 'The Prevention and Prohibition of Forced Marriages: A Comparative Approach' (2008) 57(3) *ICLQ*, 501–528.
37 Ibid. 527.

legal system, and England, a common law system, indicates many differences in the procedure adopted by each legal system to curb the practice of forced marriage . . . in both France and England civil practice and procedure is a possible tool to shape the ideology of the community without the risk of antagonizing or polarizing such communities and time will tell as to whether the criminal route favoured by Belgium, Germany and Norway will be more successful than the civil law approach of France and England.[38]

This observation offers an enticing opportunity for future comparative research.

Finally, a rather different type of comparative exercise is where the reader is left to make his or her own comparisons, having been presented with material across a range of jurisdictions. This approach is taken by a number of international organisations and indeed might be said to represent the approach taken by the UN if one reads across its many country reports. The one selected here is a report compiled by an organisation called the Child Rights International Network (CRIN). The report, published in February 2016, focusses on 'Rights, Remedies and Representation: A Global Report on Access to Justice for Children'. The report covers 197 countries, and looks at how these countries 'empower children to realise their rights or perpetuate the rights violations that they should combat'.[39] This report is the result of work by a huge team of researchers consisting of lawyers, NGOs, academics and others who worked on country reports following a template of topics for consistency of material. The country reports were then used to inform a global report, in which countries are ranked 'by scoring each country against international standards for access to justice for children'.[40] As the Executive Summary indicates 'This report represents a snapshot of how the world has tried to develop mechanisms to protect children's rights and ensure there are remedies for violations of children's rights'.[41] Going from country reports to a global report is a synthesis, but there are implied comparisons. The use of a template to compile information does have it limits – not least because what appears in principle may not apply in practice, but is a method frequently used by the International Academy of Comparative Law when it asks for country reports,[42] and clearly, where a major human rights project is being

---

38 Ibid. 527–528.
39 Individual country reports are available on the CRIN website: Child Rights International Network, 'Rights, Remedies and Representation: A Global Report on Access to Justice for Children' <http://www.crin.org> accessed 7 February 2017.
40 Ibid. 3.
41 Ibid.
42 See for example, Arnold Rainer, 'Are Human Rights Universal and Binding' in Karen Brown and David Snyder (eds), *General Reports of the XVIIIth Congress of the International Academy of Comparative Law* (New York: Springer, 2012).

undertaken, has practical advantages. If the caveats highlighted earlier in this chapter are remembered, such a report offers the comparativist a good starting point and might be used in order to make a selection of topic(s) (e.g. the role of public interest litigation in children's rights), and/or the legal systems which might be compared (determined for example, geographically or according to global ranking).

Further reading

Merris Amos, 'Transplanting Human Rights Norms: The Case of the United Kingdom's Human Rights Act' (2013) 36 *Human Rights Quarterly*, 386.

Henk Botha, 'Human Dignity in Comparative Perspective' (2009) 20 *Stellenbosch Law Review*, 171.

Mauro Bussani and Ugo Mattei (eds), *The Cambridge Companion to Comparative Law* (Cambridge: Cambridge University Press, 2012).

Israel de Jesús Butler, 'A Comparative Analysis of Individual Petition in Regional and Global Human Rights Protection Mechanisms' (2004) 23 *University of Queensland Law Journal*, 22.

David Cabrelli and Sue Farran, 'Exploring the Interfaces between Contract Law and Property Law: A UK Comparative Approach' (2006) 13(4) *Maastricht Journal of European and Comparative Law*, 403.

Child Rights International Network, 'Rights, Remedies and Representation: A Global Report on Access to Justice for Children' <http://www.crin.org> accessed 7 February 2017.

Brigitte Clark and Claudina Richards, 'The Prevention and Prohibition of Forced Marriages: A Comparative Approach' (2008) 57(3) *ICLQ*, 501–528.

Peter de Cruz, *Comparative Law in a Changing World* (Abingdon: Routledge, 2007).

René David and John Brierley, *Major Legal Systems in the World Today*, 2nd edn. (London: Stevens and Sons, 1978).

Ruby Dhand and Robert Diab, 'Canada's Refugee Health Law and Policy from a Comparative, Constitutional, and Human Rights Perspective' (2015) 1 *Canadian Journal of Comparative and Contemporary Law*, 351.

Jacques du Plessis, 'Comparative Law and the Study of Mixed Legal Systems' in Mathias Reiman and Reinhard Zimmermann (eds), *The Oxford Handbook of Comparative Law* (Oxford: Oxford University Press, 2012).

Simone Glanert (ed.) *Comparative Law – Engaging Translation* (Abingdon: Routledge, 2014).

H. Patrick Glenn, 'Comparative Law, Immigration and Human Rights' (1991) 2 *African Journal of International and Comparative Law*, 668.

H. Patrick Glenn, *Legal Traditions of the World*, 5th edn. (Oxford: Oxford University Press, 2014).

JuriGlobe, *Mixed Legal Systems*, University of Ottawa <www.juriglobe.ca> accessed 7 February 2017.

Otto Khan-Freund, 'On Uses and Misuses of Comparative Law' (1974) 37 *Modern Law Review*, 1.

Maarten Kurrenbrouwer, 'Colonialism and Human Rights. Indonesia and The Netherlands in Comparative Perspective' (2003) 21 *Netherlands Quarterly Human Rights*, 203.

Andra Le Roux-Kemp, 'The Recognition of Health Rights in Constitutions on the African Continent: A Systematic Review' (2016) 24 *African Journal of International and Comparative Law*, 142.

Jonathan Miller 'A Typology of Legal Transplants: Using Sociology, Legal History and Argentine Examples to Explain the Transplant Process' (2003) 51(4) *American Journal of Comparative Law*, 839–885.

Dominic O'Brien and Sue Farran, 'A New Dawn for Human Rights in Fiji: Learning from Comparative Lessons' (2015) 2(2) *Journal of International and Comparative Law*, 227.

Esin Örücü, 'What is a Mixed Legal Systems: Exclusion or Expansion' (2008) 12(1) *Electronic Journal of Comparative Law* <http://www.ejcl.org> accessed 7 February 2017.

Vernon Valentine Palmer, Mohamed Y Mattar and Anna Koppel (eds), *Mixed Legal Systems, East and West* (Abingdon: Routledge, 2014).

John Quigley, 'Socialist Law and the Civil Law Tradition' (1989) 37(4) *The American Journal of Comparative Law*, 781.

Peter E. Quint, 'International Human Rights: The Convergence of Comparative and International Law' (2001) 36 *Texas International Law Journal*, 605.

Arnold Rainer, 'Are Human Rights Universal and Binding' in Karen Brown and David Snyder (eds), *General Reports of the XVIIIth Congress of the International Academy of Comparative Law* (New York: Springer, 2012).

Kenneth Reid, 'The Idea of Mixed Legal Systems' (2003–2004) 78 *Tulane Law Review*, 5.

Egon Schwelb, 'Marriage and Human Rights' (1963) 12 *American Journal of Comparative Law*, 337.

Matthias Siems, *Comparative Law* (Cambridge: Cambridge University Press, 2014).

Alan Watson, *Legal Transplants: An Approach to Comparative Law* (Edinburgh: Scottish Academic Press, 1974).

Konrad Zweigert and Heinz Kötz, *An Introduction to Comparative Law* 3rd edn (Tony Weir tr.) (Oxford: Clarendon Press, 1998).

9 'Mixing methods': reflections on compatibility

Lee McConnell and Rhona Smith

1 Introduction

The purpose of this collection has been to provide an accessible, introductory overview of the principal methods employed when researching human rights. It is hoped that having considered the foregoing chapters, readers now appreciate the reflexive relationship between the types of research questions they ask and the suitability of the methods employed in order to obtain answers. As will by now be apparent, any single method has an array of potential applications, strengths and limitations. Yet, it would be artificial to attempt to silo the methods discussed completely. While certain combinations of methods will be more compatible than others, it is clear that methods in human rights research rarely operate in a vacuum. Instead, researchers are often prone to adopt a mixed approach, where different methods are blended to ensure the research questions are fully addressed, or to account for certain sub-questions, the answers to which are relevant to the understanding of the research area as a whole. This can produce more credible results as a degree of 'testing' is inbuilt by using a second or third method to corroborate or cross-check findings, or to reach a more holistic, deeper understanding of the field of study with which the primary research question is concerned. Accordingly, this final chapter reviews some of the links between the methods already discussed, highlighting where appropriate potential scope for combinations, or at the very least, methodological compatibilities. It also reflects on the practical issues that must be considered when bringing together seemingly discrete research methods.

2 Exploring methodological compatibilities

Our starting point was an overview of the development of a 'human rights based approach' to research. This is, in essence, a manifesto for research of all stripes concerning the subject matter of human rights that has developed out of the human rights movement itself, and the institutional framework of the UN. It prescribes certain principles with which researchers should ideally seek to align their work, which consist of both ethical considerations (i.e. ensuring that the research undertaken and the methods employed actually respect human rights) and normative goals (i.e. that research should ideally advance the realisation of human rights, and contribute to the capacity development of duty bearers and/or rights holders). Clearly, all of the methods presented in this book can be tailored to align with this ethos, but their compatibility is by no means automatic. Instead, care and attention by each particular researcher will be required to realise these goals as far as possible. The chapters examining empirical methods, whether qualitative or quantitative, all stress the importance of the ethical issues engaged by this type of research, from respect for privacy, confidentiality and the anonymisation of research, to respect for diversity in cultural, economic, legal and historical contexts. Empirical methods also offer a diverse range of methods by which researchers can attempt to measure and monitor human rights compliance and capacity, though as we have seen, these are not always compatible and may even point to conflicting results. In relation to the theoretical/doctrinal methods considered, there is also clear scope to keep these ethical considerations in mind as key sources and their interpretations are analysed and evaluated, and the philosophical traditions that have informed their development are externalised and critiqued.

Next, Suzanne Egan provided a reflective discussion of doctrinal approaches to human rights law, and it is clear that no matter what research question is being examined, most, if not all, pieces of legal academic writing will employ this method to some degree. As Egan describes, the approach is instrumental in providing an accurate description of what the law *is*. Whether one is interested in empirically measuring the efficacy, social experience, theoretical framings, political biases, economic effects or historical origins of a particular area of human rights law, some form of statement on the law being examined will likely be necessary. In terms of its links to legal theoretical methodologies, the doctrinal approach is often characterised as reflecting the dominant positivist approach to international law. This is a method which seeks to identify ambiguities, explore inconsistencies, and improve the determinacy and coherence of legal rules. The intersection between legal positivist theory and the doctrinal method is apparent in McConnell's discussion of the work of d'Aspremont on formalism in international law,[1] an approach which argues against the trend of deformalisation of legal sources at the international level, which is evident in the adoption of soft law, the non-binding status of commentaries from human rights monitoring bodies, and the formation of customary law via the notoriously problematic doctrine of *opinio juris*. Egan cautions the researcher against similar factors which undermine the ascertainment and description of legal doctrines in international human rights law.

---

1 Jean d'Aspremont, *Formalism and the Sources of International Law: A Theory of the Ascertainment of Legal Rules* (Oxford: Oxford University Press, 2012); Jean d'Aspremont, 'Softness in International law: A Self-Serving Quest for New Legal Materials' (2008) 19 *European Journal of International Law*, 1075.

The wider question of whether it is advisable (or even accurate) to frame law as a coherent and determinate discipline that is deducible by reason and logical analysis, and by which accurate predictions of future doctrinal developments can be made, underlies the doctrinal method. It may be argued that law itself is fundamentally chaotic and indeterminate, prone to reflect ideological biases, and that this tendency is obscured by a façade of apparently disinterested positivist/doctrinal 'ordering'. These factors permit theoretical critiques drawn from scholarship outlined in the 'critical approaches' section of McConnell's chapter.[2] In this regard, Egan expressly recognises the need for reflexivity in research engaging with the doctrinal method, a factor which correlates strongly with McConnell's call for awareness of the unarticulated theoretical assumptions at play in researchers' understandings of legal doctrines. Egan also cogently highlights the criticism that purely doctrinal analysis is too concerned with an internal point of view on the nature of law – one in which the 'system' itself is not the subject of enquiry, but its products (i.e. legal concepts and categories). While it is true that this method might permit the doctrinal legal scholar to formulate arguments regarding amendments or reform to the existing products of the legal system, it nonetheless has the potential to leave the social, political and economic factors which systemically construct or give rise to the legal order and its products unarticulated.[3] Instead, these considerations may be maligned as irrelevant, extraneous, or even, 'polluting'.[4]

As Egan notes, the doctrinal method is often not purely concerned with the identification and description of law from an internal perspective, but also permits the researcher to make normative claims surrounding the future development, interpretation or reform of the area of law being considered. Such claims might be coloured by empirical factors which demonstrate a disconnection between doctrine and practice, highlight unintended social consequences, catalogue significant human rights violations, or reveal new or emerging global phenomena. In this regard, there may be a place in doctrinal/theoretical projects for the more 'scientific', quantitative methods of human rights research such as those detailed by Landman. While these approaches might not provide the answers to the primary doctrinal/theoretical question posed in a piece of research directly, the data and analysis gathered may help to contextualise the project, or serve as the initial impetus for the researcher to investigate the legal doctrines underlying the practice in question by prompting research questions relating to the normative/doctrinal development

---

2 See Lee McConnell, Chapter 4.

3 For a Marxist account in this regard, see China Miéville, *Between Equal Rights: A Marxist Theory of International Law* (Leiden: Brill, 2005); Robert Knox, 'Marxism, International Law, and Political Strategy' (2009) 22 *Leiden Journal of International Law*, 413.

4 Gustav Bergmann and Lewis Zerpy, 'The Formalism in Kelsen's Pure Theory of Law' (1945) 55 *Ethics*, 110, 130; Roland Portmann, *Legal Personality in International Law* (Cambridge: Cambridge University Press, 2010) p. 173.

of the field of law. For instance, Egan references trends relevant to the field of inquiry, including the increasing 'privatisation' of human rights abuses and the effects produced non-state actors in a system predicated on inter-state relations.[5] A clear example of a normative argument inspired by these new international realities that is embedded within an overtly positivist-doctrinal research project is McConnell's 'Assessing the Feasibility of a Business and Human Rights Treaty'.[6] This work expressly adopts the positivist Pure Theory of Law in order to dispel social contract arguments that preclude the expansion of the subjects of international human rights obligations to include multinational corporations. In doing so, the doctrinal work not only outlines the current state-of-play in the legal regulation of non-state actors, but also highlights opportunities and governance gaps into which international human rights could potentially expand in an effort to better safeguard vulnerable communities.

Moreover, the devices employed in McConnell's article include analogical reasoning from private law and existing treaty regimes, which are key techniques or 'canons of interpretation' highlighted by Egan.[7] The relevance of this interpretive technique is also evident in Sue Farran's account of the comparative method, which is discussed in further detail below. In the comparative context, analogies may be drawn between doctrines within a single legal order, across clusters of common and civil law states, and/or between international, regional, domestic and local systems. In this regard, Egan's discussion of the elaboration of the concept of 'membership of a particular social group' in relation to domestic and international refugee law demonstrates a clear compatibility between the comparative and doctrinal methods. Other accepted canons of interpretation may boast quite distinct theoretical/philosophical roots. Egan highlights Jackson's employment of moral claims to underscore his normative statements regarding operation of the law, and the adoption of teleological interpretive methods[8] which are rooted in the classical naturalist philosophy influenced by Aristotle.[9] As readers will now appreciate, doctrinal analysis boasts a rich scope for compatibility with the comparative, theoretical, empirical and experiential/qualitative techniques outlined in the foregoing chapters of this book.

In her chapter, Sue Farran considered comparative approaches to human rights, a method that, owing to its breadth, presents considerable scope to supplement and work in harmony with other methods. Farran's acknowledgement that the comparative method often entails highlighting the experience of 'the

5 Suzanne Egan, Chapter 3.
6 Lee McConnell, 'Assessing the Feasibility of a Business and Human Rights Treaty' (2017) 66 *International and Comparative Law Quarterly*, 143.
7 Suzanne Egan, Chapter 3.
8 Miles Jackson, 'Freeing Soering: The ECHR, State Complicity in Torture, and Jurisdiction' (2016) 217 *European Journal of International Law*, 817.
9 Raymond Wacks, *Understanding Jurisprudence*, 4th edn. (Oxford: Oxford University Press, 2015) p. 16.

other' evidences a potential link with the theoretical methodology employed in research that considers the perspective of marginalised groups, a popular theme in human rights research. Such a tendency clearly aligns with the postmodernist perspectives on law outlined in McConnell's contribution, concisely described by Cook as 'exposing the subordination and marginality of alternative social visions whose relegation to the status of *exception* to the rule, *counter*-tradition or *minority* perspective can no longer by objectively justified'.[10] While the direct comparison of legal orders (e.g. common law, civil law) may not always reflect this tendency (comparisons are frequently drawn between – or indeed within – states or regional systems with comparable cultural, socio-political and economic traditions),[11] there is clear scope to focus on voices that are overlooked by the wholesale transplant of Western doctrines without tailoring to the local context. Indeed, it may be possible to highlight instances such as these and to use them to theorise continued Western imperialism in a supposedly post-colonial era.[12] Such insights high-light the inherently political nature and effects of law, against the strictly doctrinal-positivist explanations of 'analogical' reasoning that were appraised by Egan. There is also a clear overlap between these considerations and the 'law in context' considerations raised by Smith in her outline of the human rights based approach to research.

Additionally, Farran highlights the ideology of universality and equality that is embedded within the human rights project, and enables us to consider and appreciate 'why the experience of human rights is uneven'.[13] In appraising the empirical/experiential side of the comparative approach, there is clear scope for quantitative and ethnographic methods outlined by Smith and Smith, Landman, and Simmons and Feldman, to contextualise, supplement and ground this form of analysis. For instance, Landman's examination of the effects of treaty ratification on human rights observance[14] could be coupled with a comparative account of the translation of international legal principles to the local setting. Anthropological and ethnographic data on domestic legal traditions and cultures could be used to enrich this discussion still further. This compatibility between qualitative and quantitative methods in human rights research is expressly acknowledged by both Smith and Smith, and Landman, the latter noting that quantitative accounts often

---

10 Anthony E. Cook, 'Reflections on Postmodernism' (1992) 26 *New England University Law Review*, 751, 754.

11 Peter E. Quint, 'International Human Rights: The Convergence of Comparative and International Law' (2001) 36 *Texas International Law Journal*, 605, 607.

12 Andrea Bianchi, *International Law Theories: An Inquiry in to Different Ways of Thinking* (Oxford: Oxford University Press, 2016) pp. 205–226; Antony Anghie, *Imperialism, Sovereignty and the Making of International Law* (Cambridge: Cambridge University Press, 2007).

13 See Sue Farran, Chapter 8.

14 Todd Landman, *Protecting Human Rights: A Global Comparative Study* (Washington, DC: Georgetown University Press, 2005).

provide partial evidence . . . and help us build larger sets of explanation for the human rights problems we observe and study. . . . Used alongside narrative analysis, ethnographic research, forensic anthropology, testimonials, archival research and other approaches to analysing social and political phenomena, statistics and quantitative analysis have an important role to play, but not the only role.[15]

Smith and Smith affirm this, noting that open text survey questions can be used alongside quantitative closed questions to supplement, clarify or verify the quantitative data. Similarly, in the examples provided by Simmons and Feldman, each study adopts a 'multi-method' approach 'relying on a number of data collection techniques including qualitative interviews, participant observation, content analysis, focus groups, and even quantitative surveys'.[16]

In terms of legal theory, the notion of equal, universal rights discussed by Farran reflects a predominantly Western liberal legal paradigm, which is potentially blind to the differences and specific requirements of 'the other'. Farran highlights the difficulties in transplanting individualistic notions of legal rights in legal systems which give prominence to the collectivism of the community or group. In this context, the transplants of purportedly neutral liberal conceptions of rights which have attained prominence at the international level are potentially 'destabilising'.[17] Comparative approaches of the experience of groups such as women, minorities or members of various class groups even within Western liberal democracies highlight potential biases inherent within the structure of legal doctrines. Thus, the potential to couple the comparative method with theoretical models from Critical Legal Studies, Critical Race Theory, Third-World Approaches to International Law, feminism and others is clear.[18]

But it is not purely structural insights drawn from the comparative approach that can be further contextualised and explained in conjunction with legal theory. An examination of the content and application of human rights can also prove useful. Farran highlights the influence of religion in shaping the content and underscoring the validity of legal orders in various parts of the world, a factor that obviously permits theoretical insights from natural law theories. Beyond this, the notion of universality inherent in the human rights movement, and the comparison of the uneven interpretation and implementation of international standards in legal systems across the globe permits discussion of the immutability of human rights and the moral concepts they engender such as 'human dignity'. Farran highlights Botha's 'Human Dignity

15 See Todd Landman, Chapter 6.
16 See Simmons and Feldman, Chapter 7.
17 See Sue Farran, Chapter 8.
18 See generally the appropriate chapters in Andrea Bianchi, *International Law Theories: An Inquiry in to Different Ways of Thinking* (Oxford: Oxford University Press, 2016).

in Comparative Perspective' in this regard,[19] and it would prove useful for readers to consider the comparable references to dignity in the context of naturalist legal theories highlighted in McConnell's discussion of McCrudden's 'Human Dignity and Judicial Interpretation of Human Rights'.[20] Similarly, the discussions of cosmopolitan theory in Sweet's comparative analysis of the domestic constitutional arrangements of state parties to the European Convention on Human Rights provides another explicit link between theoretical perspectives and the comparative method outlined by Farran.[21]

On Simmons and Feldman's account, there is potential for both compatibility and conflict in the critical ethnography they detail, the comparative approach outlined by Farran, and the tensions surrounding universalism and relativism inherent within cosmopolitan/naturalist legal theories introduced by McConnell. While arguments against the universalising tendencies of human rights research in the anthropological tradition from which ethnography is drawn are highlighted, there is clear scope to utilise in ethnographies in order to understand the ways in which human rights have been experienced and have proven useful in particular contexts. This may in turn lead to a more considered, contextual and reflexive approach to legal comparative studies endorsed by Farran. Moreover, such empirical approaches may supplement comparative studies, helping to illuminate, amplify and empower the voice of the 'other' in the face of the dominant legal liberalism that underscores international human rights law and the continuing colonialism it potentially facilitates,[22] demonstrating still further links with 'critical' theories. Pollert, a Marxist feminist, blends ethnographical observation with qualitative interviews conducted in the 1970s.[23]

As was noted above, the experiential/quantitative data on human rights introduced by Landman, Smith and Smith, and Simmons and Feldman, while valuable in their own right, may also contextualise, supplement and even inspire doctrinal, comparative and theoretical research projects. The data revealed and the analysis undertaken in the bivariate studies described by Landman also

---

19 Henk Botha, 'Human Dignity in Comparative Perspective' (2009) 20 *Stellenborsch Law Review*, 171.

20 Christopher McCrudden, 'Human Dignity and Judicial Interpretation of Human Rights' (2008) 19 *European Journal of International Law*, 656.

21 Alec Stone Sweet, 'A Cosmopolitan Legal Order: Constitutional Pluralism and Rights Adjudication in Europe' (2012) 1 *Global Constitutionalism*, 53.

22 There is also clear scope for engagement from the perspective of feminist legal theories, as evidenced by the following literature cited by Simmons and Feldman: Lisa R. Pruitt and Marta R. Vanegas, 'CEDAW and Rural Development: Empowering Women with Law from the Top Down, Activism from the Bottom Up' (2012) 41 *Baltimore Law Review*, 263, 267; Cf Peggy Levitt and Sally Engle Merry, 'Vernacularization on the Ground: Local Uses of Global Women's Rights in Peru, China, India and the United States' (2009) 9(4) *Global Networks*, 441.

23 Anna Pollert, *Girls, Wives, Factory Lives* (London: Macmillan, 1981).

potentially reveal deeper relationships with theory and doctrine. This is because the variables against which human rights compliance can be analysed also reflect particular socio-political or economic models of social organisation (for example human rights observance in liberal democracies). Thus, empirical insights relating to human rights compliance can be further supplemented by a theoretical contextualisation of the individualistic framing of rights in legal doctrine and the political philosophy that underlies in the social order in which such rights are integrated. In the case of liberal democracies, theoretical themes of this type can be drawn from liberal legal theories, correlating particularly strongly with the work of Rawls, Téson and Slaughter.[24] Theoretical arguments concerning the relationship between variables such as 'participation' and 'due process' in the international law-making process and the inducement of human rights 'compliance' by the relevant addressees have been advanced by Franck in relation to states and recently expanded to non-state actors by scholars such as Ryngaert.[25] There is perhaps some scope to test these theoretical insights via empirical/quantitative methods in the fashion Landman describes.

Landman also offers a note of caution in his introduction to bivariate and multivariate studies seeking to uncover the relationships between multiple different variables. He notes that such studies can be prone to inferring 'spurious' relationships between the variables which upon first sight appear to be causally linked, but on further analysis may be determined by a third or fourth factor absent from the initial analysis. Thus, researchers must remain cognisant of the distinction between *correlation* and *causation* in their quantitative analyses. Recent theoretical-doctrinal literature in the field revived these concerns in the field of human rights, with scholars such as McGrogan emphasising the 'high causal density' of human societies which can make it difficult to infer accurate causal relationships between variables. Accordingly, McGrogan calls for a more descriptive *ex post facto* account focused on the quantification of violations of human rights laws.[26] Comparable quantitative

24 John Rawls, *The Law of Peoples* (Boston: Harvard University Press, 2003); Fernando Tesón, 'Kantian International Liberalism' in David R. Mapel and Terry Nardin (eds), *International Society* (Princeton, NJ: Princeton University Press, 1998); Anne-Marie Slaughter, 'International Law in a World of Liberal States' (1995) 6 *European Journal of International Law*, 503.

25 Thomas Franck, *The Power of Legitimacy Among Nations* (Oxford: Oxford University Press, 1990); Cedric Ryngaert, 'Imposing International Duties on Non-State Actors and the Legitimacy of International Law' in Cedric Ryngaert and Math Noortmann (eds), *Non-State Actor Dynamics in International Law: From Law-Takers to Law-Makers* (Abingdon: Routledge, 2010).

26 David McGrogan, 'The Problem of Causality in International Human Rights Law' (2016) 65(3) *International and Comparative Law Quarterly*, 615.

analyses are evident in Landman's description of 'events data' collected in the work of a large number of post-conflict truth and reconciliation commissions.[27]

Even from this brief reflection on the methods described in this volume, it should be clear to the reader that there is rich scope for human rights research to exploit the connections, synergies and interfaces between methods. Clearly, methods must be chosen wisely and tailored to suit the particular research questions pursued in each particular project. Caution must also be exercised where methods are prone to give rise to conflicting results/data. Nonetheless, with some careful planning, it is clear that a combination of methods may significantly enhance the quality of human rights research. It is to the practicalities of mixed methods that we now turn.

3 Practicalities

The previous chapters have explored different methods for researching and analysing human rights. However, all too often the reality is that a mix of methods are used. This may be the choice of the researcher, or requested by the funder. A range of methods may also be required to actually address adequately the research question. Human rights and fundamental freedoms do not exist in isolation as phenomena to be studied. Rather, human rights engage with duty bearers, rights holders and potentially donors or partners. This can influence the methods used to research problems. Moreover, human rights often meld into other rights and freedoms. For example, when examining voting preferences in a particular country, it is difficult to analytically isolate the rights to education, political participation and freedom of expression. Similarly, it would be difficult to deconstruct events and identify the individual rights and freedoms when examining the impact of poverty in a small rural community. Adequate standard of living, food security, infrastructure in the community, the relative standard of living of the rest of the population, cultural rights . . . the list of relevant rights and freedoms goes on. Human rights and fundamental freedoms are obviously interdependent, interrelated and indivisible. It is not therefore surprising that human rights as a subject lends itself to interdisciplinary research, permeating all disciplines and subjects, rather than being the sole preserve of one or two.

3a *Interdisciplinary and multidisciplinary*

When mixing research methods, the terms interdisciplinary and multidisciplinary often arise. Interdisciplinary research essentially brings together different approaches in an effort to forge a new approach. Multidisciplinary

---

27 See Todd Landman, Chapter 6.

research, in contrast, brings together different disciplines to approach an issue from different perspectives. The methods maintain their separate identities but researchers can collaborate and work together.

Interdisciplinary research, for lawyers, can draw on other disciplines and traditions. Socio-legal research, for example, is interdisciplinary, drawing on the research traditions of law and sociology.[28] It bridges both disciplines to create a new approach that is neither accurately described as legal nor sociological. Law is studied as a culturally specific mode of social organisation with associated implications and consequences. Many socio-legal studies address elements of law's effect on family life,[29] or other ways in which law has a societal impact. As noted, interdisciplinary research brings together different approaches (or disciplines) to forge a new way of looking at a problem or a new model of analysis. Different methodologies offer different perspectives, so drawing on different methods in a new or innovative way can create a new approach to studying human rights. Although there are some established interdisciplinary approaches, there is always scope for new combinations to be evinced.

Criminology is cross disciplinary, drawing on a range of other disciplines including law, psychology and sociology. Theories of crime and real-world experience of the criminal justice system are studied. Areas of particular interest include gender-based violence, crime and punishment, youth justice, policing and prison/detention centres. Clearly there is a strong human rights dimension in many criminological studies.[30]

It should be noted that in the social sciences, interdisciplinary research can mean using both qualitative and quantitative methods, so distinct are they from each other. In human rights, each can be used independently, but often both are used, with qualitative methods being used to deepen understanding of the data reached after a quantitative analysis. Qualitative data can often 'soften' the perceived bluntness of statistical data by providing further explanation for the statistics.

Multidisciplinary research can offer many advantages to human rights research teams. Researching a particular problem or phenomenon from multiple approaches can be illuminating, as different perspectives can help deepen understanding and even aid exploration of solutions. An example is Dawn Watkins and Mandy Burton's edited book on *Research Methods in Law*[31] which

---

28 See, for example, David Cowan and Daniel Wincott (eds), *Exploring the 'Legal' in Socio-Legal Studies* (Basingstoke: Palgrave Macmillan, 2015); Dermot Feenan (ed.), *Exploring the 'Socio' in Socio-Legal Studies* (Basingstoke: Palgrave Macmillan, 2013).

29 Richard Collier and Sally Sheldon, *Fragmenting Fatherhood – a Socio-Legal Study* (London: Bloomsbury, 2008).

30 Leanne Weber, Elaine Fishwick and Marinella Marmo (eds) *The Routledge International Handbook of Criminology and Human Rights* (Abingdon: Routledge, 2017).

31 Dawn Watkins and Mandy Burton (eds), *Research Methods in Law* (Abingdon: Routledge, 2013).

takes a single topic – law decision-making in the legal system – and explores it through some of the main methodological approaches to legal research. Although primarily a tool to demonstrate different methods deployed in legal research, it does ably deepen understanding of the topic through the different studies in the book. It also demonstrates the differences between the presented methods, and highlights the advantages of multidisciplinary research.

For human rights research, it is perfectly feasible to adopt either inter-disciplinary approaches or multidisciplinary approaches to a particular research question or phenomenon. The particular terms of reference or call for a project may dictate which approach is needed, as may the skills and experience of the research team. Of course, much can also depend on the nature of the research and the particular aim of a piece of work.

3b Triangulation

In human rights research, often researchers mix methods to add credibility to the findings or to add depth to the research. Take, for example, a research project focusing on statistical analyses of children in education, with data disaggregated by sex, race and religion to add further understanding. The researcher may decide to interview the minister of education or the local education authorities for further information on why the statistics are as they are. The researcher may also choose to analyse reports on the millennium development goals by way of background, and the UNICEF state of the world's children data to determine the extent to which the case study reflects the general trends in the state.

Quantitative and qualitative data are often used to cross-check and add depth to the other. Ted Piccone, for example, combines some quantitative data with a series of qualitative interviews to evolve an understanding of the role and function of UN special procedures.[32] Theories may then be engaged to explain the findings. Hathaway, for example, analyses quantitative data over 40 years to assess the impact of human rights treaty ratification on human rights practices within states[33] and subsequently assesses a political theory of international law in light of an analysis of reasons for states ratifying treaties.[34] When considering universal periodic review in the Human Rights Council, researchers have used diverse methods and approaches to research the topic. Examples include: UPR-info used semi-structured interviews when

---

32 Ted Piccone, *Catalysts for Change: How the UN's Independent Experts Promote Human Rights* (Washington, DC: Brookings, 2012).

33 Oona Hathaway, 'Do Human Rights Treaties Make a Difference?' (2002) 111 *Yale Law Journal*, 1935.

34 Oona Hathaway, 'Why Do Nations Join Human Rights Treaties?' (2007) 51 *Journal Of Conflict Resolution*, 588.

considering the 'butterfly' effect of the UPR recommendations[35]; McMahon analyses the recommendations in the first cycle, categorising the textual data by a level of action categorisation[36]; and Yuyun Wahyuningrum presents a personal autoethnographic reflection of involvement in the process.[37] Were such a range of research to focus on a specific issue or aspect (e.g. geographical, state specific), then clearly the results should more easily triangulate.

However, it should be noted that results obtained using different methods do not necessarily corroborate. This can cause problems. For example, a researcher trying to understand food security on an island may start with a quantitative analysis of data gathered on malnutrition in hospitals and crop yields and failures. This will provide a set of information from which deductions on food security can be made. Interviewing a select group of islanders may yield more information on the reasons behind crop failures, though equally, it may not. Similarly, qualitative data may be analysed to further the understanding of malnutrition but this may only be true for a small part of the community. Care must be taken when mixing methods and when trying to triangulate data as the result may not be the level of information you want or need. Mismatched results can sometimes be explained within the research outputs, though much depends on the specific circumstances. Often it is the research design which has caused the apparent anomaly.

Dobash and Dobash take a feminist approach to examining the phenomenon of violence against women. In a classic sociological body of work, a critique of the historical contexts, including roots, causes, frequency and prevention, was followed by over a hundred informal interviews with women in refuges in two locations and observations in situ in those refuges (designated places of safety for women victims of violence).[38] The interviewers 'became permanent fixtures in the life and activities of the refuges'[39] and the qualitative work was checked against the public information of violence against women reported to the police and courts in two cities.[40] This wide range of methods contributed to

35 UPR-Info, *The Butterfly Effect: Spreading good practices of UPR implementation* (Geneva: UPR Info, 2017) <https://www.upr-info.org/sites/default/files/general-document/pdf/2016_the_butterfly_effect.pdf> accessed 17 April 2017.

36 Edward Mcmahon, *The Universal Periodic Review: A Work in Progress: An Evaluation of the First Cycle of the New UPR Mechanismof the United Nations Human Rights Council* (Bonn: Friedrich Ebert Stiftung, 2012), <http://library.fes.de/pdf-files/bueros/genf/09297.pdf> accessed 17 February 2017.

37 Yuyun Wahyuningrum, 'Indonesia and the Universal Periodic Review: Negotiating Rights' in Hilary Charlesworth and Emma Larking (eds) *Human Rights and the Universal Periodic Review: Rituals and Ritualism* (Cambridge: Cambridge University Press, 2014).

38 Russell Dobash and Emerson Dobash, *Violence Against Wives: A Case against the Patriarchy* (New York: Free Press/Macmillan, 1979).

39 Dobash and Dobash, nx, 258. This is also an example of a pilot study then a revised full study.

40 Ibid, 260.

this classic sociological book on violence against women. These academics have continued to mix methods in their subsequent work.[41]

Triangulating results is clearly important in human rights research when empirical work is being used. To strengthen the conclusions drawn or arguments being made, triangulating results can offer benefits. Even when efforts at triangulation seem futile (e.g. the results do not seem to be corroborated), there is a benefit in reflecting on and explaining differences in results. As noted above, this could be because one method produced a very small-scale result; the second a much broader scale and extrapolation suggests that the small-scale study was atypical of the larger scale sample.

3c *Evaluation*

Evaluation is a common source of research contracts in human rights in the twenty-first century, as there is increasing pressure on funders to justify their support for various enterprises and activities. Outcomes now govern most steps of the process. Evaluation of programmes is common to establish whether the funding was successful, to determine what change, if any, resulted and to verify whether the planned outcomes were met. Programme evaluation often deploys mixed methods in an attempt to be as thorough as possible. For example, a programme aimed at increasing human rights knowledge of judges in a particular country may be evaluated by the collection of data from judgements and reports of judges, which can be analysed to determine evidence of greater knowledge than when a similar evaluation is undertaken before the training programme began. This may not tell the full story; for example, the constitution or procedural laws may not permit human rights treaties to be cited in court or mentioned in judgments. A qualitative review of data collected from interviews or questionnaires to determine the experience of the trainers, judges and programme organisers as well as other relevant partners (e.g. Ministry of Justice, Judicial Training Academy) could provide explanations of some of the information produced from a quantitative analysis and details as to what the trainings actually achieved. Such information will usually be required in evaluation reports and so a variety of methods may be required. In this example, doctrinal to understand what judges can do, quantitative to evaluate the scope of the training and statistical impact, and qualitative to explain what happened in practice.

Robson notes challenges with evaluation research which is neither rigorous nor evidence driven and notes the pressures which can be placed on the researchers.[42] A programme may not include sufficient funds for a comprehensive

---

41 For example, Russell Dobash and Emerson Dobash, 'Women's Violence to Men in Intimate Relationships' (2004) 44 *British Journal of Criminology*, 324–349 uses qualitative and quantitative approaches.

42 Colin Robson, *Real World Research*, 3rd edn. (London: Wiley, 2011) p. 179.

evaluation. For example, travel to conduct face to face interviews may not be feasible within the available budget. Skype and electronic or other telecommunication options may suffice, but the researcher may lack the country knowledge and awareness of the politics, culture and reality of the situation on the ground. The final programme evaluation may be compromised by a flawed baseline survey (at the start of the programme) or an incomplete or flawed mid-term evaluation.

Human rights development indicators, sustainable (or millennium) development goals and targets, development programme mid-term and end reviews – all draw on evaluations to a greater or lesser extent. Increasingly, a mix of methods is required to best understand the progress made, change in circumstances or benefits accrued. Which methods depends on what the researcher is trying to examine or prove. Frequently, statistical data provides a snapshot of progress towards set goals, but ethnographic data may be required to understand the real-world experiences and the practical implications of a particular change/programme.

4 Conclusions

When researching human rights, the selection of methods can involve a balance of several factors. The research question is the first port of call. Given the question, a decision on research strategy is next. Some questions indicate the method/s required to answer the question; other questions may be answered by different methods. Some researchers have their preferred method which they use for all or most of their work. Teams of researchers can bring experience in different methods to a particular problem. Researchers should be aware that different methods can result in different approaches to a problem. The choice may be influenced by who is commissioning the research, the purpose of the research and/or the practicalities of the resources available – money, staff and so on. Analysing primary documentary evidence such as treaties, laws and cases along with commentary and analysis can provide an understanding of the scope of a right or freedom. Considering that, in conjunction with a theoretical approach, can give a very deep understanding of an issue. A different insight is obtained with a review of state implementation through external reviews such as treaty body reports, universal periodic review reports, regional human rights organisation reports, UNDP millennium development goal or sustainable development goal reports, and NGO reports. The impact on the ground on real people may be better understood with the collection of qualitative data through interviews, observations and focus groups, or through quantitative analysis of questionnaires. All depends on the nature of the research question and the purpose for which the research is being undertaken. This does mean that the same issue can be examined using different methods with the results giving a variety of insights into a particular issue.

What remains constant, is the need to have a planned approach to a research study, carefully consider the theoretical underpinning, accurately reflect the legal position and then be able to justify the selection of methods. Mixing methods can be trial and error, but there remains a need for careful forethought, planning and a logical narrative to ensure that the question or phenomenon is explored in the best way.

In human rights research, the choice of methods may be influenced by the intended recipient of the research. So, using a human rights based approach, if the government as duty bearer is the intended recipient, it may be that a strong doctrinal approach will best evaluate current laws, identify gaps and suggest solutions. On the other hand, it may be that hard empirical data will be needed to persuade a government to change (or continue with) a particular policy. If the end user is a vulnerable or marginalised group, consideration needs to be given to protection of the people as well as empowerment – again, empirical data may prove a strong tool, but then so too may theories or legal doctrine. For advocacy goals, understanding legal principles will often be imperative. As is so often the case, much depends on the situation involved, the researcher, resources and the end user of the research.

As this chapter outlines, with human rights, mixed methods are often used. A researcher will use different methods to better understand the problem and identify possible solutions. Ultimately, human rights research methods can best be viewed as a toolbox – the more methods and approaches available, the easier it is to select the best options for a particular project. The one principle this book prioritises is that human rights research should be undertaken in a manner which is rigorous, does not worsen the situation of duty bearers or rights holders, and most certainly does not increase the chance of reprisals.

Index